Anstoß 1

Carole Shepherd | Angela Heidemann | Andy Giles

Teacher's Resource File

Hodder & Stoughton
A member of the Hodder Headline Group

Acknowledgement:

The authors and publishers would like to thank the following for permission to reproduce copyright materials: Hülsta Werbung, PCM 5.16, © Hülsta, Hüls GmbH & Co. KG

Orders: please contact Bookpoint Ltd, 130 Milton Park, Abingdon, Oxon OX14 4SB. Telephone: (44) 01235 827720. Fax: (44) 01235 400454. Lines are open from 9.00–6.00, Monday to Saturday, with a 24 hour message answering service. Email address: orders@bookpoint.co.uk

British Library Cataloguing in Publication Data
A catalogue record for this title is available from the British Library

ISBN 0 340 78233 1

First Published 2002
Impression number   10 9 8 7 6 5 4 3 2 1
Year   2007 2006 2005 2004 2003 2002

Copyright © 2002 Carole Shepherd, Angela Heidemann, Andy Giles

Cover photo from The Apple Agency Ltd
Typeset by Servis Filmsetting Ltd, Manchester
Printed in Italy for Hodder & Stoughton Educational, a division of Hodder Headline Plc, 338 Euston Road, London NW1 3BH by Hobbs the Printers, Totton, Hampshire

CONTENTS

(Introduction) How to use Anstoß 1

Anstoß 1 consists of:
- *the Student's Book in full colour*
- *the Teacher's Resource File*
- *3 cassettes*

This Teacher's Resource File consists of:
- *Section 1: Teacher's Notes on the Student's Book and the Photocopy Masters. This contains helpful advice for the exploitation of the material in the Student's Book, full transcripts and answers; as well as helpful advice for the exploitation of material in Section 2, transcripts and answers.*
- *Section 2: Photocopy Masters. This section is a resource file of photocopiable material, including assessment and student profile masters.*

Section 1 is divided into 8 chapters, as per the Student's Book. Each chapter gives:
- *information on suggested teaching procedures.*
- *advice on further activities.*
- *guidance on the level of the activities.*

The Teacher's Resource File contains a chapter by chapter explanation of activities in the Student's Book, and suggestions for developing:

- *additional activities –these can be used to supplement the textbook activities and are often in the form of games or other fun activities. (Identified in the book by an* **A** *.)*
- *extension activities –these are for the more able students and often focus on grammatical points. (Identified in the book by an* **E** *.)*

Der Cartoon

The cartoon story about the Anstoß-Band runs throughout the *Anstoß* series and is a fun reading and listening activity containing the core vocabulary for each Einheit.

Pupils will get to know the characters and their lives, and will want to read on and find out what happens to them in *Anstoß 1*, and later in *Anstoß 2* and *Anstoß GCSE*.

We hope that by allowing the students to hypothesise on the situations depicted and the possible meanings of the speech bubbles, *Anstoß 1* will encourage active learning and guessing strategies.

Students can also use the images as a source of cultural and contextual information. The teacher will be able to lead discussions by asking questions such as: What is different from Britain? (e.g. environment, behaviour, gestures etc.) In what situation is the language used? (e.g. friend's house, shop etc.) Who uses what sort of language to whom? (formal and informal language usage).

The story has been divided into manageable units which are related to a particular theme or topic area. The situations have been made as realistic as possible in order to encourage a high level of interest and involvement. It is helpful if you constantly refer to the expressions and words used in the stories to show that they are a useful source of language.

Each story contains quite a lot of new language so you, as the teacher, should encourage intelligent guesswork. The illustrations and the students' gradual familiarity with the characters will help to make the words more accessible.

After the students have listened to and read through the dialogues an appropriate number of times, they can be encouraged to enact the dialogues. We do not stipulate the number of times each story should be played as we feel you are the best judge of how much repetition your students require. Students should try to imitate the pronunciation and intonation of the characters they have heard on tape. As they gain in confidence, they can be encouraged to adapt the stories and even "perform" without their books in their hands.

Die Raps

Each chapter includes a number of rap songs. The song lyrics feature and revise some of the main vocabulary and grammatical structures for each topic area. The music was composed especially for *Anstoß* by German musicians in a style which we hope will capture the imagination and enthusiasm of your students. Raps were chosen because they do not require advanced musical skills and are therefore an enjoyable group activity.

Since music is a powerful memory aid, students should be encouraged not only to listen to the songs but also to sing along to them and to learn them by heart. In some cases songs are accompanied by actions. We hope this will be particularly helpful for weaker students who might need extra stimuli.

Most songs have been placed towards the end of units so that students can look forward to them when they have mastered a particular topic. They can be used as an enjoyable revision and consolidation activity. There are also comprehension and extension activities based on the songs, which require students to listen carefully to the lyrics.

Some teachers may prefer students to listen to the songs at the beginning of a new topic area. The songs can then be used as a warm-up activity. Students could memorise the key expressions and practise pronunciation. Confidence will follow as students work through the chapter and become more familiar with the expressions.

On the cassettes most songs are followed by instrumental versions of the raps. Once students have become confident with the words, they can be encouraged to sing the raps 'karaoke-style'.

More able students could be asked to invent extra verses or may want to personalise the existing lyrics by replacing certain words, they may even wish to provide their own lyrics for the songs.

Symbols

The following symbols are used in *Anstoß 1*:

indicates a Reading activity. This may also be a Listening activity – as in the case of the cartoons. Wherever possible helpful visual clues are given to promote active reading skills.

indicates a Listening activity. The transcripts for all the Listening activities, including the songs and cartoons are to be found in the grey shaded Transcript boxes. These exercises can be used with a cassette player operated by the teacher or in a language laboratory.

indicates a Writing activity. This may be a simple True / False or even a letter writing exercise. There is plenty of scope for all students to work up to the limit of their ability. Activities which are more suitable for more able students are identified with an **E** in this book.

indicates a Speaking activity. The visuals in *Anstoß* are designed to stimulate a wide range of verbal responses.

☺☺ indicates Pair work.

☺☺☺ indicates Group work.

indicates the song is recorded on tape.

reminds the students to copy the activity into their exercise books rather than writing in the textbook.

a black top hat denotes formal language.

a baseball cap denotes informal language.

indicates a quiz or game.

Sprachtipp boxes give helpful advice on grammatical structures throughout each chapter.

Vokabeltipp boxes give helpful information on new vocabulary. Much vocabulary learning can happen incidentally as the students are exposed to the language. However regular rote learning and testing of vocabulary are recommended!

Kulturtipp boxes give an insight into the culture of German-speaking countries. If there is sufficient time additional activities are given so that students can research further in their own time – either in school or local libraries or on the Internet. Suggestions for describing cultural differences are given in this book.

Aussprache . . . . boxes give helpful advice on how to pronounce words and letter combinations which English speakers find difficult.

www. boxes give useful key words for searches and also website addresses. Obviously some of these may change after the book has gone to print. We will make every effort to check these regularly and post changes on the Hodder & Stoughton website – www.anstoss.co.uk.

Wörterbuch These boxes give you useful advice on how to use a dictionary.

Erste Hilfe These boxes give vocabulary related to a specific Listening or Reading activity

Lerntipp These boxes give you some useful study tips.

Pass auf! These boxes give you advice about expressions you will need to use regularly.

Leseseiten are given at the end of each chapter to further consolidate the vocabulary introduced in the unit and to encourage further reading and 'reading for gist'.

At the end of each chapter there are two pages which sum up the grammatical structures and main expressions used in the chapter. The time spent on this section will vary according to the ability of the students. Here the teacher's sensitive response to individual needs and differences is paramount.

These pages have been designed in consultation with students, who have expressed a wish to have such information to assist them with homework assignments or when the teacher is unavailable:

Grammatik sums up the grammatical structures covered in the chapter.

 Aussagesätze sums up the key phrases which have been introduced in the chapter.

The **Teacher's Resource File** contains:

- worksheets relating to topics and exercises in the student's book
- some OHP Masters for wall display (e.g. classroom commands)
- Additional and Extension material (denoted by **A** and **E** respectively)
- Student Profile Masters. These state the objectives of each chapter and include columns for recording assessment by the student and the teacher
- Assessment Master – Test 1 (Speaking, Writing, Listening and Reading tasks based on chapters 1–4)
- End of Book Assessment Master (Speaking, Writing, Listening and Reading tasks based on a variety of topics from chapters 1–8)
- Certificate Master for End of Book Assessment, listing items covered in the assessment sheets (photocopiable masters for the school's internal use only – to promote a positive attitude to language learning and so that students feel they have achieved something, but **NOT** relating to an examination grade)
- 'Action Plan' Masters – students will fill these in after each assessment to show that they know where they need to improve (e.g. which vocabulary they still need to learn / what grammar they still need to master) and how they intend to act upon it.

Please note: although all Internet sites quoted in this book were available at the time of writing, Internet addresses are subject to change. Before using any of the sites quoted in class, please check that they are still available and suitable for classroom use.

Spiele

You will find reference to a selection of games you can play with your students in the Student's Book and in the Teacher's Resource File. Here is a selection of these which can be used with any topic area:

1. **Bitte** – a version of Simon Says, this can be used to practise classroom commands.

2. **Du bist dran** – give an instruction or command to the first student in the class or team, which has to be mimed to the next student. After having successfully guessed the answer, he / she has to provide a new instruction for the next player to mime. Best done as a chain game or race.

3. **Pelmanism** – students can make about 20–30 small cards with German words or phrases on half of them and the English equivalents on the other half. The vocabulary can relate to any topic. Shuffle all the cards and arrange them face down on a table. Students play in small groups and take turns to turn over two cards. If they turn over a matching pair, they keep the cards. If they fail to do so, then they have to replace the cards. This is obviously a good test of memory. The winner is the player who has the highest number of cards.

4. **Lotto** – this game can be adapted to most topics. Students write down numbers or draw vocabulary items or simply write a list of 5 or 6 words or phrases which have been set as a learning homework. The teacher calls out words or phrases at random, and students cross them off their lists as they are called. When all their words have been called, students shout **Lotto**! The winner must say aloud the words / phrases called to gain their prize!

5. **Zahlspiel** – write numbers or words at random on the board. Form two teams and give each team member a letter, so that each team has a member with each letter. Call out a letter and the team member from each team with that letter must come forward to the front of the class. The teacher then calls out one of the words or one of the numbers in German. The contestant who rubs the number or the word off the board first wins a point for the team.

6. **Zählenspiel** – counting round the class, but varying the method or sequence to twos, threes, backwards etc.

7. **Ja und Nein** – a version of the 'yes / no interlude' on the old TV quiz game 'Take your Pick'. A student comes to the front of the class and answers questions in German for a minute without using the words **Ja** or **Nein**.

8. **Schlachtschiffe** – Battleships can be adapted to practise any topic. It allows the vocabulary from a learning homework to be used and tested. Sitting in pairs, each student chooses 3 or 4 words or phrases, keeping them secret from his / her partner. Then partners take turns to try to guess the words written on each other's paper. After a successful guess the player gets another turn. The first one to 'sink' all his / her partner's ships (or phrases) is the winner!

Kapitel 1 Hallo!

Within the course of the next few chapters your students will be introduced to the main cartoon characters who will play in or have something to do with the Anstoß-Band. The first Resource File Masters give you blank character data cards, or **Steckbriefe**, for each of the 6 main characters in Book 1, with a picture of each character: **Heinz, Pia, Yasemin, Matthias, Laura** and **David**. Another card has been left blank for students to fill in with their own details and photo, or the details of their favourite popstar / footballer etc. The **Steckbriefe** can either be distributed at the end of the chapter, or they can be filled in as and when students learn a new piece of information about a character. They may have to wait until the later chapters to fill in all the details! The completed cards can be exploited for role plays or used as a stimulus for written work.

In order that you are able to get to know the characters, their details are given below:

Vorname: *Heinz (Pommes)*	**Nachname:** *Schuh*
Adresse: *Wiesenweg 13, Mainz*	**Telefonnummer:** *06131–224939*
	Nationalität: *Deutsch*
	Alter: *15*
	Geburtstag: *23.09.*

Aussehen: *Rote, kurze Haare, grüne Augen, mittelgroß und schlank. Ein sportlicher Junge.*
Charakter: *Frech und sportlich. Etwas faul. Immer lustig.*
Familie: **Mutter:** *Heike Schuh, 44* **Vater:** *Martin Schuh, 44* **Geschwister:** *Florian (22), lange, braune Haare. Er studiert Informatik.*
Haustiere: *keine*
Schule: *Realschule Nord* **Lieblingsfächer:** *Sport und Musik* **Sonstiges:** *Geht nicht so gern zur Schule.*
Haus / Wohnung: *neues Reihenhaus im Vorort.* *Heinz' Zimmer ist im Dachgeschoss.* **Zimmer:** *mittelgroß und unordentlich mit Fußballpostern*
Hobbys: *HipHop Musik, Fußball, Squash, Tennis, Computerspiele, Partys.*
Lieblingsessen: *Pommes mit Ketchup, Kartoffelchips, Cola.*
Rolle in der Band: *Singt und spielt Gitarre.*
Sonstiges: *Er wohnt neben Yasemin und ist im Squash-Verein.* *Sein Bruder Florian ist der Freund von Matthias' Tante Anna.*

Vorname: *Yasemin*	**Nachname:** *Akbar*
Adresse: *Wiesenweg 17, Mainz*	**Telefonnummer:** *06131–22 56 00*
	Nationalität: *Türkisch*
	Alter: *15*
	Geburtstag: *02.04.*

Aussehen: *Hübsch. Lange, dunkle Haare und dunkle Augen. Klein.*

Charakter: *Intelligent und cool*

Familie:
Mutter: *Nürgül Akbar (40)*
Vater: *Hassan Akbar (49)*
Geschwister: *Bruder Mehmet (13), Schwester Hatice (11), Bruder Tarkan (5)*

Haustiere: *1 Kanarienvogel (gelb), namens Abdul, ein Aquarium mit Fischen (gehört Mehmet), ein Meerschweinchen braun / weiß, namens Muffi.*

Schule: *Gesamtschule Stadtmitte*
Lieblingsfächer: *Mathematik, Chemie*
Mag nicht: *Religion*
Sonstiges: *Ist Mitglied im Computer-Club.*

Haus / Wohnung: *modernes Reihenhaus im Vorort mit Garten.*
Zimmer: *Kleines Zimmer im ersten Stock. Modern und hell.*

Hobbys: *Auf dem Internet surfen, Computer, Squash, lesen, Karate, Amnesty International, Mode.*

Lieblingsessen: *Eis und Milkshakes*

Rolle in der Band: *Schlagzeug*

Sonstiges: *Yasemin wohnt neben Heinz. Heinz, Yasemin und Laura sind im Squash-Verein. Yasemin und Laura sind zusammen im Computer-Club in der Schule.*

Vorname: *Pia*	**Nachname:** *Klein*
Adresse: *Barbarastraße 34, Mainz*	**Telefonnummer:** *43 12 56*
	Nationalität: *Deutsch*
	Alter: *14*
	Geburtstag: *06.12.*

Aussehen: *Gefärbte, kurze Haare, blaue Augen, groß und cool.*

Charakter: *Wild, aber auch hilfsbereit.*

Familie:
Mutter: *Elisabeth Klein (45)*
Vater: *Sascha Kowalski (50)*
Geschwister: *Markus Klein (24), Bettina (9), Andi (6)*

Haustiere: *Schlange*

Schule: *Realschule Nord*
Lieblingsfächer: *Erdkunde*
Mag nicht: *Geschichte*
Sonstiges:

Haus / Wohnung: *Wohnung im Norden der Stadt, im Erdgeschoss.*
Zimmer: *Sie teilt sich ein Zimmer mit Bettina.*

Hobbys: *Bassgitarre und Rockmusik, lesen, Briefe schreiben, schwimmen, schlafen, telefonieren.*

Lieblingsessen: *Schokolade, Yoghurt*

Rolle in der Band: *Bassgitarre*

Sonstiges: *Heinz und Pia gehen in die gleiche Klasse in der Schule.*

David Miller joins the band in Chapter 6:

Vorname: *David*	**Nachname:** *Miller*
Adresse: *Königsstraße 254, Mainz.* *Kommt aus Balerno bei Edinburgh.*	**Telefonnummer:** *34 90 22*
	Nationalität: *Schottisch*
	Alter: *14*
	Geburtstag: *09.08.*

Aussehen: *Braune, mittellange Haare. Dunkle Augen. Mittelgroß.*
Charakter: *Nett, aber frech.*
Familie: **Mutter:** *Sheila Miller (35)*   **Vater:** *Charles Miller (41)*   **Geschwister:** *Laura (15)*
Haustiere: *ein Hund, weiß, namens Bello.*
Schule: *Gesamtschule Stadtmitte*   **Lieblingsfächer:** *Musik und Kunst*   **Mag nicht:** *Chemie*   **Sonstiges:**
Haus / Wohnung: *Mietwohnung in der Stadtmitte. Hochhaus 7. Stock mit Balkon.*   **Zimmer:** *klein.*
Hobbys: *Kino, malen, Keyboard und Klavier, Tennis, schwimmen, Ski fahren.*
Lieblingsessen: *Döner Kebab*
Rolle in der Band: *—noch keine—*
Sonstiges: *Die Familie Miller ist seit einem Jahr in Mainz . Der Vater arbeitet in Mainz.*

David's sister is a friend of Yasemin:

Vorname: *Laura*	**Nachname:** *Miller*
Adresse: *Königsstraße 254, Mainz.* *Kommt aus Balerno bei Edinburgh.*	**Telefonnummer:** *34 90 22*
	Nationalität: *Schottisch*
	Alter: *15*
	Geburtstag: *19.03.*

Aussehen: *Dunkle, mittellange Haare. Blaue Augen. Sportlich.*
Charakter: *freundlich und sportlich*
Familie: **Mutter:** *Sheila Miller (35)*   **Vater:** *Charles Miller (41)*   **Geschwister:** *David (14)*
Haustiere: *Ein Hund, weiß, namens Bello.*
Schule: *Gesamtschule Stadtmitte*   **Lieblingsfächer:** *Sport und Biologie*   **Mag nicht:** *Französisch*   **Sonstiges:** *Mitglied beim Computer-Club.*
Haus / Wohnung: *Mietwohnung in der Stadtmitte. Hochhaus 7. Stock mit Balkon.*   **Zimmer:** *klein.*
Hobbys: *Rad fahren, Badminton, Squash, Partys, tanzen, Internet.*
Lieblingsessen: *Salate, Obst, Schokolade*
Rolle in der Band: —
Sonstiges: *Sie wohnt seit einem Jahr in Mainz. Der Vater arbeitet in Mainz.*   *Laura ist mit Heinz und Yasemin im Squash-Verein.*

Laura likes Matthias, an Austrian boy who is staying with relatives in Mainz:

Vorname: *Matthias*	**Nachname:** *Hasler*
Adresse: *bei Anna Meyer* *zu Hause:* *Haslerhof, Am Berg 7, Salzburg / Österreich*	**Telefonnummer:** **Handy:** *0173–334 76 76*
	Nationalität: *Österreicher*
	Alter: *16*
	Geburtstag: *05.07.*
Aussehen: *Sieht gut aus, blonde, mittellange Haare, blaue Augen, groß, sportlich.*	
Charakter: *hilfsbereit, sportlich*	
Familie: **Mutter:** *Maria Hasler (35)* **Vater:** *Anton Hasler (36)* **Geschwister:** *Lena (13)*	
Haustiere: *in Salzburg einen Hund – Bärli, 2 Katzen – Max und Moritz. Ein Pferd – (braun) Mara.*	
Schule: *Mozart-Gymnasium* **Lieblingsfächer:** *Biologie und Sport* **Mag nicht:** *Deutsch* **Sonstiges:**	
Haus / Wohnung: *Im Urlaub bei Anna Meyer, seiner Tante* **Zu Hause:** *ein Bauernhaus auf dem Land* **Zimmer:** *mittelgroß*	
Hobbys: *Fahrrad fahren, spielt Fußball im Verein, reiten, Ski fahren, Snowboard fahren, Tiere, Fotografie, Musik hören.*	
Lieblingsessen: *Spätzle mit Käsesoße. Vegetarier!*	
Rolle in der Band: —	
Sonstiges: *Besucht seine Tante Anna Meyer oft in Mainz. (Anna ist die Freundin von Heinz' Bruder, Florian.)*	

Einheit A Wie geht's?

Unit 1A will introduce:
- *simple greetings and responses*
- *asking people how they are and responding*

PCMs 1.1 and 1.2 accompany this section.

1 Die Geburtstagsparty (1)

By starting with a birthday party, the students immediately encounter **Herzlichen Glückwunsch zum Geburtstag**. This means that whenever it is someone's birthday they will be able to wish him / her Happy Birthday in German – always a popular activity among students!

The cartoon and accompanying listening activity can be used as a warm-up exercise, but will also be exploited actively throughout the chapter, so you will be able to refer back to the key words in the cartoon to consolidate and revise vocabulary. Depending on the ability range and interest of your class you may wish to play the tape once, twice or several times.

Transcript

David:	Guten Tag, Frau Schuh! Guten Tag, Herr Schuh!
Laura:	Guten Abend, Herr und Frau Schuh!
Herr und Frau Schuh:	Guten Abend, David und Laura! Kommt rein!
Frau Schuh:	Wie geht es dir, Laura?
Laura:	Danke, sehr gut. Und wie geht es Ihnen?
Frau Schuh:	Es geht mir gut, Laura.
Laura:	Für Sie!
Frau Schuh:	Oh, danke schön. Das ist ja nett!
David und Laura:	Hallo Heinz!
Heinz:	Hallo David! Hallo Laura! Alles klar? Kommt mit!
David:	Alles klar. Wie geht's dir?
Heinz:	Mir geht's toll.
David und Laura:	Herzlichen Glückwunsch zum Geburtstag!
Heinz:	Danke!

2 Partnerarbeit: Lies den Cartoon und hör noch einmal zu!

This exercise is intended to make learners aware of different registers of language. David and Laura use the informal **Hallo** when greeting their friend. The other two greetings are used to greet the adults and are more formal. This could encourage some cross-cultural comparison. Students could think about how they greet their friends and relatives, and how they greet people they do not know – what words / gestures they use.

Answers

	Frau Schuh	Heinz
Hallo		X
Guten Tag	X	
Guten Abend	X	

Vokabeltipp Hallo!

This table provides students with a summary of core 'Greetings' vocabulary and its usage. It can be exploited in a number of ways. Students could shake hands when they enter the classroom. A clock or the symbols used in the book could be used as cues for when to use which greeting.

The icon of the baseball cap is used to indicate 'informal' language, the icon of the black top hat is used to indicate 'formal' language.

Kulturtipp Saying hello and goodbye

If students are allowed to explore the cartoon for cultural differences they may come up with several:

- German houses look different. Terraced houses are often fairly modern. There are very few red brick terraced houses compared to Britain.
- Laura gives Mrs Schuh some flowers. When you visit someone in Germany it is considered polite to bring a small gift for the hostess, often flowers or chocolate. Wine, on the other hand, is rarely brought, as it is considered the host's privilege to choose the drinks. You may want to point out that children are not expected to bring presents and that you do not bring presents if you see someone very frequently. Even a very generous German would find that a bit too much.
- The guests do not bring birthday cards. These are generally only sent if you cannot say 'Happy Birthday' in person.
- The children may notice that Heinz takes his guests downstairs into the party cellar. It is worth pointing out that most German houses have large cellars which are not only used

for storage purposes but in a number of other ways, such as the teenagers' **Partykeller**, father's **Hobbykeller**, where the DIY gets done, or as a **Waschkeller** for washing and drying laundry.

A number of words have been included which are not in the story but which you may want to comment on:

Grüß dich, Servus and **Ciao** – these are very common among young people nowadays

Grüß Gott – this is commonly used in the South of Germany and in Austria

Gruezi – is often used in Switzerland.

3   Hör zu! Guten Tag!   A

This consolidates the pronunciation of the Greetings.

Transcript
1   Guten Morgen, Gabi. (sound of alarm clock)
2   Guten Tag, Frau Müller. (church bell tolling 3 times)
3   Guten Abend, Herr Klein. (clock chiming 6 times)
4   Gute Nacht, Mama. (yawn)
5   Tschüs! Auf Wiedersehen! (slamming door, fading footsteps)

4   Hör zu! Was sagt man?   A

This consolidates the pronunciation of the greetings. Students should be encouraged to decide which is the correct greeting for the time indicated by the sound effects.

Transcript
1   (sound of alarm clock)
2   (church bell tolling 3 times)
3   (clock chiming 6 times)
4   (yawn)
5   (slamming door, fading footsteps)

Answers
1   Guten Morgen   4   Gute Nacht
2   Guten Tag   5   Auf Wiedersehen!
3   Guten Abend

5   Schreib was!   Anagramme   E

A fun activity to encourage spelling German words correctly.

Answers
1   BIS BALD   3   GUTEN TAG
2   AUF WIEDERSEHEN   4   GUTE NACHT

PCM 1.1   Sieh dir die Bilder an. Sag was!   A

This short exercise practises Greetings once more.

Vokabeltipp Wie geht's?

It is important to explain carefully the difference between the two forms of 'you' used here. The questions and answers can be practised by you asking the question and one student responding and then asking the same question to a different student, who in his / her turn responds then asks another student, and so on. This activity will be referred to from now on as a 'weave'.

Sprachtipp

nicht
This item introduces this very useful little word!

6 / 7   Hör zu! Wie geht's?

These exercises practise the key phrases of this unit and may require some more discussion about formal / informal register e.g. **du** can be used with adults whom you know well.

Transcript
A
Herr Schuh: Guten Morgen, Heinz.
Heinz: Guten Morgen, Papa.
Herr Schuh: Wie geht es dir?
Heinz: Mir geht es schlecht.
Herr Schuh: Oh!

B
Pia: Hallo, Laura.
Laura: Hallo, Pia.
Pia: Wie geht's?
Laura: Danke, prima.
          Und wie geht's dir?
Pia: Mir geht's klasse.

C
Frau Schuh: Guten Tag, Frau Klein!
Frau Klein: Guten Tag, Frau Schuh!
              Wie geht es Ihnen?
Frau Schuh: Danke, mir geht es gut.
              Wie geht es Ihnen?
Frau Klein: Danke, nicht so gut.

Answers

Name:	⏰	⏰	⏰	🎩	🎩	☺	😐	☹
A								
Heinz	x				x			x
B								
Pia		Any		x		x		
Laura		Any		x		x		
C								
Frau Schuh	x				x	x		
Frau Klein	x				x			x

PCM 1.2   Hör zu! Begrüßungen

This short exercise practises the formal and informal greetings once more.

Transcript

Woman 1:	Auf Wiedersehen, Frau Karstens!
Woman 2:	Tschüs!!!
Man 1:	Gute Nacht, Ben. Schlaf gut!
Man 2:	Gute Nacht, Papa!
Woman:	Guten Morgen, Herr Gruber! Wie geht es Ihnen heute Morgen?
Man:	Gut, gut! Danke. Guten Morgen!
Man:	Guten Abend, Maja. Wie geht's?
Woman:	Guten Abend!
Woman:	Guten Tag, Tatjana, guten Tag, Olaf!
Man + Woman:	Guten Tag!

Answers

1E, 2D, 3A, 4C, 5B.

8   Partnerarbeit: Sag was!

This exercise can be used to encourage speaking with a partner. Students can rely heavily on cues and repetition, but more able students can be encouraged to make up both sides of the conversation with or without visual cues. This exercise can also be used as a writing task, with the students writing out the dialogues prior to acting them out in class or recording them on tape.

9   Schreib was! Füll die Lücken im Cartoon

This is an extension activity. It requires comprehension of the individual components of the new expressions.

Answers

<u>Guten</u> Morgen Peter! Wie geht es <u>dir</u>?

Guten Morgen, Frau Meier. Nicht <u>so gut</u>.

<u>Hallo</u> Bettina! <u>Wie</u> geht's?

Hallo, Suvira! Mir <u>geht</u> es <u>prima</u>!

Guten <u>Tag</u>, Klara! <u>Alles klar</u>?

Danke, <u>mir</u> geht's gut.

Einheit B   Wie heißt du?

Unit 1B will introduce:
- *giving your name and asking for others' names*
- *the concept of formal and informal German*
- *the alphabet and spelling names*
- *some useful classroom phrases*

PCMs 1.3 – 1.6 accompany this section.

1   Die Geburtstagsparty (2)

This cartoon consolidates the previous unit by introducing ways of saying your name in German. Students should be encouraged to develop guessing strategies. They could hypothesise about what might happen next before moving on to the next picture. Students could try to give the next line from memory.

Transcript	
Heinz:	Das ist David.
David:	Hallo!
Matthias:	Hallo David. Ich bin Matthias.
Pia:	Wie heißt du?
Laura:	Ich heiße Laura. Und wie heißt du?
Pia:	Ich bin Pia.
Yasemin:	Heißt du David?
Pierre:	Nein, ich heiße Pierre.
Laura:	Du, Pia! Wer ist das?
Pia:	Das da? Das ist Matthias aus Österreich.
Laura:	Matthias!

 **Vornamen** **A**

This internet site gives the current most common first names in German. Students could be encouraged to compare these with their own names and the names of their friends. You may choose to give your students a 'German' name for use during the German class and to use them initially for practice of „Wie heißt du?"

2   Lies den Cartoon noch mal. Wie sagt man das auf Deutsch?

Allow students to guess before giving them the correct answers. You may write the expressions on the board or OHT.

Wer ist das?   Das ist . . .
Wie heißt du?   Ich heiße . . . / Ich bin . . .

sein

This item introduces two parts of the important verb 'to be'.

3   Schreib was!   **E**

This grammatical exercise practises the **bin** and **ist** forms of the verb 'to be'.

Answers
1   Ich <u>bin</u> Pierre.
2   Er <u>ist</u> Heinz.
3   Das <u>ist</u> Yasemin.
4   Das <u>ist</u> Heinz.

Lerntipp   My name is . . .

This box encourages students to see which pieces of vocabulary they need to learn.

PCM 1.3   Wie heißt du?

This item consolidates the useful phrases needed in introductions.

Students can complete the speech bubbles for the characters in the band and practise saying these sentences, and then do a drawing of either themselves or a partner / friend and fill in the speech bubble: **Ich heiße / Ich bin** . . . The drawings can then be kept by the students or used as an attractive classroom display. The phrases: **Wie heißt du? Ich heiße / Ich bin** . . . could be practised orally in a number of ways including weaves, chants and ball games (the person who catches the ball has to give his / her name and ask the next question).

PCM 1.4   Hör zu! Wer hat gute Laune?

This exercise practises greetings and gives students ways of identifying how people are feeling.

Transcript	
Man:	Wie geht's?
Woman:	Gut. Es geht mir gut.
Man:	Wie heißt du?
Woman:	Ich heiße Ling.
Woman 2:	Hallo, wie heißt du?
Man 2:	Ich heiße Pablo.
Woman 2:	Wie geht's, Pablo?
Man 2:	Prima! Es geht mir toll!
Man 3:	Wie ist dein Name?
Woman 3:	Ich bin Anke.

Man 3:	Tag, Anke. Wie geht's?
Woman 3:	Danke, sehr gut. Mir geht's klasse!
Woman 4:	Wie heißt du denn?
Man 4:	Mein Name ist Mark.
Woman 4:	Geht es dir nicht gut?
Man 4:	Nein, mir geht es schlecht, sehr schlecht!
Woman 4:	Oh je!
Man 5:	Bist du Katrin?
Woman 5:	Ja, richtig. Ich bin Katrin.
Man 5:	Wie geht es dir? Geht es dir gut?
Woman 5:	Nein, leider geht es mir heute nicht so gut.

Answers

1D, 2C, 3B, 4A, 5E

Spiel: HipHop   E

A game called **HipHop** could be played to practise asking for and stating names. The game requires a large space without obstacles where students can run without hurting themselves, such as a hall or the playground.

All stand in a circle. The teacher stands in the middle and initiates the game.

If the teacher shouts **HIP!** and points at a student, this student has to ask the player on his / her right: **Wie heißt du?** The person on the right has to respond in German.

If the teacher shouts **HOP!** and points at a student, this student has to ask the player on his / her left: **Wie heißt du?** The person on the left has to respond in German.

If the teacher shouts **HIP HOP!** all students swap places as quickly as they can.

Once the game is established a student can take over the role of caller. When the caller shouts **HIP HOP!** he / she grabs another player who then becomes caller.

If the game is to be played in a restricted space like a classroom you could omit the swapping places element!

4   Schreib was und sag was!

This is a simple writing and speaking exercise to familiarise the students with the expressions and the characters.

Answers

1	Das ist Heinz.	3	Das Matthias.
2	Das ist David.	4	Das ist Yasemin.

5   Hör zu und schreib was! Wie heißt du?   E

This listening exercise is designed to consolidate existing vocabulary and to introduce other, more formal, phrases. It is also useful to practise the spelling of German names.

Transcript

1

Matthias:	Hallo, wie heißt du?
Laura:	Hallo. Ich heiße Laura. Laura Miller.

2

Matthias:	Hallo, wie heißt du?
Pia:	Hallo. Ich bin Pia Klein.

3

Matthias:	Guten Morgen. Wie heißen Sie?
Frau Klein:	Ich bin Frau Klein. Mein Vorname ist Elisabeth. Mein Nachname ist Klein.

4

Matthias:	Guten Tag. Wie heißen Sie?
Herr Schuh:	Guten Tag. Ich bin Herr Schuh. Herr Martin Schuh.

5

Matthias:	Hallo, wie heißt du?
Heinz:	Hallo. Ich heiße Heinz. Mein Nachname ist Schuh.

Answers

	Vorname	Nachname
1	Laura	Miller
2	Pia	Klein
3	Elisabeth	Klein
4	Martin	Schuh
5	Heinz	Schuh

Sprachtipp

du and Sie

It is important that students grasp the basic concept of polite vs. familiar forms. They should address the teacher and other adults in polite language. Model dialogues could be practised: students could practise in pairs taking turns to role play the characters from the cartoon, their own parents, celebrities or even other teachers.

6   Hör zu! Wie heißt du? oder Wie heißen Sie?   E

This exercise consolidates the **Sprachtipp** by giving a scenario where a French boy, Pierre, muddles up **du** and **Sie**. It is important that the students realise that this is a mistake which is easy to make, and that they have to be careful if they visit a German-speaking country. Although adults are generally sympathetic if they make a mistake, it is always worthwhile knowing the correct way to address someone!

Transcript

Pierre:	Hallo! Ich bin Pierre. Ich komme zur Party.
Frau Schuh:	Guten Abend. Wie heißt du?
Pierre:	Ich heiße Pierre. Und wie heißt du?
Frau Schuh:	Ich bin Frau Schuh, Heinz' Mutter.
Pierre:	Wie geht es dir, Frau Schuh?
Frau Schuh:	Hier ist Heinz.
Heinz:	Hallo Pierre. Sagst du 'Du' zu meiner Mutter?
Pierre:	Ja. Ist das nicht richtig?
Heinz:	Nein! Das ist falsch. Du sagst 'Frau Schuh' und 'Sie'.
Pierre:	Oh, entschuldigung, Frau Schuh!
Frau Schuh:	Macht nichts.
Herr Schuh:	Hallo! Wer ist denn das?
Pierre:	Ich bin Pierre. Und wer bist du . . .
Heinz:	Sie! Wer sind Sie!!!
Pierre:	Ach ja! Wer sind Sie?
Herr Schuh:	Ich bin Herr Schuh, Heinz' Vater.
Pierre:	Wie geht es dir – Nein! Wie geht es <u>Ihnen</u>, Herr Schuh?
Herr Schuh:	Danke, gut.

Answers

1 Pierre uses **du** to Mrs Schuh.
2 He should have used **Sie**, because she is an adult and someone he does not know.

7 Quiz: Wie heißen Sie?   E

This exercise can be done as a homework activity involving friends and family, since the students themselves may not know everybody featured. Otherwise, the teacher may give them the names but let them find out which picture they belong to by using the library or the Internet.

Apart from the obvious use as a cue for formal questions and answers (written and spoken), it serves as an introduction to German culture by making students aware of some famous Germans.

It is possible to extend this exercise by encouraging students to collect more information about these and other prominent figures from German-speaking countries.

If they have access to the Internet, the full names of the celebrities will suffice as search words in most big search engines to lead them to a large number of fan pages for actors and football stars etc. Search engines such as 'Altavista' allow the searcher to enter the language they want the information in.

Aussprache •

Students should be aware of the necessity of good pronunciation in order to be understood. The **ch** sound is very important, as it does not sound like the English 'ch'.

Hör zu und wiederhole!

This exercise may be used in a language lab or as a chant.

Transcript

Ich – nicht – schlecht – sprechen
Nacht – acht – Sprache – Mittwoch – Buch

8 Hör zu! Das Alphabet

Students should be encouraged to pronounce the letters after the speaker.

Transcript

A B C D E F G H I J K L M N O P Q R S T U V W X Y Z
ä ö ü ß

9 Hör zu! Lied: ABC

This song is available on tape and should be practised with the class to help memorise the letters. If the teachers or the students can play and have access to a musical instrument, they may also play the song themselves.

Transcript

ABCD
EFGH
IJKL
MNOP
QRST
UVW
XYZ!

Aussprache •

This item introduces 3 letters which often cause confusion: A, E and I and explains the correct pronunciation of these letters.

PCM 1.5   Das Alphabet

This sheet, can be used as an OHT or photocopied for the students to draw and colour in.

The students will not have met all these words, but with your help, they can illustrate the word, or colour the ones that are already drawn in. This is a good way to start vocabulary-building skills. It can also be used for pronunciation practice and to expand the students' vocabulary. For more able pupils it also practises gender and encourages students to always learn words with the **der / die / das**.

Students could be further encouraged to draw their own alphabet for wall display, tracing from the master copy. More able students may wish to make up their own, using a dictionary! They could be given the imaginary task of making up an alphabet booklet for a Kindergarten class in Germany. If your school has a link with a German school, the students may be able to send their alphabets to the school to distribute to small children. Alternatively, contact the Goethe Institute (see useful addresses on the Anstoß website: www.anstoss.co.uk) and ask if there are any primary schools in your area where children are studying German.

10　Hör zu! Am Telefon

This listening exercise practises the alphabet and introduces a few useful classroom expressions. Students should be encouraged to spell their own names and to play spelling games, such as 'hangman'. As an extension activity students could be encouraged to write out their own telephone conversations with a partner.

> **Transcript**
> A: Hallo?
> B: Hallo! Ist das Lebowski? Janina Lebowski?
> A: Wie bitte?
> B: Ist das Janina Lebowski?
> A: Levinski?
> B: Wie bitte? Nein, Lebowski!
> A: Wie schreibt man das?
> B: L – E – B – O – W – S – K – I.
> A: Und der Vorname?
> B: Janina, J – A – N – I – N – A.
> A: Entschuldigung. Langsamer bitte.
> B: J – A – N – I – N – A.
> A: Aha, ich wiederhole: Vorname: J – A – N – I – N – A, Nachname L – E – B – O – W – S – K – I. Richtig?
> B　Ja, das ist richtig. Janina Lebowski.
> A: Und wie heißen Sie?
> B: Ich?
> A: Ja, Sie.
> B: Ich heiße Mustafa Atatürk.
> A: Entschuldigung. Wie schreibt man das bitte?
> B: Einen Moment: M – U – S – T – A – F – A. Das ist der Vorname. Und mein Nachname ist Atatürk: A – T – A – T – U – Umlaut – R – K.

> A: Ich wiederhole: M – U – S – T – A – F – A, und dann A – T – A – T – U – Umlaut – R – K. Ist das richtig?
> B: Ja, das stimmt.
> A: Herr Atatürk, was kann ich für Sie tun?
> B: Ich möchte mit Janina Lebowski sprechen.
> A: Ach so. Janina Lebowski ist nicht hier. Hier ist Gertrude Hinterhuber.
> B: Hinterhuber? Wie schreibt man das? . . . . . .

Answers
1　JANINA　　　LEBOWSKI
2　MUSTAFA　　ATATÜRK

Spiel: Buchstabentanz　　E

The game **Buchstabentanz** could be played as an extension activity. The game is best played in a large space without obstacles where students can 'dance' without hurting themselves, such as a hall or the playground. The game is similar to musical chairs.

Students have to dance as long as the music plays. When the music stops the teacher shouts out a letter of the alphabet. All students have to sit down except for those whose name begins with that letter. Anyone who makes a mistake is 'out' and could help the teacher identify others who hesitate as the game speeds up. The winner is the last person left in the game!

Vokabeltipp　Wie schreibt man das?

Since the aim is to use as much German in class as possible, some basic classroom phrases have been summarised here. It may be useful to create big posters with such phrases and to put them up on the walls. Students should be encouraged to use these phrases. A photocopiable master (Im Klassenzimmer, PCM 1.6) is also available in Section 2 and includes other useful classroom commands.

PCM 1.6　Im Klassenzimmer

You may like to use these instructions as wall or OHP display items or give them to the students as reference material.

11　Partnerarbeit. Du bist dran: Sag was!

This item encourages students to ask other students their names in a weave, pair or group activity.

12 Gruppenarbeit: Autos   **A**

This exercise can be exploited as project work. Students can look for pictures of these cars in magazines or access the companies' web sites. They should be encouraged to compare the difference between the German and the English pronunciation e.g. VW. These are easily accessible via the main search engines by typing in the name of the maker, or type of car e.g. VW, BMW, Porsche, Rover, Bentley, Mercedes.

 Deutsche Autos

This box gives the current Internet addresses for the German car manufacturers listed.

13 Schreib was! Dialog   **E**

This exercise will stretch more advanced students and provide a nice written summary.

Answers

1   Tag
2   heißt
3   Ich
4   wie
5   heiße
6   das
7   schreibt
8   Ich
9   geht
10   Danke
11   es
12   Prima
13   Auf
14   tschüs
15   bald

Einheit C   Wo wohnst du?

Unit 1C will introduce:
- *simple phrases for discussing where students live*
- *basic geography and information about German-speaking countries*
- *verb endings*

PCMs 1.7 – 1.12 accompany this section.

1   Lies den Cartoon und hör zu! Die Geburtstagsparty (3)

The story continues and will be exploited in subsequent exercises. Students will be able to speculate on what happens next.

Transcript

Matthias:	Hallo! Ich bin der Matthias. Und wie heißt du?
Laura:	Ich heiße Laura.
Matthias:	Wohnst du in Mainz?
Laura:	Nein, Ich wohne in Balerno. Das ist in Schottland. In der Nähe von Edinburg. Ich bin Schottin! Und wo wohnst du?
Matthias:	Ich komme aus Österreich, aus Salzburg. Ich wohne jetzt in Mainz.
Laura:	Oh! . . . Wo ist Salzburg?
Matthias:	Das ist im Westen von Österreich.
Matthias:	Heinz macht Musik. Willst du tanzen, Laura?
Laura:	Wie bitte? Was heißt „tanzen" auf Englisch?
Matthias:	„Tanzen" heißt 'dancing'!
Laura:	Jaaaa! Bitte.

2   Partnerarbeit: Laura und Matthias

Can also be used as a listening exercise and a cue for role plays in conjunction with the related **Vokabeltipp**.

Answers

Name	Stadt	Land
Laura	Balerno	Schottland
Matthias	Salzburg	Österreich

 Vokabeltipp

This item introduces the key questions and answers of this unit. It can be exploited at various levels – as a simple Reading / Speaking exercise for the 'core' language and as an extension activity for those students who are able to work out how to say 'north', 'east' etc.

PCM 1.7 Partnerarbeit: Sag was! Mach' ein Interview!

This item encourages the students to take part in simple role play conversations, based on the vocabulary introduced so far.

PCM 1.8 Europa

Photocopiable map of Europe, with names in German. This can be used as a handy reference tool.

3 Woher kommen sie?

This exercise exploits the information given in the **Kulturtipp** box.

Answers

Name	Stadt	Land
Daniela	Berlin	Deutschland
Johann	Wien	Österreich
Maria	Bern	Schweiz
Steffi	Vaduz	Liechtenstein

4 Gruppenarbeit: Ortsnamen

Students will probably come up with many different answers. Here are just a few suggestions:

Köln – Cologne; München – Munich; Basel – Basle; Schwarzwald – Black Forest.

This exercise can also be exploited for spelling practice or as a timed game where teams compete to find the places named by the teacher or the opposing team.

Students might come across older maps of Germany still showing East Germany as a separate country. You may want to give a very brief history of the reunification in 1989. Here are some key dates and events:

8 / 5 / 1945	End of 2nd World War. USA, USSR, France and Great Britain entered Germany as 'occupying forces'.
23 / 5 / 1949	**Bundesrepublik Deutschland** was founded. People had a free vote.
7 / 10 / 1949	**Deutsche Demokratische Republik** was founded. People could only vote for one party. More and more East Germans moved to the West.

13 / 8 / 1961	The Berlin Wall was erected literally overnight as a barrier between two parts of the city. The wall was patrolled by heavily armed guards. It was to remain there for 28 years.
In the 1980s	Gorbatschow was introducing 'Glasnost' and 'Perestroika' to Russia. The East Germans campaigned for more freedom.
Autumn 1989	Many East Germans left the country by pretending to take a holiday in Hungary.
9 / 10 / 1989	The Berlin Wall fell.
18 / 3 / 1990	There were free elections in East Germany.
3 / 10 / 1990	Re-unification of Germany.

You may wish to tell the students about the two key words used to describe the fall of the Berlin Wall:

die Wiedervereinigung and **die Wende**, and to show pictures of that historical time.

As an extension exercise, students could be asked to choose a major German city (or German-speaking country) and collect information / pictures from travel brochures or the Internet to create colourful classroom displays.

Kulturtipp Deutschsprachige Länder

The maps are to be used to encourage the students to be aware of the countries where German is spoken, as well as for them to learn how to say where they come from.

5 Sag was! Partnerarbeit: Wo ist . . . A

This is a speaking exercise consolidating the language just learned. Students have to 'hunt' for the places on the map. Students should work in groups.

Answers

1 München ist im Süden von Deutschland.
2 Wien ist im Osten von Österreich.
3 Zürich ist im Norden der Schweiz.
4 Berlin ist im Osten von Deutschland.
5 Hamburg ist im Norden von Deutschland.
6 Köln ist im Westen von Deutschland.
7 Graz ist im Osten / Süden von Österreich.
8 Salzburg ist im Westen von Österreich.
9 Basel ist im Norden der Schweiz.
10 Bern ist im Westen der Schweiz.

6 Hör zu! Wo wohnt er? Wo wohnt sie?

This exercise consolidates the students' cultural knowledge. It can be used in the language lab as an independent activity. The object of the activity is to allow students to 'explore' where other towns are. Pia, Yasemin and Matthias all now live in Mainz.

Transcript

1 Das ist Heinz. Er wohnt in Mainz. Mainz ist eine Stadt im Westen von Deutschland, in der Nähe von Frankfurt.

2 Das ist Pia. Sie wohnt in Greifswald. Das ist im Nord-Osten von Deutschland.

3 Das ist Matthias. Er kommt aus Salzburg. Das ist im Westen von Österreich.

4 Das ist Yasemin. Sie wohnt in Bremen. Das ist im Norden von Deutschland, in der Nähe von Hamburg.

Answers

1 Heinz wohnt in Mainz. Mainz ist eine Stadt im Westen von Deutschland, in der Nähe von Frankfurt.

2 Pia wohnt in Greifswald. Das ist im Nord-Osten von Deutschland.

3 Matthias kommt aus Salzburg. Das ist im Westen von Österreich.

4 Yasemin wohnt in Bremen. Das ist im Norden von Deutschland, in der Nähe von Hamburg.

PCM 1.9 Hör zu! Wo wohnen sie?

This item encourages students to link place names and countries.

Transcript
Eins
Woman: Hallo! Ich heiße Ursel! Ich wohne in Bern. Das ist eine Stadt in der Schweiz. Ich bin Schweizerin.

Zwei
Man: Guten Tag! Ich heiße Alexis. Ich komme aus Athen. Das ist die Hauptstadt von Griechenland. Ich bin Grieche.

Drei
Woman: Hi! Ich bin Joyce. Ich komme aus Seattle. Das ist im Westen der USA. Ich bin Amerikanerin.

Vier
Boy: Hallo! Mein Name ist Liam. Ich komme aus Leeds in England. Ich bin britisch.

Fünf
Woman: Guten Morgen! Ich heiße Magda. Ich wohne in Warschau. Ich komme aus Polen. Zu Hause spreche ich Polnisch.

Sechs
Man: Tag! Ich bin Pieter. Ich wohne in Amsterdam. Das ist die Hauptstadt der Niederlande. Ich komme aus den Niederlanden.

Answers
1 F ii **2** C iv **3** E vi **4** D i **5** B v **6** A iii

7 Sag was! Du bist dran! Wo wohnst du?

To be used in conjunction with the photocopiable master of the UK. As an extension activity students could be asked to arrange themselves according to the distance they live away from the school or the distance to their birthplace (**Woher kommst du?**). Students could also prepare their own written summary about themselves and then make a file of the whole class.

PCM 1.10 Großbritannien

Photocopiable map of the British Isles, with names in German. This can be used as a handy reference tool.

Spiel: Landsleute

As an additional activity students could play the game **Landsleute**.

Each player should be given a card with the name of a country. There can be several cards for each country: e.g 5 × Deutschland, 5 × Großbritannien, 5 × Österreich, etc.

Cards should be shuffled and then one given to each student. Students have to look at the card to see which country they have and then put the card face down on the table, so that the others cannot see. Then they have to look for their fellow countrymen by asking everyone in the class: „Woher kommst du?" All questions and answers must be in German. The game ends when everyone has found their countrymen and the country is 'united'.

Vokabeltipp Länder

This item should be used in conjunction with the photocopiable map of Europe. When students practise telling each other where they come from they may need some additional vocabulary, such as **Pakistan**, **Indien**, etc. As an extension activity you could ask students to try and find as many famous people as they can who come from Germany, France, Italy etc.

PCM 1.11   Spiel: Wortsuche   A

This item is a fun way of reinforcing the names of the countries. Students should be encouraged to write down the names of the countries they find.

Answers
(horizontal)
Deutschland (row 1)
England (r. 5)
Italien (r.6)
Niederlande (r.11, backwards)
(vertical)
Spanien (column 3)
Schweiz (c.5)
Irland (c.8)
Frankreich (c.12, backwards)
(diagonal)
Polen (c.6, r.3)

8   Hör zu! Hallo!

As an extension activity, students could be asked to make up the questions that precede these statements.

Transcript
1 Yasemin:
Hallo, ich heiße Yasemin Akbar.
Das schreibt man Y A S E M I N, A K B A R.
Ich komme aus der Türkei. Ich bin Türkin.
Aber jetzt wohne ich in Deutschland. Ich wohne in Bremen.

2 Pierre:
Guten Tag, ich bin Pierre Didier.
Das schreibt man P I E R R E, D I D I E R.
Ich bin Franzose.
Ich wohne in Tours. Das ist in der Mitte von Frankreich.

Answers

Vorname	Yasemin	**Vorname**	Pierre
Nachname	Akbar	**Nachname**	Didier
Nationalität	Türkin	**Nationalität**	Franzose
Wohnort	Bremen	**Wohnort**	Tours

9   Quiz: Deutschsprachige Länder   E

If the teacher has access to any authentic materials from these countries, such as coins or pictures, this may be a good point to introduce them. This is also a good time to inform the students that the euro is the currency in Germany and Austria, but the Swiss have kept the Swiss franc as the English have kept the pound – for the moment.

	Deutschland	**Österreich**	**die Schweiz**	**Liechtenstein**
Map	Berlin	Wien	Bern	Vaduz
Flag				
Capital	Berlin	Wien	Bern	Vaduz
Currency	Euro	Euro	Franken	Franken
Language(s)	Deutsch	Deutsch	Deutsch	Deutsch
			Französisch	
			Italienisch	

Vokabeltipp Sprichst du Deutsch?

This item provides helpful constructions for students.

10 Quiz: Woher kommt das Auto? Buchstabiere!   **E**

This activity practises the countries.

Answers

D	Deutschland
A	Österreich
CH	Schweiz
F	Frankreich
I	Italien
GB	Großbritannien

Note: here are some useful internet sites for German-speaking countries and cities:

Tourism in Germany (in English)
    http://www.germany-tourism.de
Berlin website with virtual sightseeing
    http://www.berlin-info.de
City guide to Munich
    http://www.muenchen-tourist.de
City guide to Mainz
    http://www.uni-mainz.de/UniInfo/Stadt
Tourism in Austria (in English)(good photos)
    http://www.austria-tourism.at
Lots of useful links about Vienna and Austria
    http://www.magwien.gv.at

PCM 1.12   Spiel: Wo ist die Party?   **E**

This activity is available on a photocopiable master and gives the more able students practice in using the signs to achieve a goal.

Answer
Students should arrive at Heinz' house.

Sprachtipp

This item explains the grammar point used in Ex 11.

11 Schreib was!

This item encourages the student to look back at what he / she has read to practise the present tense of verbs.

Answers
1 Ich heiße Laura.
2 Wohnst du in Mainz?
3 Nein, ich wohne in Balerno.
4 Ich komme aus Österreich.

12 Schreib was! Verben   **E**

This item gives further practise of the verbs given in the chapter.

Answers
1 Ich komme aus Wien.
2 Er heißt Pierre.
3 Ich wohne in Basel.
4 Du kommst aus Schottland.
5 Sie heißt Pia.
6 Wie heißt du?
7 Heinz wohnt in Mainz.
8 Matthias kommt aus Österreich.
9 Laura wohnt in Balerno.
10 Yasemin kommt aus Deutschland.

13 Partnerarbeit: Sag was! Ein Interview   **E**

This exercise uses the questions introduced in this section. Students may need to revise the phrases beforehand. Some students may need to see the phrases written on an OHT or on the board. More able students can make up their own cards, using either known celebrities or fictitious characters.

Leseseiten

These colourful postcards give the students a different approach to the vocabulary introduced in the chapter, plus a little more besides. The students should be encouraged to match up the postcard and the picture of the town from which they are writing. They will be gradually introduced to more and more 'real' situations as the book progresses.

Aussagesätze and **Grammatik**

These pages are useful quick references for students working alone or in pairs – on a classwork or homework assignment. They are also useful for revision purposes, as they sum up the important grammar and vocabulary of the chapter.

Kapitel 2 Wir lernen uns kennen

Zahlen und Daten

Unit 2A will introduce:
- *numbers 1-31*
- *the months and the seasons*
- *giving your age and stating your birthday*
- *stating your telephone number*

PCMs 2.1 – 2.5 accompany this section.

1 Lies den Cartoon und hör zu! Die Telefonnummer

This cartoon serves as a first introduction to numbers and giving your telephone number in German. The subsequent exercises exploit this vocabulary. The students can speculate about the story: will Laura ring Matthias? What does Matthias think of Laura? Who is the blonde girl?

Transcript

Matthias:	Heinz ist gut!
Laura:	Und du tanzt gut, Matthias!
Matthias:	Das ist mein Handy. Einen Moment, Laura!
Matthias: (on phone)	Matthias Hasler! Hallo, Anna. Ja, okay! – Tschüs!
Frau Schuh:	Hallo Laura und David! Eure Mutter ist da!
Laura:	Oh je! Wie ist deine Telefonnummer?
Matthias:	Meine Nummer ist 0173 – 334 76 76. Ruf mich an, okay?
Laura:	Ja! Tschüs, bis bald!

2 Partnerarbeit. Wie sagt man das auf Deutsch?

This exercise exploits the key words used in the unit.

Answers
Wie ist deine Telefonnummer?
Meine Nummer ist . . .

Vokabeltipp Telefonnummern

This tip reminds the students about formal and informal language and shows them how you ask for a telephone number.

Vokabeltipp Die Zahlen

This is also available on tape for chants and language lab work. The numbers are extremely useful for pronunciation practice as they contain many important sounds, notably "**ie**" and "**ei**" (see below).

Transcript
null / eins / zwei / drei / vier / fünf / sechs / sieben / acht / neun / zehn / elf / zwölf / dreizehn / vierzehn / fünfzehn / sechzehn / siebzehn / achtzehn / neunzehn / zwanzig / einundzwanzig / zweiundzwanzig / dreiundzwanzig / vierundzwanzig / fünfundzwanzig / sechsundzwanzig / siebenundzwanzig / achtundzwanzig / neunundzwanzig / dreißig

Aussprache •

Pass auf! It is important to practise the difference between "**ie**" and "**ei**" sounds early to avoid interference from English. The numbers in the following exercise are an ideal opportunity to do so!

3 Hör zu! ie oder ei?

This item practises the difference between "**ie**" and "**ei**" pointed out in the **Sprachtipp**.

Transcript
Eins, sieben, drei, vier, sie, Frankreich, Wien, Rhein, Österreich, kein, Auf Wiedersehen, Wie, heißt, nein, hier.

4 Sag was! Wie viele?

The objective of this exercise is to practise saying the numbers. It is not the intention to practise plurals here – these will come later.

5 Hör zu! Die Fußballergebnisse   **A**

If internet access is available, students could be encouraged to download and print out images from some of the German clubs mentioned in the table or to find out what colour their shirts are.

Useful Searchwords: **Fußballbundesliga, DFB**

Transcript
Und hier die Fußballergebnisse:
Spiel 1:   FC Bayern München gegen Borussia Dortmund eins zu null.

Spiel 2: Schalke 04 gegen Kaiserslautern zwei zu eins.

Spiel 3: Herta BSC Berlin gegen Leverkusen unentschieden eins zu eins.

Spiel 4: MSV Duisburg gegen den FC Hansa Rostock drei zu null.

Spiel 5: SV Werder Bremen: VfB Stuttgart vier zu zwei.

Answers

Spiel 1	1:0		Spiel 4	3:0
Spiel 2	2:1		Spiel 5	4:2
Spiel 3	1:1			

6 Hör zu! Die Rakete **A**

This is a launch countdown which can either be chanted by students standing in a circle or sitting at a table. If possible, students start to chant the numbers crouching down low. After **null** (zero) they all drum on the tables or slap their knees faster and faster, making launching noises until the rocket takes off. Everybody jumps up, with their hands in the air shouting: **Jaaaaa!!!** As an alternative the students could start off counting very softly and then gradually increase the sound until they reach **null – Jaaaaa!**

Transcript
Starte die Rakete
zehn, neun, acht, sieben, sechs, fünf, vier, drei, zwei, eins, null – Jaaaaa!

7 Partnerarbeit: Sag was **E**

This task is best performed with a partner, where one asks the questions and the other answers. It can also be done as an individual task, or be exploited for further extension activities – the teacher reads out a number and the student writes it down.

8 Gruppenarbeit: Nationale Telefonnummern **E**

This task encourages practical research skills. Students can find country codes in the telephone directory (international codes) or from directory enquiries international numbers (153). Students should be told to ask permission before ringing this service as it is not free of charge! You may also wish to discuss the cost of international calls vs. local calls.

Answers

Germany – 0049	Switzerland – 0041	Mainz – 0049-6131
Austria – 0043	Bremen – 421	Salzburg – 0043-662

Vokabeltipp **Wie alt bist du?**

This tip introduces the vocabulary for giving your age.

9 Hör zu! Wie alt ist . . . ? **A**

This activity provides more practice with numbers in the form of giving your age.

Transcript

Frau Schuh:	Guten Tag, Frau Osman.
Frau Osman:	Guten Tag, Frau Schuh. Herzlichen Glückwunsch zum Geburtstag!
Frau Schuh:	Danke!
Frau Osman:	Wie alt sind Sie denn?
Frau Schuh:	Ich bin 31, und Sie?
Frau Osman:	Mein Geburtstag ist am 6. Januar. Ich bin 30 Jahre alt.
David:	Herzlichen Glückwunsch zum Geburtstag, Matthias. Wie alt bist du heute?
Matthias:	Ich bin 16. Und wie alt bist du, David?
David:	Ich bin 14 Jahre alt. Mein Geburtstag ist am 9. August.

Answers

1	Frau Schuh?	Sie ist 31 (Jahre alt.)
2	Frau Osman?	Sie ist 30 (Jahre alt.)
3	Matthias?	Er ist 16 (Jahre alt.)
4	David?	Er ist 14 (Jahre alt.)

Vokabeltipp **Das Datum**

This tip introduces the numbers required for dates. Teachers should stress that the numbers listed here are really just the numbers they have already learned + **-ten** / **-sten** and that there is really not too much to learn.

10 Hör zu! Lied: Monate

The song practises the months of the year. Students could sing / clap along with the song and stand up when they hear the month they are born in.

Transcript
Wann ist dein Geburtstag? Wie alt bist du?
Wann bist du geboren? Wie alt bist du?

Im Januar, im Januar –
steh auf, steh auf, steh auf!
Im Februar, im Februar –
steh auf, steh auf, steh auf!

Wann ist dein Geburtstag? Wie alt bist du?
Wann bist du geboren? Wie alt bist du?

Im März, im März –
steh auf, steh auf, steh auf!
Im April, im April –
steh auf, steh auf, steh auf!

Wann ist dein Geburtstag? Wie alt bist du?
Wann bist du geboren? Wie alt bist du?

Im Mai, im Mai –
steh auf, steh auf, steh auf!
Im Juni, im Juni –
steh auf, steh auf, steh auf!

Wann ist dein Geburtstag? Wie alt bist du?
Wann bist du geboren? Wie alt bist du?

Im Juli, im Juli –
steh auf, steh auf, steh auf!
Im August, im August –
steh auf, steh auf, steh auf!

Wann ist dein Geburtstag? Wie alt bist du?
Wann bist du geboren? Wie alt bist du?

Im September, im September –
steh auf, steh auf, steh auf!
Im Oktober, im Oktober –
steh auf, steh auf, steh auf!

Wann ist dein Geburtstag? Wie alt bist du?
Wann bist du geboren? Wie alt bist du?

Im November, im November –
steh auf, steh auf, steh auf!
Im Dezember, im Dezember –
steh auf, steh auf, steh auf!

Vokabeltipp Die Monate

Encourage the students to look at the similarities to the English months:

- 4 are the same: April, August, September and November
- 2 lose one letter at the end: Januar und Februar
- 5 have only one letter different: Mai, Juni, Juli, Oktober and Dezember

but it is a good idea to compare the differences in pronunciation.

Kulturtipp Die Monate

Here you could discuss differences between English-speaking countries:

e.g. the word "purse" means a handbag to an American.

Ask them if they can think of words that are only used in their local area.

Vokabeltipp Mein Geburtstag

This tip gives further advice on the formal and informal expressions.

---

11 Sag was! Wann hast du Geburtstag?

An opportunity for the students to say when their birthday is.

---

12 Quiz: Wann ist Ihr Geburtstag?

This exercise introduces the difference between my birthday is . . . and your (formal) birthday is . . . but it can be exploited in various ways – for instance as a reading comprehension, where the students have to write the date of each person's birthday in number format.

Answers

Einstein: 14. März 1879   Schiffer: 25. August 1970
Schumacher: 3. Januar 1969   Graf: 14. Juni 1969

---

13 Hör zu! Lied: Geburtstagslied   A

Most students will know the Happy Birthday tune and they will be now be able to sing this one whenever a member of the class has a birthday. Students are often keen to sing Happy Birthday as they usually are familiar with the tune. It also introduces **"Viel Glück"**.

Transcript
Zum Geburtstag viel Glück!
Zum Geburtstag viel Glück!
Zum Geburtstag, lieber Heinz
Zum Geburtstag viel Glück!

PCM 2.1   Schreib was! Wann haben sie   E
Geburtstag?

Answers
1   Helga hat am zwölften April Geburtstag.
2   Andreas hat am siebten Dezember Geburtstag.
3   Susanne hat am ersten Mai Geburtstag.
4   Peter hat am dreiundzwanzigsten August Geburtstag.
5   Maria hat am einunddreißigsten Juni Geburtstag.
6   Jan hat am siebten Juli Geburtstag.

PCM 2.2   Was passt zusammen?   E

This is a simple matching exercise, making full use of the key expressions learned.

Answers
1   Wie geht es dir?   J   Mir geht es gut.
2   Woher kommst du?   D   Ich komme aus der Schweiz.

3	Wo wohnst du?	A	Ich wohne in Hamburg.
4	Wie heißt du?	C	Ich heiße Hannah.
5	Wo ist das?	F	Das ist im Süden von Österreich.
6	Wie alt bist du?	B	Ich bin 11 Jahre alt.
7	Wie heißen Sie?	G	Ich bin Frau Meier.
8	Wann ist dein Geburtstag?	I	Am 12. Februar
9	Wie ist deine Telefonnummer?	E	Meine Nummer ist 23 66 98.
10	Sprechen Sie Deutsch?	H	Ja, ein bisschen.

PCM 2.3 Hör zu! Mein Geburtstagskalender   E

Here students have to listen carefully in order to match the names with the correct months. This item practises the months of the year and also prepares students for GCSE-style questions.

Transcript

Im Januar und November sind gar keine Geburtstage bei uns in der Familie. Im Oktober und Dezember sind auch keine Geburtstage.

Oma Gitta hat im Februar Geburtstag.

Und Oma Birte hat im Mai Geburtstag.

Meine Mutter und meine Freundin Eva sind beide im September geboren.

Mein Vater und mein Opa haben im selben Monat Geburtstag: Beide im April.

Mein Bruder Steffen hat im März Geburtstag. Hassan ist auch im März geboren.

Im Juni ist Tante Lubas Geburtstag, aber im Juli hat keiner Geburtstag.

Sascha und Timo sind im selben Monat geboren wie ich. Wir haben alle drei im August Geburtstag.

Ja, mein Geburtstag ist am 19. August, Saschas ist am 22. August und Timo hat am 27. 8. Geburtstag!

Answers

Januar	—
Februar	Oma Gitta
März	Steffen, Hassan
April	Papa, Opa
Mai	Oma Birte
Juni	Luba
Juli	—
August	Sascha, Timo, ich
September	Mama, Eva
Oktober	—
November	—
Dezember	—

Spiel: Zwillinge   A

In order to practise asking for and stating birthdays, the game **Zwillinge** could be used as an additional activity. The game is best played in an open space, like a hall or playground, however it could be played in a confined space like a classroom if students are allowed to ask questions in turn, rather than walking around the room.

You will need to prepare sufficient pairs of cards for the number of students in the class. If there is an odd number of students, make one set of three cards and explain that there is one set of **Drillinge** (triplets). Write one birthday on each pair of cards (e.g. 2 × **2. Juli**, 2 × **5. März**, etc.). Shuffle all the cards and give one to each student.

All students then must try to find their **Zwilling**, i.e. the person who has been given the same birthday as themselves. The phrases needed are:

Wann hast du Geburtstag?   **Mein Geburtstag ist am . . . .**

The game is over when everyone has paired up.

Vokabeltipp Die Jahreszeiten   A

The seasons are brought in here mainly for passive use, but you may wish to exploit the words for wall displays based on the weather appropriate for each season.

PCM 2.4 Schreib was! Jahreszeiten und Monate   A

This is an additional activity which gives students of all abilities a chance to revise the spelling of the months of the year.

PCM 2.5 Schreib was! Haben oder sein?   E

This item revises the 2 very important verbs "haben" and "sein".

Answers

1	hast	5	bist
2	ist	6	habe
3	ist	7	hat
4	ist	8	bist

14 Sag was! Heinz und Band auf Tour   E

This involves more practice with dates and a more challenging speaking activity. It could also be used as a writing activity for the more able.

Answers

1 Am neunundzwanzigsten Februar
2 Am zweiten März

3 Am siebzehnten März
4 Am fünfzehnten März
5 Am zehnten März
6 Am fünften März
7 Am dritten März

 Deutsche Musik – Charts und Tourdaten

The internet addresses could be used to discuss the number of American / English songs in the German charts and to further practise pronunciation and dates.

15 Hör zu! Die Top Ten in Deutschland   E

Top Ten is actually the word used by young people in Germany. The German term **Hitparade** is reserved for more traditional **Schlagermusik**.

Students may want to write their own Top Ten modelled on this recording. They could either use fictitious songs and musicians or the current chart hits or even their own favourites.

Transcript

Guten Abend! Und hier die Top Ten aus Deutschland vom 8. September.
Auf dem zehnten Platz – Die Doofen mit *Wie heißt du?*
Auf dem neunten Platz ist Marlene mit *Hallo Hubert!*
Auf Platz acht – Die Mädchenband mit dem Lied *Ich und du.*
Auf dem siebten Platz – Tik-Tak-Toe mit *Bis bald, Alter.*
Auf Platz sechs – Heinz und Freunde – *Die Nummer Eins.*
Auf Platz fünf ist die Deutsch – Englische Freundschaft mit *Sprichst du Deutsch?*
Auf Platz vier – Berlin Boys mit *A – L – I Ali.*
Auf dem dritten Platz – Die toten Hosen mit *Im Norden ist es kalt.*
Auf dem zweiten Platz – Herbert und Hubert – *Ich weiß nicht.*
Und ganz oben auf dem ersten Platz – die Joe Doll Band mit *Anstoß!*

Answers
Datum: 8. September

Platz	Musiker(in)
10	Die Doofen
6	Heinz und Freunde
1	Joe Doll Band
5	Deutsch-Englische Freundschaft
3	Die toten Hosen
2	Herbert und Hubert
7	Tik-Tak-Toe
4	Berlin Boys
8	Die Mädchenband
9	Marlene

16 Hör zu! Lotto   E

In Germany the national lottery has existed for much longer than in Britain and is very popular. Many people play regularly. The drawing of the numbers is transmitted on national television just like in Britain. This could lead to a discussion of the pros and cons of lotteries and the similarities / differences to British lottery slips.

The teacher needs to be aware that certain religions do not approve of the lottery. A sensitive approach is obviously called for (depending on who is in the class).

The students could also draw their own Bingo cards. The teacher or other students can draw numbers from a hat. Alternatively a large board with numbers (e.g. 1–30 / 40 / 50 etc) can be used to test the student's knowledge of the numbers!

Transcript and Answers
Die Lottozahlen für Samstag, den 28.9.
4, 13, 1, 30, 27, 18 Zusatzzahl: 11

17 / 18   Eine E-mail aus Deutschland   E

The writing task should be modelled closely on the 'received' e-mail. If the school has links to any German schools, similar e-mails / letters could be exchanged between schools.

Answers
Vorname:	Katja
Nachname:	Heller
Stadt:	Regensburg
Land:	Deutschland
Alter:	12
Geburtstag:	26. Juni
E-mail-Adresse:	K.Heller@abc.co.de

19 Lied: Der Heinz- und Pia-Rap

This song is mainly intended to help the students to remember the important words and phrases introduced up to now. It contains the core phrases of the first two chapters set to music. Students could be encouraged to sing or to clap along. An instrumental version of this song has been provided. Students can write their own rap or change words / expressions. They could for instance insert their own names, ages and towns e.g. „Hallo, Guten Tag, ich bin die Jenny. Ich bin die Jenny Jones, und wie heißt du?"

Transcript

Heinz:	Hallo, Guten Tag, ich bin der Heinz.
	Ich bin der Heinz Schuh, und wie heißt du?
Pia:	Hallo, lieber Heinz, ich bin die Pia,
	Ich bin die Pia Klein, wie geht es dir?
Heinz:	Mir geht es gut; mir geht es prima!
	Und wie geht es dir? Alles klar, liebe Pia?
Pia:	Heinz, lieber Heinz, mir geht's wunderbar!
	Mir geht es toll, lieber Heinz, ja, ja.
Heinz:	Sag' mal Pia, wo kommst du her?
Pia:	Ich komme aus Greifswald, das ist am Meer.
	Und wo wohnst du, wo wohnst du Heinz?
Heinz:	Ich wohne hier; ich wohne in Mainz.
Heinz:	Ich bin die Nummer Eins,
	Ich bin der Heinz!
	Ich bin fünfzehn Jahre.
	Ich komme aus Mainz.
Pia:	Ich bin die Pia;
	Ich wohn' in Greifswald,
	Und ich bin vierzehn Jahre alt.
	Auf Wiederseh'n Heinz, Tschüs, bis bald!
Heinz:	Tschüs, liebe Pia, auf Wiedersehn! Mach es gut, ich muss jetzt gehn'.

Answers

Vorname:	Heinz
Nachname:	Schuh
Stadt:	Mainz
Alter:	15
Vorname:	Pia
Nachname:	Klein
Stadt:	Greifswald
Alter:	14

Einheit B   Wo ist es?

Unit 2B will introduce:
- *genders and articles*
- *classroom objects*
- *asking where something is and answering*

PCMs 2.6 – 2.11 accompany this section.

1   Lies den Cartoon und hör zu! Lauras Traum

This cartoon includes the core phrases from this chapter. It also introduces some classroom vocabulary. The students could speculate as to whether Laura will be late for school, whether David will / will not give his sister the telephone number and whether Laura will / will not phone Matthias.

Transcript

Reporter:	Guten Tag. Darf ich ein Interview machen? Wie heißt ihr?
Heinz:	Ich bin der Heinz Schuh. Das ist Pia Klein am Bass. Und das ist Yasemin Akbar am Schlagzeug.
Reporter:	Und wo kommt ihr her?
Pia:	Ich komme aus Greifswald. Heinz kommt aus Mainz. Und Yasemin kommt aus der Türkei.
Reporter:	Toll! Wie alt seid ihr?
Matthias:	Pia ist 14, ich bin 16 und Yasemin ist 15 Jahre alt.
Laura:	Oh je! Ich komme zu spät! Heute ist Schule.
Laura:	David, hilf mir! Bring mir die Schultasche? Wo ist das Buch? Und das Heft?
David:	Die Tasche ist hier.
Laura:	Danke, David! . . .
	Wo ist Matthias Telefonnummer???!!!
David:	Ich weiß nicht.

2   Gruppenarbeit. Sieh der Bild 6 im Cartoon auf Seite 30 an

This is intended as a speaking exercise. The colour coding is paving the way for awareness of noun genders.

Lerntipp   Vokabeln lernen

The teacher may ask the class what they are doing to memorise the new vocabulary and share ideas for remembering things. Vocabulary books, index cards, sample sentences or labelling things in their own house are very effective. Pictures of the relevant items may be helpful – students could be referred to the alphabet PCM (1.5) and the **die / der / das** with the words.

Wörterbuch

Dictionary skills need to be learned right from the beginning in order to make students responsible for their own learning. This is a first introduction to German dictionaries. Make a set of dictionaries available to the class and let them discover features for themselves. Point out the many pitfalls of wrong translations (e.g. President Kennedy's famous "I am a doughnut" speech) and discourage the students from buying the first cheap dictionary they can find or asking the parents to invest in an expensive one which they might not use! Above all discourage the use of current on-line translation tools which do not give accurate renderings of the original. Indeed, a good idea is to use one of these in class – get the children to translate a nursery rhyme into German and then back again into English – they will soon see the problems!

3 Finde den Artikel im Wörterbuch und suche im Bild **E**

The class will need a set of dictionaries for this exercise. You may want to use large coloured labels for the objects in your own classroom. You can either stick them on yourself or let students do the labelling. "Post-it" stickers are ideal because they are simple to remove and do not leave a mark.

Answers
Buch, n.; Heft, n.; Bleistift, m.; Buntstift, m.; Kuli, m.; Radiergummi, n.; Anspitzer, m.; Mappe, f.; Tasche, f.; Lineal, n.; Jacke, f.; Kreide, f.; Tafel, f.; Stuhl, m.; Tür, f.; Fenster, n.; Poster, n.; Kassette, f.

Sprachtipp

der, die, das
This Sprachtipp consolidates the previous item and encourages students to look back through the Chapter and to find the nouns themselves. This is an ideal time to encourage the use of vocabulary books and dictionaries. Short, regular tests of vocabulary, including the correct use of the definite article can be used to encourage good habits! Students should be advised to note down and learn nouns with the definite article rather than the indefinite article. They should now be able to see that the masculine and neuter indefinite article are identical and therefore the gender can best be seen from the **der**, **die**, **das** form.

PCM 2.6 Gruppenarbeit mit dem Wörterbuch

This item provides you with a PCM of the page in the Pupil's Book so that they can colour in the items according to their gender. It thereby reinforces the grammatical item on genders.

PCM 2.7 Spiel: Was ist das? **A**

Hopefully the students will be able to connect the dots and write the answer. They may enjoy making up their own dot-to-dot items for Kindergarten aged children.

Answer:
Der Stuhl

4 Sag was! Ist das ein…? **E**

This is a speaking exercise drilling classroom vocabulary and practising the new words **kein** and **keine** in a fun way.

As an extension activity you may wish to practise this further orally with classroom objects e.g. hold up a ruler and say: „**Ist das ein Heft?**"

Answers
1 Ja, das ist ein Tisch.
2 Ja, das ist ein Heft.
3 Nein, das ist kein Kuli. Das ist ein Poster.
4 Nein, das ist kein Lineal. Das ist eine Kassette.
5 Nein, das ist kein Tisch. Das ist ein Stuhl.
6 Nein, das ist keine Tür. Das ist ein Fenster.
7 Nein, das ist keine Mappe. Das ist eine Jacke.
8 Ja, das ist eine Tür.
9 Nein, das ist kein Bleistift. Das ist ein Kuli.
10 Nein, das ist keine Kreide. Das ist eine Tafel.

5 Was sucht der Lehrer? Hör zu und kreuze an!

This listening exercise practises the skill of identifying a word from a list of classroom objects.

Transcript	
Eins	**Vier**
Teacher: Wo ist das Buch?	Teacher: Wo ist die Tasche?
Student: Hier!	Student: Da!
Zwei	**Fünf**
Teacher: Wo ist der Kuli?	Teacher: Wo ist das Radiergummi?
Student: Da!	
Drei	Student: Hier!
Teacher: Wo ist die Kreide?	
Student: Hier!	

Answers
1 D (book), **2** A (biro), **3** B (chalk), **4** B (bag), **5** A (rubber)

PCM 2.8   Hör zu! Was braucht Peter?

Students have to listen carefully for the things Peter needs.

Transcript

Ich muss zur Schule! Oh je! Ich brauche mein Buch. Wo ist mein Buch?
Und mein Heft. Ich brauche mein Heft.
Und wo ist meine Jacke? Meine Jacke ist weg!
Und wo sind mein Kuli und meine Buntstifte? Ich kann meinen Kuli und die Buntstifte nicht finden!!!
Oh je!!!

Answers
The following items should be coloured in: book, exercise book, coat, biro, colour pencils.

PCM 2.9   Spiel: Piratengold   **E**

A game to use numbers and get an initial idea of following directions! Weaker students may need help with the directions!

Answer:

F	R	A	N	K	F	U	R	T

PCM 2.10   Spiel: Schiffe versenken   **E**

A German version of battleships, this item revises numbers and letters of the alphabet. Students should sit opposite each other so that they cannot see each other's sheets. They should hide all their ships in the first grid. The number and length of ships each player has is indicated below the first grid.

3 Schnellboote (speed boats), **2 Kreuzer** (cruisers), **2 Schlachtschiffe** (battleships), **1 Flugzeugträger** (aircraft carrier).

Ships can be placed horizontally or vertically but not diagonally. Ships cannot touch each other anywhere. Players take turns trying to discover the location of the other player's ships. The first player calls out a grid reference (e.g. A 2). The second player then responds:

Wasser – if there is no ship on that field.
Treffer – if there is a ship on that field.
versenkt – if all fields occupied by that ship have been hit.

If a player scores a hit, he or she has another turn. If not it is the other player's turn.

The second grid is used to record the location of the other player's ships.

The player who "sinks" all his opponent's ships first wins the game.

6   Partnerarbeit: Sag was!   **E**

Students should be encouraged to make up their own role plays, based on the phrases from the chapter. PCM 1.7 accompanies this exercise.

Aussprache •

It is important to practise the correct pronunciation of the "**e**" sounds which English speakers tend to avoid.

PCM 2.11   Kreuzworträtsel   **E**

A different way of revising what they have learned!

Answer:

Leseseiten •   **E**

These colourful posters give the students a different approach to the vocabulary introduced in the chapter, plus a little more besides. The students should be encouraged to check details on the poster carefully. The exercises are designed to resemble GCSE-style questioning.

Answers

Wie ist die Telefonnummer von / vom . . .
1 0251-30 23 60   **3** 0234 / 76 74 50
2 (0231) 16 35 11

Wann ist . . . in . . .
1 am 5. Mai   **3** am 21. August
2 am 16. September   **4** am 4. April

Richtig oder Falsch?
1 Richtig   **3** Richtig   **5** Falsch
2 Falsch   **4** Falsch

Was passt zusammen?

Münster	Dekadenz	4. April
Bochum	Bap	27. Februar
Dortmund	Technoparty	14. März

Aussagesätze and Grammatik

These pages are useful quick references for students working alone or in pairs – on a class work or homework assignment. They are also useful for revision purposes, as they sum up the important grammar and vocabulary of the chapter.

Kapitel 3   Freunde und Familie

Einheit A   Wie siehst du aus?

In Unit 3A students learn how to:
- *describe people*
- *ask what someone looks like*
- *describe people's characters*
- *ask what sort of character someone has*

PCMs 3.1 and 3.2 accompany this section.

1   Lies den Cartoon und hör zu! Der Telefonanruf

The story continues. Students could read up to scene 5 (with the lower part covered up) and guess what will happen next. Who do they think the blonde is? Do they think the blonde is Matthias' girlfriend / competition for Laura? Should Laura ring Matthias or wait for him to contact her?

Transcript	
Yasemin:	Matthias ist wirklich süß! Und so nett!
Laura:	Matthias hat eine Freundin!
Yasemin:	Wie heißt sie?
Laura:	Ich weiß nicht. Aber sie ist doof!
Yasemin:	Wie sieht sie aus?
Laura:	Sie hat lange, blonde, lockige Haare. Sie ist sehr hübsch.
Yasemin:	Und du hast braune, glatte Haare. Das ist auch sehr schön!
Laura:	Danke! Du bist meine beste Freundin, Yasemin.
Yasemin:	Vielleicht ist sie Matthias' Schwester. Komm, ruf' an!
Laura:	Ich weiß nicht . . . Ich habe Angst . . .
Anna:	Ja, Anna Meyer, guten Tag.

2   Partnerarbeit. Leute beschreiben

Here **er** and **sie** are being practised with a separable verb. It may help prepare students for the next exercise if they look at the way the girls in the cartoon describe Anna and Laura. Pupils should be able to work out the answers from the cartoon.

Answers

Wie sieht sie aus?   Wie sieht er aus?

Vokabeltipp   Haare und Augen beschreiben

You may have some students with slightly more unusual hairstyles in your class. Here is some extra vocabulary you might need:

- **eine Dauerwelle** (a perm)
- **gefärbte Haare** (coloured hair)
- **weiße** (white) / **lila** (purple) / **pinke** (bright pink) **Haare**

Complexion is not featured in this vocabulary box because some students might feel uncomfortable discussing their skin colour / complexion. Here is some extra vocabulary should it be requested:

- **Er / Sie hat helle** (light) / **dunkle** (dark) **Haut** (skin).

You may ask the class if they can identify descriptions of students or teachers using the **Vokabeltipp**.

As an extension exercise you could carry out a poll in class. Create 2 charts – one for eye colour and one for hair colour – and stickers with the following written on them:

blaue   grüne   braune   graue   schwarze Augen   schwarze   braune   rote   blonde graue   Haare

The poll can then be one or both of the following:

a. Wie sehe ich aus?
Students place a sticker with their names in the relevant columns (one for hair and one for eyes).
Fragen:
Wie viele Schüler haben blonde Haare?
Wie viele Schüler haben braune Augen? etc.

b. Mein Traumpartner
Students place stickers in the columns with the colours they favour in their ideal partner. You could have separate charts for boys and girls e.g.:

Der Traummann / die Traumfrau hat . . .
Augen und . . . Haare.

3   Sag und schreib was! Mein Lieblingsstar

This exercise should encourage students to use the vocabulary given to describe their favourite stars. Additional pictures for this exercise could come from magazines about music, sports or films or the Internet. This could also be turned into a homework assignment and students could create posters with descriptions for wall display.

Spiel: Ballspiel **E**

A further reinforcement activity is a simple ball game. You will need a soft ball and category cards.

Create 3–5 cards for each category (number will depend on the number of children in your class). Shuffle the cards and place the stack upside-down on a table. The first player picks up a card and reads it out aloud. He / She throws the ball to another player. This player must respond to the question asked. Then that player picks another card and continues . . .

Categories:

Name:	Wie heißt du?
Alter:	Wie alt bist du?
Geburtstag:	Wann hast du Geburtstag?
Wohnort:	Wo wohnst du?
Haare:	Wie sieht dein Haar aus?
Augen:	Wie sehen deine Augen aus?
Aussehen:	Bist du klein oder groß?
Charakter:	Wie bist du?

4 Hör zu! Kriminelle gesucht **E**

This exercise will appeal to the more creative students who will enjoy drawing pictures of the criminals described. It will probably be necessary to practise the key words prior to drawing the posters.

> **Transcript**
> Achtung! Achtung! Die Polizei sucht drei gefährliche Kriminelle.
> Bert Böse hat rote, lange Haare und braune Augen. Er hat einen Schnurrbart.
> Karlotta Klau hat kurze, gerade, schwarze Haare. Sie hat blaue Augen und eine rote Brille.
> Rudi Ratte hat grüne Augen, einen braunen Bart und Glatze.
> Bitte helfen Sie der Polizei.

 Vokabeltipp Wie sieht er / sie aus?

You could ask students to arrange themselves according to height and then each one say which group they belong to (**groß**, **mittelgroß**, **klein**), if you think they will feel comfortable with that.

Lerntipp Neue Wörter lernen

Students may like to discuss what strategies they use / could use to learn new words.

5 Sag was! Zeugen **A**

This is a straightforward speaking exercise for pairs, and should be manageable for all levels. Students should swap roles.

Answers

Peter Pistole hat braune, kurze Haare und graue Augen.
Max Messer hat graue, mittellange Haare und schwarze Augen.
Klaus Klau hat kurze rote Haare und grüne Augen.
Kurt Schlagemann hat lange, blonde Haare und blaue Augen.
Günther Motz hat graue Augen und blonde, kurze Haare.
Hein Heimlich hat grüne Augen und lange, braune Haare.

Wörterbuch **E**

This exercise practises early dictionary skills. Students should be encouraged to describe the pictures – both orally and in written form. A brief explanation of the accusative after **haben** may be required.

Answers

eine Glatze	bald head
ein(en) Bart	beard
ein(en) Schnurrbart	moustache
eine Brille	glasses
(Kontaktlinsen	contact lenses!)

Wörterbuch Adjektive **E**

This encourages early dictionary skills. You may want to explain other abbreviations your pupils find. Please check with your own set of dictionaries, as abbreviations vary from publisher to publisher.

Answers

Bart (noun)
blond (adj.)
wohnen (verb)
jung (adj.)
Brille (noun)
heißen (verb)
lang (adj.)

Spiel: Augenzeugen **E**

For this extension activity you will need to prepare photos, drawings or pictures of people. You could use cuttings from magazines or let students do their own drawings. The more striking the features of the people depicted the better.

Divide students into pairs: the eye witness (**Augenzeuge**) and the police officer (**Polizist**).

Shuffle the pictures face down and hand one to each group. The eyewitness looks at his / her picture for 15 seconds. The time can be counted out by the police officer. Then the eye witness hands the picture to the police officer.

The police officer then asks the witness questions e.g.: „Wie sieht der Mann / die Frau aus?"

The witness must describe the person without looking at the picture again. The police officer can ask for more details and check whether the information is correct. The eye witness wins a point if he / she is able to answer all the questions correctly. When the questioning is over, he / she can look at the picture again. Roles can then be reversed with new pictures.

6 Sag was! Wie siehst du aus?

This speaking exercise could also be used as a written homework assignment or in combination with IT-skills. Students could even scan in pictures of themselves and their family / friends.

7 Wer ist das?

This exercise applies and revises the above vocabulary.

8 Schreib was! Sieh die Bilder an

This item has two possible responses: the simple **ja** / **nein** and the more detailed answer (which of course will be more useful later for examinations). The idea is to encourage students to expand on their answers – so they do not simply answer "yes" or "no".

9 Spiel: Zwanzig Fragen   **E**

In order to play this game students need to have mastered the above vocabulary, including forming yes / no questions. For classes that need more help, these words can be put on the board.

Vokabeltipp Charakter

In order to familiarise themselves with these new words students could take turns acting out the characteristics. Or students could be asked to guess the words from a mime done by the teacher and then they can take turns miming.

10 Hör zu! Danas Freunde

This could be used in a language lab as a cued speaking exercise. Play the first part of the sentence and the sound, and let students guess the correct adjective. Then play some more of the tape so that the students hear the key word, which they can then repeat.

Transcript
1 Das ist Susanne. *[sound of yawning]* Sie ist ein bisschen langweilig.
2 Das ist Jan. *[sound of laughter]* Jan ist sehr lustig.
3 Hier ist Nicole. *[sound of sporting activity]* Sie ist total sportlich.
4 Und das ist Gregor. *[sound of music]* Er ist ganz cool.
5 Und das bin ich. *[sound of applause]* Ich bin echt nett.

Answers
1b / 2a / 3c / 4c / 5b

 Haare und Aussehen

Some tips for would-be hairdressers and those who like fashion, with some useful expressions for those who want to expand their own vocabulary.

11 Schreib was! Wie ist er? Wie ist sie?

The pictures here could be used for a speaking exercise prior to getting students to write their views on these people. Allow them to check back for the correct spelling.

12 Schreib was! Ganz oder gar nicht?

A straightforward gap filling exercise. Students can use the **Sprachtipp Ganz oder gar nicht**. There are a number of possiblities for each gap, therefore no definitive answers are given here. If students struggle with the amount of choice available to them, you can limit the possible answers to:

– **nicht**   + **sehr**

 **ß ≠ B**

The German **scharfes S** or **esszett (ß)** and the letter **B** are easily confused, especially by beginners.

Projekt   Meine Band   E

Students could be encouraged to invent a band. They could:

- create a display including a picture of each band member and a short summary of personal details (name, age, where they live, appearance . . .)
- design a poster featuring the band and announcing tour dates.
- give a short presentation to the class introducing their band.

As students acquire more vocabulary the displays can be extended.

13 Hör zu! Meine Traumfrau   E

This listening exercise is a little more demanding since learners are not just listening for individual words but have to understand whole sentences. More able students should be able to appreciate the ironic ending. You may want to ask why Tina hit Martin. Tina is obviously keen on Martin, but he only has eyes for Maria. You could encourage more able students to correct the false statements and even to write their own imaginative dialogues based on this example.

Transcript

Tina:	Martin??? Wie sieht deine Traumfrau aus?
Martin:	Hm . . . sie ist nicht groß und nicht klein. Mittelgroß! Sie ist ganz hübsch. Sie hat eine Brille, braune Augen und lange, braune Haare.
Tina:	Lockige Haare oder gerade Haare?
Martin:	Nein, nicht gerade. Sehr lockige Haare.
Tina:	Wie ich?
Martin:	Ja, wie du, Tina!
Tina:	Und wie ist sie?
Martin:	Nett. Sie ist total nett, Tina.
Tina:	Ist sie total sportlich?
Martin:	Sportlich? Nein, sie ist gar nicht sportlich. Sie ist total faul.
Tina:	Faul? Ich bin nicht faul. Ich bin ganz sportlich!!!
Martin:	Du? Ja, du bist sportlich, Tina. Aber Maria ist nicht sportlich. Maria ist total faul!
Tina:	Maria? Maria!!! Wer ist Maria?!
Martin:	AU!

Answers

1 F (mittelgroß)
2 R
3 R
4 F (braune Augen)
5 F (lockig und braun)
6 R
7 F (nicht sportlich)
8 F (nicht Tina, sondern Maria)

PCM 3.1   Fragebogen: Mein Traum

This item revises the important words for describing friends and family.

PCM 3.2   Spiel: Was passt nicht?

This is a straightforward odd-man-out exercise.

Answers

1	freundlich	does not refer to hair
2	klein	is not a trait of character
3	Haare	is not a person
4	lockig	does not refer to figure
5	kurz	does not begin with the letter "b"
6	groß	is an adjective and not a noun

Einheit B   Haustiere

In Unit 3B students will learn to talk about:
- *whether they have any pets*
- *what the pets look like*

PCMs 3.3 – 3.6 accompany this section.

1   Lies den Cartoon und hör zu!
Der Spaziergang im Park

This cartoon serves as an introduction to the vocabulary in this unit. Students could read the beginning and then guess how it continues. They can discuss the story and practise the vocabulary.

You could discuss some of the following questions in English:

- Which pets do they have?
- How are Laura and Matthias feeling about this chance encounter?
- What is Anna's connection to Matthias? . . . and to Florian?
- Do you think Matthias likes Laura? What makes you think this?
- Have they ever had an embarrassing moment involving a pet?

Transcript

Laura:	Ach Bello! Matthias ist so nett!
Laura:	Bello!
Matthias:	Laura!
Laura:	Matthias!
Laura:	Hast du Haustiere?
Matthias:	Ich habe einen Hund. Er ist ein Bernhardiner und heißt Bärli.
Heinz:	Laura! Das ist mein Bruder Florian und das ist seine Freundin Anna.
Matthias:	Anna, das ist Laura!
Laura:	H...h...hallo.
Anna:	Aha! Laura aus Schottland, richtig? Ich bin Matthias' Tante.

2   Haustiere beschreiben

This item encourages vocabulary building and focuses on the most important sentences in the story. You could ask for further items e.g. How do you say I have 2 cats / I don't have any pets etc.

Answers

Hast du Haustiere?

Ich habe einen Hund.

Vokabeltipp Haustiere

Some students may have different animals. Here is a list of some more pets:

die Wüstenmaus	gerbil
die Schlange	snake
das Meerschweinchen	guinea pig
der Papagei	parrot
die Maus	mouse
der Kanarienvogel	canary
die Schildkröte	tortoise
der Wellensittich	budgerigar
die Wasserschildkröte	terrapin
das Pony	pony

You could bring a photo of a pet / allow students to bring photos of their pets and discuss these animals. Students could also create small collages of animals e.g. one for **die Katze** with things associated with cats (food, pictures, toys); another for **der Hund** etc.

S p r a c h t i p p

Akkusativ (1)
A first introduction to the Accusative case. They only need to understand boys are "odd man out"!!

3   Hör zu! Tiere   `A`

A The animal sounds will help the students to remember the vocabulary. As an extension activity, students could be asked to pretend to be an animal. The other students have to guess which animal it is and say the name in German.

Transcript
1 Miriam hat einen Fisch.
2 Bettina hat eine Katze.
3 Jan hat eine Ratte.
4 Max hat ein Pferd.
5 Irene hat einen Vogel.
6 Anne hat keine Haustiere.
7 Benjamin hat einen Hund.

Answers

1	einen Fisch	5	einen Vogel
2	eine Katze	6	keine Haustiere
3	eine Ratte	7	einen Hund
4	ein Pferd		

B Students should be encouraged to move about the classroom and to speak to different partners. You can allocate certain pets to certain students / groups, or let all students gather the information, depending on the size of your group. The results can be made into an attractive wall display to remind students of the names of the animals.

PCM 3.3 Schreib was! Grammatik! Ein oder einen?

The following items further practise the indefinite article and the accusative case.

Answers

1	einen	5	ein
2	ein	6	einen
3	ein	7	einen, einen
4	einen	8	ein

Sprachtipp

Plural

This item introduces the idea of the plural and briefly shows how it differs from the English plural. There is no need to go into any great detail here.

4 Schreib was! Wie heißt der Plural?

An exercise on dictionary skills and plurals!

Answers

1	ein Hund	zwei Hunde
2	ein Haustier	zwei Haustiere
3	ein Pferd	zwei Pferde
4	ein Vogel	zwei Vögel
5	ein Fisch	zwei Fische
6	eine Ratte	zwei Ratten

Vokabeltipp Beschreib deine Haustiere

As well as giving vocabulary, this box also emphasises genders and the fact that **die** words should be referred to as **sie**; **das** words as **es**; and **der** words as **er**. Other features students may want to describe:

grau**e** Streifen – stripes
weiß**e** Tupfen – spots
ein**e** hell**e** / dunkl**e** Mähne – a light / dark mane
ein**en** hell**en** / dunkl**en** Schweif – a light / dark tail (of horses and ponies)
ein**e** weiß**e** Pfote / weiß**e** Pfoten – a white paw / white paws

5 Hör zu! Meine Haustiere   E

This listening exercise is longer and more complex than the previous one. You may want to introduce it when you are happy that your students are familiar with the vocabulary on pets. More able students could write a role play modelled on these taped interviews.

Transcript
Eins

Interviewer:	Wie heißt du?
Tayfun:	Ich heiße Tayfun.
Interviewer:	Hast du Haustiere, Tayfun?
Tayfun:	Ja, ich habe Haustiere.
Interviewer:	Aha. Und was für Tiere hast du?
Tayfun:	Ich habe zwei Hamster und einen Vogel.
Interviewer:	Wie sieht der Vogel aus?
Tayfun:	Er ist blau und grün.
Interviewer:	Und wie heißt er?
Tayfun:	Der Vogel heißt Kalif.
Interviewer:	Und die Hamster?
Tayfun:	Die heißen Ali und Baba. Sie sind sehr lustig.
Interviewer:	Danke, Tayfun.

Zwei

Interviewer:	Guten Tag. Wie heißen Sie, wenn ich mal fragen darf?
Frau Seiffert:	Ich bin Frau Liselotte Seiffert.
Interviewer:	Frau Seiffert, haben Sie Haustiere?
Frau Seiffert:	Oh ja, ich habe 3 Katzen.
Interviewer:	Wie heißen die Katzen?
Frau Seiffert:	Mitzi, Karlo und Findus.
Interviewer:	Und wie sehen die Katzen aus?
Frau Seiffert:	Die Mitzi, ja, die ist schwarz und weiß. Der Karlo ist ganz rot, also rot-braun, ja? Und der Findus, der Findus, ja, der ist so grau.
Interviewer:	Vielen Dank, Frau Seiffert.

Drei

Interviewer:	Guten Tag, wie heißt du?
Julia:	Ich heiße Julia.
Interviewer:	Und du?
Julia:	Das ist mein Bruder Sascha.
Sascha:	Hallo!
Interviewer:	Sascha, Julia, habt ihr Haustiere?
Julia:	Nein, nein, ich habe keine Haustiere, . . . aber mein Bruder Sascha hat ein Tier.
Sascha:	Ja, ich habe eine Ratte!
Interviewer:	Eine Ratte? Hmmm . . . und wie heißt sie?
Sascha:	Monster, meine Ratte heißt Monster. Sie ist klein und total cool. Echt süß!
Julia:	Nein, deine Ratte ist total doof!!! Iiigitt!
Interviewer:	Eh . . . danke.

Answers

Name	Pets	Pets' names
Tayfun	2 hamsters	Ali, Baba
	blue / green bird	Kalif
Frau Seiffert	black & white cat	Mitzi
	brown cat	Karlo
	grey and white cat	Findus
Julia	no pets	
Sascha	rat	Monster

PCM 3.4 Lies was! Was ist mein Tier?

This is a matching exercise to practise pets and descriptions.

Answers

Katja Huber   D
Fridolin Kaiser   A
Birgit Koch   C
Hassan Ergül   B

PCM 3.5 Spiel: Tier-Labyrinth

This item and the one below give more practice with the words for pets.

Answers

2 Kaninchen, 1 Pferd, 1 Vogel, 1 Schildkröte

PCM 3.6 Spiel: Welches Tier war das?

Answers

A) Katze
B) Pferd
C) Vogel
D) Hamster
E) Kaninchen
F) Hund

---

6 Lies was! Vermisst! E

For this exercise it is only necessary to recognise key words, not to understand every word.

---

7 Schreib was! Mach ein Poster. E

This exercise is modelled on the previous text in Exercise 6, but requires students to handle phrases independently. It will appeal to the more creative students and may lend itself to word processing.

---

8 Sag was! Tiere E

This exercise is suitable for more able students. They could also look at one of the Internet sites listed and describe an animal from one of the sites.

Spiel: Katze und Maus A

This game is best played with all players sitting in a circle in a large room or playground. Each student is given a card with the name and / or picture of a pet animal. If more animals are needed, the teacher may have to introduce the names of some farm and wild animals, or play in two smaller groups. Alternatively there could be two animals of each type. The teacher should call out the names of two animals e.g. „Die Katze jagt die Maus."

The students who have these animals now have to chase each other clockwise around the outside of the circle. The chaser tries to tap the chased animal before it can get back to its space.

After the game has been established, the role of caller can be taken over by a student.

---

9 Sag was! Du bist dran

This exercise allows students to talk about their own pets / dream pets. You may wish to bring along a few pictures of pets for students who do not have any. If the school has IT-facilities, students could also create posters about their own pets or pets from a local animal sanctuary.

---

10 Spiel: Wortschlange E

An opportunity to practise the key words of this unit in a fun way!

Answers

Katze / Hund / Vogel / Fisch / Pferd / Ratte / Hamster
Solution: Mein Haustier ist lieb.

 **Haustiere**

Some useful sites for various animals. Students may not yet be able to understand all the German, but they should be able to pick out the key vocabulary for animals and colours.

Einheit C   Meine Familie

In Unit 3C students will learn how to:
- *talk about their relatives*
- *talk about their family tree*
- *say the numbers 30–100*

PCMs 3.7 – 3.10 accompany this section.

1   Lies den Cartoon und hör zu! Tante Anna

Matthias and Laura are discussing their families. Students could say if they have / know of anybody who has aunts and uncles who are the same age as or even younger than their nephews / nieces.

Transcript

Laura: Ist Anna wirklich deine Tante?

Matthias: Ja. Meine Mutter ist 35. Sie hat 3 Schwestern und einen Bruder. Tante Guste ist 31, Tante Klara ist 29, Onkel Peter ist 26 und Tante Anna ist 20.
Anna wohnt in Mainz. Ich bin hier zu Besuch.

Laura: Ach so!
Hast du auch Geschwister?

Matthias: Ja, ich habe eine Schwester. Sie heißt Lena und ist 13 Jahre alt. Sie ist ganz schön blöd!

Laura: Mein Bruder David ist auch manchmal doof.

2   Lies was! Matthias' Stammbaum

This family tree can be used in conjunction with the cartoon. You may wish to return to the tree and exploit it in more detail once students have acquired all the vocabulary in this section. It can serve as a cue for speaking and writing activities.

3   Schreib was! Matthias' Familie

Please stress that **Familie** is pronounced differently from "family"! You may want to remind students that the emphasis is on the second syllable and the final **-e** is pronounced.

Answers

Maria Hasler 35
Guste Meyer 31
Klara Meyer 29
Peter Meyer 26
Anna Meyer 20
Lena Hasler 13

Sprachtipp

Akkusativ (2)

This item continues to introduce the accusative case, this time with **der**.

4   Schreib was! Was sehen sie? Füll die Lücken aus.   **E**

This item practises the accusative of the definite article.

Answers

1   Du siehst <u>den</u> Cartoon.   4   Wir sehen <u>den</u> Vogel.
2   Er sieht <u>den</u> Stammbaum.   5   Sie sehen <u>die</u> Hunde.
3   Sie sieht <u>das</u> Kaninchen.   6   Ich sehe <u>die</u> Katze.

Vokabeltipp 30–100

You could play Bingo or any other number game to consolidate the numbers 1–100. You could, for example, play the page race. Say a page number between 1 and 100: „Schlagt Seite X im Buch auf!" The winner is the first person to find the page and name one of the exercises on it – provided the book has been treated with respect!

Spiel: Böse sechs

This game is played with dice; the aim of the game is to be the first to reach 100. Each player should throw the dice and add up the numbers in German. The score should be written down and the dice passed to the next player. The player may add to his / her score at each turn. If a player throws a **sechs** he / she loses all the points he / she gained in the previous round. All scores / numbers must be said in German.

5   Sag was! Wie alt sind sie?

Students will find the necessary information in the cartoon:

Answers

1   Frau Hasler ist 35 Jahre alt.   4   Tante Guste ist 31 Jahre alt.
2   Tante Anna ist 20 Jahre alt.   5   Lena ist 13 Jahre alt.
3   Onkel Peter ist 26 Jahre alt.

6   Schreib was! Ergänze die Sätze

This activity is based on Matthias' family tree and reinforces key vocabulary for the family members.

Answers

1   Matthias' Schwester heißt Lena.
2   Matthias' Tanten heißen Guste, Klara und Anna.

3 Matthias' Onkel heißt Peter.
4 Matthias' Vater heißt Anton.
5 Gustes Bruder heißt Peter.
6 Marias Mutter heißt Magda.
7 Matthias Großmutter heißt Magda.
8 Lenas Großvater heißt Hans.

7 Schreib was! Beschreib Matthias' Familie

This activity is also based on Matthias' family tree.

Answers
1 Lena ist <u>die Schwester</u> von Matthias.
2 Anton Hasler ist <u>der Vater</u> von Matthias.
3 Maria Hasler ist <u>die Mutter</u> von Matthias.
4 Magda Meyer ist <u>die Großmutter</u> von Matthias.
5 Tony Huber ist <u>der Onkel</u> von Matthias.

Vokabeltipp Meine Familie

This item summarises the core vocabulary and structures introduced in this unit. Words have been colour-coded to indicate gender. Plurals are also listed where it is felt they may be needed. Students may need to be reminded of the appropriate endings for possessive adjectives and indefinite articles. Please remind students of the pronunciation of **Cousin** and **Cousine**.

Kulturtipp Kosenamen

Allow students to think of pet names used in English before discussing the German terms listed.

8 Sag was! Beschreib deine Familie

An opportunity for the students to present their own family – they could bring in a photo or create a cartoon picture of their family on paper or on computer.

Sprachtipp

Possessive adjectives
This item introduces the nominative and accusative forms of the possessive adjectives and explains that they behave like **ein**.

9 Schreib was! Mache Sätze

This item practises both the possessive adjectives and the accusative case. A large number of sentences are possible, but students need to be aware that they do not use the accusative case after **das ist.**

PCM 3.7 Schreib was! Meine oder deine?

The next two exercises give the students more practice with the possessives.

Answers
a) deine	c) meine	e) Ihre	g) meine	i) seine
b) sein	d) ihre	f) ihre	h) deine	j) ihre

PCM 3.8 Schreib was! Mit oder ohne E?

Answers
a) meine	e) mein	i) deine
b) seine	f) meine, ihr	j) unser
c) unsere	g) Ihre	
d) ihr	h) mein, meine	

Vokabeltipp Beziehungen

Some useful phrases for relationships e.g. married / divorced / living together.

Lerntipp ist oder sind?

A reminder of the third person singular and plural of the important verb **sein**.

10 Schreib was!   ist oder sind?

This item reinforces the item in the **Lerntipp** and practises the third person singular and plural of **sein**.

Answers
1 Karl und Lena <u>sind</u> geschieden.
2 Romina <u>ist</u> ledig.
3 Mein Bruder <u>ist</u> verheiratet.
4 Herr und Frau Kraus <u>sind</u> geschieden.
5 Meine Tante <u>ist</u> verheiratet.

11 Schreib was! Mann und Frau. Was passt zusammen?

An exercise to encourage vocabulary building in pairs!

Answers

1	Mutter	d	Vater
2	Schwester	e	Bruder
3	Oma	g	Opa
4	Tante	h	Onkel
5	Lebenspartnerin	f	Lebenspartner
6	Freundin	a	Freund
7	Mama	c	Papa
8	Cousine	b	Cousin

12 Hör zu! Welche Familie ist es?

In this listening exercise students need to match the keywords to the pictures. Not all of the families described are traditional families. For weaker students it may be advisable to look at and describe the pictures prior to listening. You may have to remind some students of the word **Lebenspartner** and the fact that they have to count the speaker as one of the people shown in the picture.

Transcript
Eins:
Ich habe eine ganz kleine Familie. Ich habe keine Geschwister. Ich bin ein Einzelkind. Meine Eltern sind geschieden. Das ist mein Vater und das bin ich.
Zwei:
Ich habe eine große Familie. Das ist meine Mutter und das ist mein Stiefvater. Ich habe drei Brüder und eine Schwester.
Drei:
Ich habe eine große Familie. Das ist Mama und das ist ihr Lebenspartner, Frank. Ich habe drei Schwestern, aber ich habe keinen Bruder.
Vier:
Meine Familie ist nicht so groß. Ich habe eine Mutter, aber keinen Vater. Das ist mein Bruder. Er ist total cool. Und das bin ich.
Fünf:
Meine Familie ist mittelgroß. Das sind meine Eltern. Sie sind verheiratet. Das bin ich und das ist meine Schwester Leah.

Answers
1 C, 2 B, 3 D, 4 A, 5 E

PCM 3.9   Quiz: Onkel, Mutter, Opa – Wer ist das?

This PCM gives students another opportunity to practise "family" vocabulary.

Answers
A) Großvater
B) Schwester
C) Mutter
D) Onkel
E) Vater

13 Hör zu! Pias Familie

Although the text is quite complex, the tasks are quite straightforward, so weaker students should have no trouble doing them.

Transcript
Ich heiße Pia Klein. Mein Vater ist Erwin Klein. Meine Mutter heißt Elisabeth. Meine Eltern sind geschieden.

Ich habe einen großen Bruder. Er heißt Markus Klein. Papa Erwin ist der Vater von Markus.
Meine Mutter ist jetzt mit Sascha Kowalski verheiratet. Sascha ist mein Stiefvater. Er ist total nett.
Ich habe zwei kleine Geschwister, einen Halbbruder und eine Halbschwester. Bettina ist neun und Andi ist sechs. Sascha ist der Vater von Bettina und Andi. Meine kleine Schwester Bettina ist manchmal doof!
Markus hat eine Lebenspartnerin. Sie heißt Renate. Markus und Renate sind nicht verheiratet. Sie haben ein Baby, ein kleines Mädchen. Es heißt Sophia und ist 1 Jahr alt. Sie ist total süß! Ich bin die Tante von Sophia!

Answers
1	Vater	7	Geschwister
2	Mutter	8	Schwester
3	geschieden	9	Lebenspartnerin
4	Bruder	10	Baby
5	verheiratet	11	Mädchen
6	Stiefvater	12	Tante

14 Schreib was! Ergänze Pias Stammbaum

Answers
A – Elisabeth, B – Sascha, C – Renate, D – Bettina, E – Andi, F – Sophia

15 Schreib und sag was! Meine Familie

This speaking and writing exercise allows students to describe their families. It is suitable for all levels. While weaker students may stick to basic structures, more able students should try and define relationships within their families (aunts, uncles etc). If they have more unusual family trees you may need to assist them with the necessary vocabulary. If students would prefer not to share their real family trees (for whatever personal reasons) you could suggest an imaginary family tree instead.

Projekt: Stammbaum

Each group has the task to produce a family tree for an imaginary family. They have to make a display with pictures and the following information for each member of the family:

Name, Alter, Geburtstag, Haarfarbe, Augenfarbe, Haustiere

They should try to make their family as interesting as possible. At the end of the session, each group has to present their family to the class.

Spiel: Familienfeier

This activity could be played by one large group or several small groups. The teacher needs to prepare a family tree. Each group then pretends to be members of the same family who are meeting for a family gathering. Before the game begins, one member of the group is sent out of earshot. He / she will arrive late at the party. The rest of the group decide who they want to be and who the latecomer is (e.g. **Mama, Onkel Karl, Baby Tina**). The latecomer is called back. He / she is suffering from memory loss and has to find out who he / she is by asking questions which can be answered by yes or no, e.g. „**Bin ich dein Vater?**", „**Ist das deine Frau?**", „**Bist du ein Kind?**".

The group can help by acting out their roles. Couples could hold hands, children could pretend to play or if the newcomer is an elderly person, he or she could be offered a chair and treated accordingly.

PCM 3.10   Spiel: Kreuzworträtsel

Answers

		¹F	I	²S	C	H	E				
³G				C					⁴B		
E			⁵H	A	M	S	T	E	R		
L				N					I		
⁶B	R	A	U	N		⁷B			L		
				R		L			L		
⁸H	A	A	R	E		⁹A	U	G	E	N	
U			B			U					
N			A		¹⁰P				¹¹V		
D			R		F		¹²R		O		
	¹³K	A	T	Z	E		O		G		
					¹⁴R	A	T	T	E		
					D				L		

In Unit 3D your students will learn how to write:
- *an e-mail to a penfriend*
- *a letter in German*

PCMs 3.11 – 3.14 accompany this section.

1   Lies den Cartoon und hör zu! Brieffreundin gesucht!

Here Heinz is lying to Trish. She sees through his boasting and taunts him by asking for a photo. How will Heinz get himself off the hook? This could lead to a discussion of the dangers of the Internet. At the end of this unit students could be encouraged to establish their own penfriend links via e-mail or to put profiles of themselves and their classmates onto the school website.

Transcript

Heinz: Hallo Mädchen! Ich suche eine Brieffreundin. Schreibt mir!

Trish: Hallo, ich bin Trish aus England. Wie siehst du aus, Heinz?

Heinz: Hallo Trish! Ich sehe sehr gut aus. Ich bin blond, groß und sportlich. Ich bin ein Traumtyp!

Trish: Toll! Ich bin schlank, hübsch und echt cool. Ich habe lange, schwarze, krause Haare und tolle, braune Augen . . . Hast du ein Foto, Heinz?

 **Internet-Adressen**

This can lead to a discussion about e-mail addresses: which you can see clearly are from Germany (.de) and which are international (.com).

Aussprache   AU •

An opportunity to practise the vowel sound **au**.

Transcript

Hör zu und widerhole: Traumtyp: Klaus, Augen blau, sucht Frau!

Haustier weg: Maus, grau.

 Brieffreunde und Chatlines   **E**

As long as they have been warned about Chatlines and are being supervised, the students may find it fun to look at sites suitable for young German students of their own age.

2 Schreib was! -er, -e, -es, -en oder keine Endung? **E**

This item practises adjectival endings.

Answers

1 Ich habe blaue Augen.
2 Sie ist ein sportliches Mädchen.
3 Heinz ist ein blöder Junge.
4 Wir haben einen netten Freund.
5 Das ist eine schöne Katze!
6 Sie sieht die weiße Katze.
7 Ich sehe die schwarzen Hunde.
8 Er sieht den netten Junge.

Sprachtipp

Adjektive
This item explains adjectival endings very simply.

Vokabeltipp Briefe schreiben

This draws on all the core structures introduced in units 1–3. Students should not move on before they have got a good grasp of this vocabulary. Letter writing is an important skill for examinations.

You will need to tell the students to put the town and date in the top right hand corner of the letter.

You should point out that their address does not go on the letter, but on the envelope – in the top left hand corner or on the back.

Ask students to note the position of the sender's address and the recipient's house number on the sample envelope given. You should also comment on the postcode and the letter **D** before the code. Finally, students will need to remember whether the person they are writing to is male or female: **Liebe** is used to address a female, **Lieber** a male.

3 Schreib was! Schreibe einen Brief. Fülle die Lücken aus.

This letter writing exercise is suitable for all abilities as students just need to fill gaps and the words are given below. More able students could write a letter modelled on the one given here using the vocabulary suggested in the **Vokabeltipp** above.

Answers
Bern, den 29. März
Liebe Rebecca!
Wie geht es dir?
Ich heiße Lena. Ich komme aus der Schweiz und ich suche eine Brieffreundin. Willst du mir schreiben?
Ich wohne in Bern. Das ist in der Mitte der Schweiz. Wo wohnst du?
Ich bin 12 Jahre alt. Wie alt bist du?
Ich habe blonde Haare und grüne Augen. Ich bin sehr sportlich. Und du? Wie siehst du aus?
Ich habe zwei Brüder. Sie sind 8 und 14. Hast du Geschwister?
Ich habe einen Hund. Er ist braun. Hast du Haustiere?
Schreib mir bald.
Deine Lena

Sprachtipp

Groß oder klein?
Capitals are so important in German! It is important to establish good writing practices!

sie, sie oder Sie?
The different meanings of **sie** cause problems. It is important for students to be able to distinguish between them.

4 Schreib was! Groß oder klein?

This exercise provides good practice with capital letters. Weaker students will need help with this exercise, but the words should be familiar to them.

Answer:
Hallo!
Ich heiße Jan und ich wohne in Österreich. Ich suche einen Brieffreund. Ich bin 13 und ich mag Tiere. Ich habe einen Hamster und drei Vögel. Ich habe schwarze Haare und blaue Augen und ich bin sehr groß. Ich habe keine Brüder, aber eine Schwester. Hast du Geschwister? Bis bald.
Dein Jan

5 Schreib was! sie, sie oder Sie?

This activity encourages discussion about what **sie** means in these sentences.

Answers

1 she
2 you (formal, singular)
3 she / it (refers to an animal)
4 they
5 you (formal, plural)
6 they

6 Der Marsmännchen-Rap

This song is suitable for all levels and revises basic descriptions. Your students can sing the whole song or just join in for the chorus. The song practises first and third person singular use.

Transcript

1
Sag was! Sag was! – Wie siehst du aus?
Ich habe grüne Haare, grüne, grüne Haare.
Alle: Er hat grüne Haare, grüne, grüne Haare??!!
2
Sag was! Sag was! – Wie siehst du aus?
Ich habe rote Augen, rote, rote Augen.
Alle: Er hat rote Augen, rote, rote Augen??!!
3
Sag was! Sag was! – Wie siehst du aus?
Ich habe eine Glatze, eine, eine Glatze.
Alle: Er hat eine Glatze, eine, eine Glatze??!!
4
Sag was! Sag was! – Wie siehst du aus?
Ich habe einen Schnurrbart, einen, einen Schnurrbart.
Alle: Er hat einen Schnurrbart, einen, einen Schnurrbart??!!
5
Sag was! Sag was! – Wo kommst du her?
Ich komme, ich komme, ich komme vom Mars!
Alle: Er kommt, er kommt, er kommt vom Mars!!!
Piep, piep, piep, piep . . .

7 Mache selber einen Rap **E**

You will find an instrumental version of this song on your tape. Let students create their own Martian-Rap and perform it karaoke-style or record it in a language laboratory.

PCM 3.11 Der Marsmännchen-Rap

Let the students listen to the tape again and then colour in the little man from Mars.

PCM 3.12 Rap: Klaus Chaos sucht eine Brieffreundin **E**

This nonsense song revises some of the main phrases of this unit and helps to consolidate vocabulary.

A way of summing up what they have learned in the chapter in a fun way!

Transcript

1
Meine Oma hat 'nen Schnurrbart,
und mein Opa sieht gut aus.
Meine Schwester mag Kaninchen.
Meine Tante, die heißt Klaus.

2
Meine Mutter ist sehr groß,
und mein Vater ist echt klein.
Mein Hamster ist sehr sportlich,
und mein Bruder, der heißt Hein.
3
Ich habe einen Onkel,
der hat ein blaues Pferd.
Ich hab' 'ne coole Brille.
Bitte, bitte schreibe mir!

Answers
from left to right:
1 Hamster
2 Onkel
3 Tante
4 Oma
5 Vater
6 Mutter
7 Opa
8 ich
9 Bruder
10 Schwester

PCM 3.13 Lied: Onkel Jörg hat einen Bauernhof

This item can be sung to the tune of *Old Macdonald had a farm*:

Transcript
Onkel Jörg hat einen Bauernhof, I-Ei, I-Ei, Oh!
Und auf dem Hof gibt's einen Hund, I-Ei, I-Ei, Oh!
Er macht Wau-Wau hier und Wau-Wau da,
hier ein Wau, da ein Wau, überall ein Wau-Wau.
Onkel Jörg hat einen Bauernhof, I-Ei, I-Ei, Oh!
. . . ein Katze . . . Sie macht Miau . . .
. . . ein Pferd . . . Es macht Wieher . . .
. . . ein Kaninchen . . . Es macht Hoppel . . .
. . . einen Fisch . . . Er macht Blub-Blub . . .
. . . eine Maus . . . Sie macht Piep-Piep . . .

PCM 3.14 Lied: Bruder Jakob

The French song *Frères Jacques* has been translated into many languages, including German:

Transcript
Bruder Jakob, Bruder Jakob,
Schläfst du noch, schläfst du noch?
Hörst du nicht die Glocken? Hörst du nicht die Glocken?
Ding, ding, dong! Ding, ding, dong!

Leseseiten

These colourful adverts for penfriends give the students a different approach to the vocabulary introduced in the chapter. The exercises are designed to resemble GCSE style questioning.

Answers

Wer spricht?	Wer ist's?
1 Timo	**1** Eugen
2 Inga	**2** Eva
	3 Aleks
	4 Eugen
	5 Katharina
	6 Timo

Aussagesätze and **Grammatik**

These pages are useful quick references for students working alone or in pairs – on a class-work or homework assignment. They are also useful for revision purposes, as they sum up the important grammar and vocabulary of the chapter.

Kapitel 4 In der Schule

Einheit A   Meine Fächer

Unit 4A will introduce how to say:
- *the school subjects and what you think of these subjects*
- *what your favourite subjects are*
- *the time of day and the days of the week*

PCMs 4.1 – 4.7 accompany this section.

1   Mein Lieblingsfach

The cartoon introduces some school subjects and expressions of opinion. There is a discussion about school between Heinz, who hates school, and Pia who likes the subjects that she studies.

Transcript

Heinz:	Schule ist doof!
Pia:	Wieso? Was gefällt dir nicht?
Heinz:	Mathe ist viel zu schwierig!
Pia:	Nein, Mathe ist doch ganz einfach.
Pia:	Kunst ist toll!
Heinz:	Das gefällt mir nicht.
Pia:	Und Biologie? Das ist interessant.
Heinz:	Schrecklich!
Heinz:	Und Erdkunde ist schrecklich langweilig.
Pia:	Erdkunde? Das ist mein Lieblingsfach!
Heinz:	Du bist ja nicht normal!!

Vokabeltipp   Meine Schulfächer

Here are some other subjects your students may ask for:

Business Studies – **Wirtschaftswissenschaften**

Drama – is not taught at German schools. It could be translated as **Theaterstudien**

Graphics – is not a separate subject in Germany. It should be translated as **Kunst**

2   Schreib was! Pias Fächer

This short exercise makes the students look carefully at the cartoon to check which subjects Pia likes.

Answers

1	Mathe	3	Biologie
2	Kunst	4	Erdkunde

3   Hör zu! Welche sechs Schulfächer sind das?

This activity practises the school subjects a little more.

Transcript

Eins:

Teacher:	Eins, zwei, drei und . . .

Zwei:

Teacher:	Good morning.
Children:	Good morning Mr Weidemann.
Teacher:	Open your books at page 23.

Drei:

Teacher:	Jens, wie viel ist vierzehn plus fünf?
Jens:	Eh . . . neunzehn?
Teacher:	Richtig. Steffi. Wie viel ist zweiundzwanzig minus sieben?

Vier:

Students:	Martin, Martin! – Tooor!!!

Fünf:

Teacher:	Hier sind drei Säugetiere: Das ist ein Hund, das ist eine Katze und das ist ein Pferd. Wer kennt noch mehr Säugetiere? Ja, Carola?
Student:	Mäuse und Hamster sind auch Säugetiere.

Sechs:

Teacher:	Wo ist Italien? Ja, Sarah?
Girl:	Italien ist im Süden von Europa. Am Mittelmeer.
Teacher:	Gut. Und wie heißt die Hauptstadt von Italien? Ja, Robin.
Boy:	Die Hauptstadt von Italien heißt Rom.

Answers

1	Musik	4	Sport
2	Englisch	5	Biologie
3	Mathe	6	Erdkunde

Aussprache   TH •

German speakers do not pronounce **TH** like the English, instead they pronounce it **T**.

Transcript

Heinz:	Mathe ist viel zu schwierig!
	Mathe, Thomas, Thorsten, Theresa.

Vokabeltipp   Wie gefällt dir . . . ?

This box gives some most useful questions and answers relating to opinions about school subjects.

4 Schreib was! Sieh dir den Cartoon nochmal an. Richtig oder falsch?

This activity uses the cartoon again to consolidate both school subjects and opinions.

Answers

1 F
2 R
3 F
4 R
5 F
6 F
7 R
8 F
9 R

5 and PCM 4.1 Sag was! Wie gefallen dir deine Schulfächer?

Please use PCM 4.1. Students should write the names of the people interviewed in the top row. Under each name they should write a number between 1 and 10 depending on the answer. The final column should be used for adding up. Results for each subject can then be compared and entered on a summary sheet. Here are some useful phrases for discussing the results:

Wie viele Punkte hat <u>Mathe</u>?
Wie viele Leute finden <u>Mathe</u> gut / nicht so gut?

6 Sag was! Was magst du lieber? Mache Sätze mit einem Partner. **E**

This activity practises the comparison **lieber als** ("than").

Vokabeltipp Lieblingsfächer

This box gives some useful expressions relating to school subject preferences.

7 Hör zu! Mein Lieblingsfach. Was passt zusammen?

This activity gives further practice in understanding opinions about subjects.

Transcript
1)

Petra:	Na, Yussuf. Findest du Schule gut?
Yussuf:	Ja. Schule ist in Ordnung. Und du?
Petra:	Es geht. Was ist denn dein Lieblingsfach, Yussuf?

| Yussuf: | Ich habe zwei Lieblingsfächer. Ich finde Chemie toll. Und mir gefällt Englisch sehr gut. Und du, Petra? Was sind deine Lieblingsfächer? |
| Petra: | Mein Lieblingsfach, . . . warte mal . . . hm . . . ja, ich mag Informatik sehr gern. Ja, Informatik ist mein Lieblingsfach. |

2)

Megan:	Hallo Jakob. Sag mal, wie findest du eigentlich Technologie?
Jakob:	Technologie? Das mag ich nicht so gern. Mein Lieblingsfach ist Sozialkunde. Das finde ich interessant. Und du, Megan?
Megan:	Technologie ist mein Lieblingsfach! Sozialkunde finde ich zu langweilig.

Answers

1	Petra	Informatik
2	Yussuf	Chemie, Englisch
3	Megan	Technologie
4	Jakob	Sozialkunde

8 Sag was! Was ist dein Lieblingsfach? Mache ein Diagramm für deine Klasse.

The students are asked to make a wall chart showing their favourite subjects cf. Exercise 5 & PCM 4.1. Students could use coloured stickers to indicate favourite subjects.

Vokabeltipp Lehrer

This activity revises character descriptions – this time in order to describe teachers. You should point out the difference between **Lehrer** and **Lehrerin** before starting Ex. 9.

9 Hör zu! Warum? **E**

This exercise is more demanding and requires the students to express their opinion in full sentences.

Transcript

Thomas:	Wie findest du Informatik, Miriam?
Miriam:	Ich finde Informatik nicht so gut, Thomas.
Thomas:	Warum?
Miriam:	Ich finde Informatik echt schwierig. Und du?
Thomas:	Ich mag Informatik. Es ist total interessant. Es ist mein Lieblingsfach.
Miriam:	Hast du eine Lehrerin oder einen Lehrer in Informatik?
Thomas:	Ich habe eine Informatik-Lehrerin. Sie ist sehr lustig und echt nett. Und du, Miriam?
Miriam:	Ich habe auch eine Lehrerin. Sie ist aber ein bisschen langweilig und gar nicht lustig.

Thomas:	Was ist denn dein Lieblingsfach?
Miriam:	Ich mag Kunst lieber als Informatik. Kunst ist mein Lieblingsfach!
Thomas:	Warum?
Miriam:	Kunst ist interessant und ganz einfach.
Thomas:	Ich finde Kunst gar nicht einfach. Ich finde es schwierig.
Miriam:	Hast du eine Kunst-Lehrerin, Thomas?
Thomas:	Nein, ich habe einen Lehrer. Und du?
Miriam:	Ich auch. Mein Lehrer ist in Ordnung. Er ist ziemlich cool. Und wie ist dein Lehrer?
Thomas:	Er ist ganz nett.

Answers

Miriams Lieblingsfach ist <u>Kunst</u>.

Thomas' Lieblingsfach ist <u>Informatik</u>.

Miriam findet Informatik <u>nicht so gut</u>.

Thomas findet Informatik <u>interessant</u>.

Miriam hat <u>eine Lehrerin</u> in Informatik.

Sie ist <u>langweilig</u>.

Thomas hat <u>eine Lehrerin</u> in Informatik.

Sie ist <u>lustig</u>.

Miriam findet Kunst <u>ganz einfach</u>.

Thomas findet Kunst <u>schwierig</u>.

Miriam hat <u>einen Lehrer</u> in Kunst.

Er ist <u>cool und in Ordnung</u>.

Thomas hat <u>einen Lehrer</u> in Kunst.

Er ist <u>nett</u>.

There are other possibilities!

10 Sag was! Mach einen Dialog nach dem Modell oben. **E**

Students are invited to write dialogues based on those they have just heard in Exercise 9. They should write out the dialogues before performing them.

PCM 4.2   Hör zu! Wie findest du . . . ?

This item practises opinions about school subjects.

Transcript

Boy:	Ich mag Biologie. Biologie finde ich gut.
Girl:	Mathe finde ich total langweilig. Ja, echt langweilig!
Boy:	Erdkunde ist mein Lieblingsfach. Ich finde Erdkunde toll!
Girl:	Mir gefällt Französisch gar nicht. Ich finde Französisch total doof!
Boy:	Informatik ist in Ordnung. Es geht.
Girl:	Ich mag Deutsch nicht so gern. Deutsch gefällt mir nicht so gut.

Answers

1 – b – C	4 – e – D
2 – f – A	5 – c – B
3 – a – E	6 – d – F

Vokabeltipp Die Uhrzeit

Time on the hour from 01.00 to 24.00 is introduced here. An introduction to more complex times will follow in Einheit B.

Kulturtipp Wie spät ist es in Deutschland?

This box gives more help with the 24 hour clock system and also explains that the German-speaking countries are one hour ahead of us.

11 Wie viel Uhr ist es in . . . ?

Apart from practising the structures introduced previously, this activity ties in with the demands for cross-curricular activities. Students could discuss time zones with their geography teacher and possibly get a map of the world showing time lines. Knowing what time it is in other parts of the world is useful if you are "chatting" on the web. You need to know what time is best to call!

PCM 4.3   Schreib was! Wie spät ist es?

This item gives further practice of the clock (hours only).

Answers

1 Es ist drei Uhr.

2 Es ist sechzehn Uhr.

3 Es ist zwölf Uhr.

4 Es ist neunzehn Uhr.

5 Es ist fünfzehn Uhr.

6 Es ist zwei Uhr.

7 Es ist achtzehn Uhr.

8 Es ist fünf Uhr.

9 Es ist einundzwanzig Uhr.

10 Es ist ein Uhr.

PCM 4.4   Schreib was! Wann hast du Mathe?

This item practises time and subjects.

Answers

1 Um neun Uhr habe ich Deutsch.

2 Um zwölf Uhr habe ich Mathe.

3 Um acht Uhr habe ich Sport.

4 Um ein Uhr habe ich Kunst.

5 Um elf Uhr habe ich Geschichte.

6 Um zwei Uhr habe ich Biologie.

7 Um neun Uhr habe ich Erdkunde.

8 Um zehn Uhr habe ich Musik.

Vokabeltipp Die Wochentage

This box gives the days of the week. The **Pass auf!** box gives the other word for Saturday – **Sonnabend** – still frequently used in certain areas of German-speaking countries.

12 Lied: Laurenzia

This song practises the days of the week and may appeal to the more energetic students! Germans normally stand in a circle while singing the song. Each time you sing Laurenzia and each time you sing a day of the week you bend your knees!

Transcript

1. Laurenzia, liebe Laurenzia mein,
   wann werden wir wieder zusammen sein?
   Am Montag.
   Ach wenn es doch erst wieder Montag wär,
   und ich bei meiner Laurenzia wär,
   am Montag.
2. Laurenzia, liebe Laurenzia mein,
   wann werden wir wieder zusammen sein?
   Am Dienstag.
   Ach wenn es doch erst wieder Montag, Dienstag wär,
   und ich bei meiner Laurenzia wär,
   am Dienstag.
3. Laurenzia, liebe Laurenzia mein,
   wann werden wir wieder zusammen sein?
   Am Mittwoch.
   Ach wenn es doch erst wieder Montag, Dienstag,
   Mittwoch wär,
   und ich bei meiner Laurenzia wär,
   am Mittwoch.
4. Laurenzia, liebe Laurenzia mein,
   wann werden wir wieder zusammen sein?
   Am Donnerstag.
   Ach wenn es doch erst wieder Montag, Dienstag,
   Mittwoch, Donnerstag wär,
   und ich bei meiner Laurenzia wär,
   am Donnerstag.
5. Laurenzia, liebe Laurenzia mein,
   wann werden wir wieder zusammen sein?
   Am Freitag.
   Ach wenn es doch erst wieder Montag, Dienstag,
   Mittwoch, Donnerstag, Freitag wär,
   und ich bei meiner Laurenzia wär,
   am Freitag.
6. Laurenzia, liebe Laurenzia mein,
   wann werden wir wieder zusammen sein?
   Am Samstag.

Ach wenn es doch erst wieder Montag, Dienstag,
Mittwoch, Donnerstag, Freitag, Samstag wär,
und ich bei meiner Laurenzia wär,
am Samstag.
7. Laurenzia, liebe Laurenzia mein,
   wann werden wir wieder zusammen sein?
   Am Sonntag.
   Ach wenn es doch erst wieder Montag, Dienstag,
   Mittwoch, Donnerstag, Freitag, Samstag, Sonntag wär,
   und ich bei meiner Laurenzia wär,
   am Sonntag.

13 and PCM 4.5 Das Launenbarometer

Make copies of PCM 4.5 for each individual to insert their own **Launenbarometer** and that of their friends. You could then make a big wall chart where students can display their results. Discuss what makes a day good or bad, and why particular days are better or worse than others. Strategies for improvement could then be discussed!

Spiel: Wolf und Schafe   A

Wolf und Schafe is an additional activity which can be used to practise numbers and the time. It is the German version of the English game "What's the time, Mr Wolf?".

A large space such as a hall or a playground is ideal for this game.

One student is **Herr Wolf** and stands or sits on one side of the room. The rest of the students are the sheep and start on the opposite side of the room.

The sheep shout: „Wie spät ist es, Herr Wolf?" The wolf answers „Es ist . . . . Uhr." (only full hours).

The sheep then take the same number of steps as the time called towards the other end of the room. The wolf tries to get the sheep close to him / her, but if a sheep manages to reach the wolf with the number of steps called, the wolf is caught and that sheep becomes the new wolf.

When the wolf thinks the sheep have come close enough to catch, he / she answers the call „Wie spät ist es, Herr Wolf?" with: **„Essenszeit!"** He / she then tries to catch a sheep, which then becomes the next wolf.

Einheit B   Mein Schultag

Unit 4 B will introduce:
- *more about the clock*
- *when school starts and finishes*
- *what lessons you have when*
- *some useful classroom phrases*

PCMs 4.8 – 4.12 accompany this section.

1   Heinz ist spät dran

Heinz saunters in late for school. The teacher could explain about times of the school day in Germany (some days may start later than others). The students may discuss what happens if they are late.

Transcript

Pia:	Mensch Heinz, du kommst zu spät!
Heinz:	Wieso? Wie viel Uhr ist es denn?
Pia:	Viertel vor zehn.
Heinz:	Ich komme nicht zu spät. Die Schule beginnt am Donnerstag um fünf vor zehn.
Pia:	Richtig, aber heute ist Mittwoch!
Heinz:	Oh je!!! Was haben wir jetzt?
Pia:	Mathe.
Heinz:	Oh nein, ich habe die Hausaufgaben vergessen ... Lass mich abschreiben, Pia!
Pia:	Nein!
Heinz:	Doch, bitte!
Pia:	Nein!
Heinz:	Aua!
Pia and Heinz:	Mist!
Herr Schulze:	Guten Morgen, alle zusammen.
Klasse:	Guten Morgen, Herr Schulze!
Herr Schulze:	Dana Kaufmann?
Dana:	Hier.
Herr Schulze:	Heinz Schuh?
Heinz:	Hier.
Herr Schulze:	Pia Klein?
Pia:	Hier!

 *Kulturtipp* **Schule**

This item gives the children some information about German and Austrian schools. If you have a link with a school in a German-speaking country, this would be a good time to get the students to find out more information about the type of school it is.

S p r a c h t i p p

Die Uhrzeit

It is a good idea to revise the numbers 1–60 in order to be able to count to 60 minutes. The time of day is best practised with a large clock with moveable hands. The more complicated expressions:

fünf vor halb drei (2.25 Uhr) and **fünf nach halb drei** (2.35 Uhr)

are not included in the Student's Book but can be introduced if the teacher so wishes.

Vokabeltipp **Wann ist Schule?**

To avoid confusion the number of possible expressions has been limited to a few simple ones. Other ways of expressing the time will be introduced later.

PCM 4.6   Schreib was! Wie spät ist es?

This item practises minutes past and to the hour. Questions 6 and 9 practise the half hour.

Answers

1	Es ist Viertel nach sechs.	6	Es ist halb drei.
2	Es ist Viertel vor fünf.	7	Es ist zehn vor acht.
3	Es ist zwanzig nach zwölf.	8	Es ist fünf nach fünf.
4	Es ist zwanzig vor sieben.	9	Es ist halb zehn.
5	Es ist zehn nach drei.	10	Es ist Viertel vor zwei.

PCM 4.7   Schreib was! Tage und Monate

This item revises the days of the week and the months of the year.

Answers	Answers
Montag	Januar
Dienstag	Februar
Mittwoch	März
Donnerstag	April
Freitag	Mai
Samstag	Juni
Sonntag	Juli
	August
	September
	Oktober
	November
	Dezember

2 Schreib was! Uhr oder Stunde? Fülle die Lücken.

Answers

1 Es ist zehn <u>Uhr</u>.
2 Die erste <u>Stunde</u> ist Deutsch.
3 Die dritte <u>Stunde</u> ist Biologie.
4 Das ist meine <u>Uhr</u>.

3 Lies was! Pias Stundenplan
4 Sieh dir Pias Stundenplan an. Wann sind die Stunden?

Students could be asked to write and display their own timetables and to write when their lessons start and finish. For extra practice students could refer to a television listings magazine in order to tell each other at what time a programme is on: e.g. „Eastenders ist von . . . bis . . .“

Answers

1 Die erste Stunde ist von 8.05 bis 8.50.
2 Die zweite Stunde ist von 8.55 bis 9.40.
3 Die dritte Stunde ist von 9.55 bis 10.40.
4 Die vierte Stunde ist von 10.45 bis 11.30.
5 Die fünfte Stunde ist von 11.55 bis 12.40.
6 Die sechste Stunde ist von 12.45 bis 13.30.

5 Sieh dir Pias Stundenplan an und fülle die Lücken aus: „beginnt" oder „endet"? **E**

Students should insert the correct word. Again this could lead to cultural comparisons as Pia's day does not always start and end at the same time.

Answers

1 Die Schule <u>beginnt</u> am Dienstag um 7.15 Uhr.
2 Die Schule <u>endet</u> am Montag um 12.40 Uhr.
3 Die Schule <u>beginnt</u> am Donnerstag um 9.55 Uhr.
4 Die Schule <u>endet</u> am Samstag um 9.40 Uhr.
5 Die kleine Pause <u>beginnt</u> um 9.40 Uhr.
6 Die große Pause <u>endet</u> um 11.55 Uhr.

6 Hör zu! Schule in Deutschland und England **A**

In this listening exercise school routines in English and German schools are compared and contrasted. It can be exploited still further by asking students to contrast and compare the school day in both countries, especially break times. It is also worth noting that German pupils don't wear school uniforms and don't have lunch in school. If your students correspond with a school in a German-speaking country, students could exchange a description of their school hours.

Transcript

Yasemin:	Hallo Claire, wie geht's?
Claire:	Prima. Und dir? Wie gefällt dir die Schule in Deutschland?
Yasemin:	Mir geht's gut. Ich finde meine Schule gut.
Claire:	Wie heißt deine Schule?
Yasemin:	Ich gehe auf die Gesamtschule Nord.
Claire:	Wann beginnt die Schule in Deutschland?
Yasemin:	Viel zu früh! Die Schule beginnt am Mittwoch und Freitag um halb acht!
Claire:	Um halb acht? Meine Schule beginnt erst um neun Uhr!
Yasemin:	Ich habe am Dienstag auch um neun Uhr Schule, Claire.
Claire:	Und wann ist am Montag und Donnerstag Schule?
Yasemin:	Die Schule beginnt am Montag und Donnerstag um Viertel nach acht. Am Samstag ist um fünf vor zehn Schule.
Claire:	Am Samstag? Hast du am Samstag auch Schule, Yasemin?
Yasemin:	Ja. Leider! Ich habe am Samstag aber nur zwei Stunden Deutsch. Die Schule endet am Samstag um halb zwölf.
Claire:	Ich habe am Samstag keine Schule! Wann ist die Schule aus?
Yasemin:	Die Schule ist am Montag und Dienstag um zwanzig nach eins aus. Am Mittwoch und Freitag ist die Schule um halb eins aus. Und die Schule endet am Donnerstag schon um halb zwölf.
Claire:	Um halb zwölf? Ich habe jeden Tag bis Viertel nach drei Schule. Das ist nicht fair, Yasemin. Ich habe von zehn nach zwölf bis zwanzig nach eins Pause. Wann hast du Pause?
Yasemin:	Ich habe zwei Pausen, Claire. Die kleine Pause ist nur 10 Minuten: von Viertel vor zehn bis fünf vor zehn. Die große Pause ist eine Viertelstunde lang: von halb zwölf bis Viertel vor zwölf.
Claire:	Hm. Das ist nicht so gut . . .

Answers

1   R
2   F – Die Schule beginnt am Mittwoch und Freitag <u>um 8.30 Uhr</u> (7.30 Uhr).
3   F – Die Schule beginnt am <u>Donnerstag</u> (Dienstag) um 9 Uhr.
4   R
5   F – Am Samstag ist um <u>10.05 Uhr</u> (9.55 Uhr) Schule.
6   R
7   F – Die Schule ist am Montag und Dienstag um <u>1.15 Uhr</u> (1.20 Uhr) aus.
8   F – Am Mittwoch und Freitag ist die Schule um <u>1.30</u> (12.30 Uhr) aus.
9   F – Am Donnerstag endet die Schule um <u>10.30</u> (11.30 Uhr).
10 F – Die kleine Pause ist von <u>9.50 Uhr bis 10.05 Uhr</u>. (9.45 – 9.55 Uhr).
11 F – Die große Pause ist <u>vier Stunden</u> lang. (eine Viertel Stunde).

7 and PCM 4.8 Ergänze Yasemin und Claires Stundenpläne

Please copy the timetables, so that the students can fill them in, based on the information they have already heard in Exercise 6, or ask the students to draw two blank forms in their exercise books. They will probably need to listen to this a number of times in order to get all the details. First they could try and listen just for the times Yasemin gives, then for the times Claire gives. Weaker students will need help here, perhaps by giving them the correct times (see above) on an OHT and asking them to select the correct one each time.

8 Sag was! Stundenpläne E

The students should first look back at Exercise 3 and describe Pia's timetable again, and then describe their own. For the purpose of this exercise it would be helpful if the students had already written out their own timetable in German.

9 Schreib was! Ergänze die Sätze E

This exercise practises the present tense of some common verbs.

Answers
1 Ich <u>heiße</u> Pia.
2 Er <u>beschreibt</u> seine Familie.
3 Du <u>hast</u> heute Geburtstag.
4 Ihr <u>wohnt</u> in der Stadtmitte.
5 Tante Katrin und Onkel Hans sind verheiratet. Sie <u>leben</u> zusammen.
6 Hans und Jürgen sind gute Freunde – sie <u>finden</u> Mathematik interessant.

Sprachtipp

Personal pronouns
This tip introduces the students to all the personal pronouns. They will, in fact, have encountered many of them prior to this. The tip also reminds the students of the present tense of the verb **wohnen**.

10 Schreib was! Bilde Sätze (1) E

This activity encourages more able students to make up sentences from the words in the 3 columns.

11 Schreib was! Bilde Sätze (2) E

This activity encourages more able students to make up their own sentences from the verb forms given.

PCM 4.9 Grammatik. Schreib was! Ich und du

This item practises the personal pronouns.

Antwort
1	ich	6	Sie
2	du	7	ihr
3	wir	8	sie
4	sie	9	es
5	er		

PCM 4.10 Schreib was! Finde das richtige Ende.

This item practises the verb endings for the present tense.

Answers
1 Wie findest du Mathe?
2 Wo wohnt Klaus?
3 Pierre kommt aus Frankreich.
4 Ich finde Deutsch interessant.
5 Wir wohnen in Wien.
6 Ich wohne in Deutschland.
7 Kommst du aus England?
8 Ich komme aus der Schweiz.

Vokabeltipp Wann habt ihr Mathe? E

These expressions encourage the students to use more German.

12 Hör zu! Welcher Tag ist es? E

The students should listen to Pia and Heinz describing their day at school. By listening carefully and looking at Pia's timetable, the students ought to be able to work out which day they are describing.

Transcript
Eins:
Pia: Was haben wir heute?
Heinz: In der ersten Stunde haben wir Mathe. In der zweiten Stunde haben wir Musik. Wir haben auch Englisch und eine Doppelstunde Sport. Die Schule ist heute um halb eins aus.
Zwei:
Heinz: Wann beginnt heute die Schule?
Pia: Um fünf nach acht.

Heinz: Was hast du in der ersten Stunde?

Pia: Englisch. Und ich habe in der zweiten Stunde Deutsch.

Heinz: Und was hast du in der letzten Stunde?

Pia: Ich habe in der letzten Stunde Französisch.

Drei:

Pia: Was habt ihr morgen?

Heinz: Wir haben eine Doppelstunde Kunst und eine Doppelstunde Deutsch. Die Schule beginnt erst um fünf vor zehn!

Pia: Klasse!

Vier:

Heinz: Wann beginnt morgen die Schule?

Pia: Morgen haben wir eine Vorstunde Informatik.

Heinz: Oh je! Und was haben wir dann?

Pia: Wir haben in der ersten und zweiten Stunde Französisch.

Heinz: Français avec la belle Madame Leroc. Oh-la-la!

Pia: Heinz, du bist doof!

Heinz: Und du bist langweilig! Was haben wir in der vierten Stunde, chérie?

Pia: Da haben wir Physik.

Heinz: Und wann ist die Schule morgen aus?

Pia: Die Schule endet schon um halb zwölf.

Heinz: Sehr gut!!!

Fünf:

Pia: Was hast du heute in der ersten Stunde?

Heinz: Ich habe Erdkunde bei Herrn Meier. Der ist so langweilig!

Pia: Und in der fünften Stunde?

Heinz: Ich habe in der fünften Stunde Religion. Das ist in Ordnung.

Pia: Und in der letzten Stunde?

Heinz: Englisch. We haff English wiz Mister Conrad! He speaks verry funny English!

Pia: Ist die Schule heute erst um halb zwei aus?

Heinz: Jaaa.

Answers

1	Freitag	4	Dienstag
2	Montag	5	Mittwoch
3	Donnerstag		

13 Sag was! Beschreib den Stundenplan **E**

This item allows the students a chance to discuss their timetables. If they have not already made out their own timetable, please copy from the blank photocopiable master provided (PCM 4.8).

14 Sag was! Mein Traumstundenplan **E**

Students should work with a partner and then report to the teacher or their group what their ideal timetable would look like.

Aussprache Die Umlaute • • • • • • • • • • • • • • •

Transcript

ä, Ä Wie spät ist es?
      Das Mädchen gefällt mir. Sie ist Engländerin.

ö, Ö Schildkröten und Vögel sind blöd.
      Hör zu, in Köln ist es schön.

ü, Ü Fünf Brüder im Süden von München: Tschüs!
      Grün für Nürgül.

Lerntipp Umlaute

If your students have access to computers this would be an opportunity to let them find out how to type the special characters in German. Your school system may have special provisions for that. You may even have a German spell-check. You can also use the following international ASCII codes which should work in most word processing environments, including e-mail.

ä = ALT + 132
ö = ALT + 148
ü = ALT + 129
ß = ALT + 225
Ä = ALT + 142
Ö = ALT + 153
Ü = ALT + 154

There is no capital version of ß. You use SS instead. Some on-line dictionaries allow you to cut and paste accented characters, when you are looking up a word.

e.g. Langenscheidt:

http://t1.sail-labs.com/t1probe.html

---

15 Hör zu! Umlaut oder kein Umlaut?

This activity encourages the students to listen out for the umlauted characters

Transcript

• **a oder ä?**
1 In der Nähe der Niederlande
2 März im Harz
3 Martha und Änne
4 Schulfächer: Mathe, Informatik, Französisch

• **o oder ö?**
1 Österreich und Köln sind schon schön.
2 Zwölf Onkel hören Monika zu.
3 Otto und Jörg sprechen Französisch.

• **u oder ü?**
1 Fünfzehn hübsche Müller und ein süßer Hund.
2 Mein Bruder ist Türke.
3 Müde aber lustig in Zürich.

- **ä, ö, oder ü?**
1 Köln
2 Würzburg
3 Düsseldorf
4 Tübingen
5 Dänemark
6 Brüssel
7 Göttingen
8 Lübeck
9 Rumänien
10 Malmö

Vokabeltipp 100–1 000 000

This item introduces the numbers from 100 to a million. These numbers could be added to your wall display, or could be used in a game of bingo with "higher" numbers! It is worth reminding the students about the fact that German-speaking countries use spaces or points instead of commas and commas instead of points.

Vokabeltipp In der Klasse (1)

This section introduces some extremely useful classroom vocabulary which either you or the students may like to copy out in a larger version for wall display!

Sprachtipp

Imperativ
Following the useful classroom vocabulary, this item introduces some imperatives which you may use or want the students to use when giving each other instructions.

Vokabeltipp In der Klasse (2)

This item builds on the **Sprachtipp** and gives the sort of instructions the pupils may hear in class.

16 Hör zu! Welches Bild passt?

The students have to match the pictures to the expressions in the **Vokabeltipp** box.

Transcript
A Komm nach vorne!
B Entschuldigung, ich habe mein Buch vergessen.
C Steht auf!
D Schließt das Buch!

E Es tut mir Leid, ich bin zu spät.
F Setzt euch!
G Entschuldigung, ich habe meinen Stift vergessen.
H Öffnet das Buch!

Answers
A 5, **B** 8, **C** 1, **D** 4, **E** 6, **F** 2, **G** 7, **H** 3

17 Spiel: Bitte!

This game is similar to "Simon says". The teacher gives instructions to the students. If he / she begins the command with **Bitte!** the students have to follow it. If he / she leaves out **Bitte!**, they should not do anything. The teacher can pretend to act on the command, even when he / she did not say **Bitte!**. Anyone who acts on a command without **Bitte!** is out.

18 Wortschlange: Finde die Schulfächer. Was bleibt übrig?

An activity to practise the school subjects.

Answers

MATHE	INFORMATIK
DEUTSCH	RELIGION
BIOLOGIE	KUNST
ENGLISCH	GESCHICHTE
ERDKUNDE	CHEMIE

After finding the subjects in the snake, the students should also find:

Solution: MEIN LIEBLINGSFACH IST DEUTSCH

PCM 4.11   Spiel: Schulrennen

On a large piece of card draw a winding line, then draw a circle on each end with **Anfang** and **Ende**. Place 30-50 spots on the line at equal distances. Make every 5th spot bigger or of a different colour.

Cut out two sets of game cards for each group (see PCMs) and place them in a stack face down on the table.

Students choose a counter and start rolling the dice. When he / she lands on a coloured spot, the student has to draw a card from the stack and must answer the question in German. When all cards have been used up they can be re-shuffled.

The player who reaches the finish first wins the game.

These are the questions that are on the PCM:

Wie gefällt dir Mathe?
Wie findest du Deutsch?

Was ist dein Lieblingsfach?
Welches Fach gefällt dir nicht?
Wer ist dein Lieblingslehrer?
Wer ist deine Lieblingslehrerin?
Wie heißt dein(e) Deutschlehrer(in)?
Wie findest du dein(e) Englischlehrer(in)?
Wie spät ist es?
Wann beginnt die Schule?
Wann ist die Schule aus?
Wann ist Pause?
Wann hast du Sport?
Wann hast du Kunst?

19 Hör zu! Lied: Der Schul-Rap

Students should listen to the song and, if possible, follow the words in the book. It will help them remember some key phrases from this chapter!

Transcript

Wie spät ist es?
Wie viel Uhr ist es?
Es ist Montag,
zehn nach zehn.
Es ist Montag –
ich muss zur Schule geh'n!
            Oh nein, oh nein!!!

Guten Morgen, guten Tag.
Entschuldigung, ich komme zu spät.
Ich habe keine Hausaufgaben;
ich habe sie vergessen!
            Oh nein, oh nein!!!

Ich hab' um acht Uhr Mathe.
Ich finde Mathe doof.
Ich hab' um neun Uhr Deutsch.
Deutsch ist viel zu schwer.
            Oh nein, oh nein!!!

Ich hab' um zehn Uhr Englisch.
Ich mag Englisch nicht.
Ich hab' um elf Uhr Pause.
Das gefällt mir gut!
            Oh ja, oh ja!!!

Ich hab' um zwölf Uhr Musik.
Ich finde Musik toll!
Um ein Uhr ist die Schule aus.
Das find' ich gut, jawohl!
            Oh ja, Hurra!!!!

PCM 4.12   Der Schul-Rap – Was passiert?

This item encourages the students to listen carefully to the song and to answer the questions given.

Answers

3, 8, 5, 7, 2, 1, 4, 6

Answers

1	R	6	R
2	R	7	F
3	F	8	F
4	F	9	R
5	R		

www. Lernen in Deutschland

Encourage the students to try and look at a web site (e.g. http://www.learnetix.de) where German pupils get help with their school subjects e.g. German, English and Maths, and meet them in the chat room.

Leseseiten

These lively opinions about teachers give the students a different approach to the topic introduced in the chapter. They include some difficult vocabulary but should be accessible with help from the teacher. The exercises are designed to resemble GCSE style questioning. „**Mach eine Liste: Wie soll ein guter / schlechter Lehrer sein?**" and „**Und du, was meinst du: Wie soll ein Lehrer sein?**" allow the students to express their own opinions. This is an important skill for Writing and Speaking examinations.

Richtig oder falsch?
Answers
1. F
2. R
3. R
4. R

Mach eine Liste: wie soll ein guter / schlechter Lehrer sein?

This item gives the students the opportunity to use the vocabulary they have learnt.

Wer spricht?
Answers
1 Anja
2 Sasha
3 Kevin
4 Tina
5 Insa

Aussagesätze and Grammatik

These pages are useful quick references for students working alone or in pairs – on a classwork or homework assignment. They are also useful for revision purposes, as they sum up the important grammar and vocabulary of the chapter.

Test 1

Test 1 provides you with Speaking, Listening, Reading and Writing material based on material in *Anstoß 1*.

I Sprechen – Rollenspiele

This item gives you a choice of two role plays and a selection of questions to conduct a short oral examination with your students.

II Lies was! In der Zeitung

This short Reading item is designed to resemble questions which could be found on a Foundation Tier paper.

Answers

1	R	1	Erwin Schindelka
2	F	2	Norbert
3	R	3	Dustin
4	F	4	51 cm
5	R	5	Jan und Christoph
		6	Bernd und Andrea Wietzke

III Hör zu! Besuch! Schreibe die Worte

Students need to listen out for specific details in order to be able to recognise these people:

Transcript

Boy: Wie siehst du aus, Sally?
Girl: Ich bin ziemlich groß und sportlich.
Boy: Und deine Haare?

Girl: Ich habe lange, blonde Haare.
Boy: Sind sie glatt?
Girl: Nein, meine Haare sind lockig.
Boy: Deine Augen?
Girl: Ich habe eine Brille und braune Augen. Und wie siehst du aus?

Transcript

Girl: Hallo, Onkel Bob.
Man: Hallo, ich komme morgen.
Girl: Wie siehst du aus, Onkel Bob?
Man: Ich bin klein und lustig.
Girl: Und deine Haare?
Man: Ich habe keine Haare. Ich habe eine Glatze, aber ich habe einen roten Bart.
Girl: Und wie sehen deine Augen aus?
Man: Ich habe blaue Augen.
Girl: Bis morgen, Onkel Bob!

Answers

Sally: groß, sportlich, lange, blonde, lockige Haare, Brille, braune Augen

Onkel Bob: klein, lustig, Glatze, Bart, blaue Augen

IV Schreib was!

Students are invited to write what they can about their family and their school as these are the main topics covered up to now. No specific details are identified, but it is hoped that each student will now be able to write some sentences from memory on either of these topic areas.

(**Kapitel 5**) **Mein Zuhause**

Unit 5 A will introduce:
- *house locations*
- *types of houses*
- *how to describe where you live*

PCMs 5.1 – 5.5 accompany this section.

1   Ich wohne hier

The cartoon introduces some simple descriptions of where people live, with Heinz boasting to Trish about his imaginary luxury homes. Trish spots what he is doing immediately and calls his bluff.

Transcript

Heinz: Hallo Trish! Hier ist mein Foto! Das bin ich.
         Das ist mein Haus in Südfrankreich. Es ist in der Nähe von Cannes.
         Es hat einen Garten und einen Swimmingpool. Toll, was?!
         Das ist meine Luxus-Wohnung in Mainz, in der Innenstadt.
         Sie ist in einem Hochhaus, im zwanzigsten Stock. Echt cool!
         Und wo wohnst du?

Trish: Hallo Heinz! Ich wohne hier. Deine Trish

2   Gruppenarbeit

This short exercise encourages students to search for the key expressions in the cartoon.

Answers
- Das ist mein Haus.
- Das ist meine Wohnung.
- Wo wohnst du?
- Ich wohne hier.

3   Schreib was! Wo wohnt Heinz?

This item requires a little more information, but is not too demanding, as it mainly requires students to lift the answer from the text. Some text manipulation is required i.e. to avoid replying "Das ist mein Haus" – so weaker students may require some assistance here.

Answers

These are suggested answers only – obviously students may use other expressions.

1   Das Haus in Südfrankreich ist in der Nähe von Cannes. Es hat einen Garten und einen Swimmingpool.
2   Die Luxus-Wohnung in Mainz ist in der Innenstadt. Sie ist in einem Hochhaus, im zwanzigsten Stock.

(**Vokabeltipp**) Haus oder Wohnung (1)

This item gives the basic key phrases for the unit and includes dative case endings. This leads onto the introduction of the dative case.

S p r a c h t i p p

Dativ (1)

This item briefly explains the concept of the dative of the indefinite article.

4   Lies was! Wer wohnt hier?

This exercise consolidates the item on the dative case.

Answers

Jan wohnt in einem Wohnblock. (Picture 2)
Frau Knapp wohnt in einer Wohnung / in einem Hochhaus. (Picture 3)
Herr Braun wohnt in einem Haus. (Picture 1)

(**Vokabeltipp**) Im Haus

This item brings in other items your students may wish to describe.

S p r a c h t i p p

Es gibt

This item reminds students of the need to use the accusative case after **es gibt** and gives a few examples.

5   Schreib was! Kreuze an: Was hat das Haus?

This item encourages students to look at the visual clues and provides a good basis for the following exercise.

Answers

1   Garten, Garage, eine Etage
2   Balkon, drei Etagen
3   Garten, Balkon, zwei Etagen

6 Sag was! Hat dein Haus . . . ?

This item ensures that students make use of the pictures and practise describing houses.

Vokabeltipp **Wo ist dein Haus?**

This item gives the necessary vocabulary for describing where a house is situated.

7 Schreib was! Wo wohnst du?

This item consolidates the above and ensures practice with the descriptions. Students could also be encouraged to describe where they live.

Answers
1 D
2 A
3 C
4 B

Vokabeltipp **Haus oder Wohnung (2)**

This item gives the basic key phrases for the unit and includes dative case endings. This leads onto further information about adjectival endings in the dative case.

PCM 5.1 Hör zu! Mein Haus

This item consolidates the work on houses. Students have to listen for the words describing features of houses and flats (Garage, Garten, Balkon, etc.). It is suitable for all levels.

Transcript

Frau Moser:	Grüß Gott! Ich heiße Moser. Ich wohne in einem alten Haus. Es gibt eine Zentralheizung. Dann ist mir im Winter immer warm. Ja, mein Haus hat eine Zentralheizung.
Susanne:	Ich bin die Susanne. Wir wohnen in einem Haus auf dem Land. Unser Haus hat einen Balkon. Der Balkon ist echt prima!
Herr Jansen:	Mein Name ist Jansen, Klaus Jansen. Ich habe ein Auto. Ich bin froh, dass mein Haus eine Garage hat. Ja, es gibt eine große Garage für mein Auto.
Robert:	Ich bin der Robert. Ich wohne in einem Hochhaus. Das Hochhaus ist ziemlich groß. Es gibt sechs Etagen! Ja, sechs Etagen! Und ich wohne ganz oben!

Answers

Frau Moser	D
Susanne	B
Herr Jansen	C
Robert	A

PCM 5.2 Sag was! Was gibt es hier?

This simple speaking exercise prepares students for more complex tasks. Students have to substitute the icon for the suitable word. As an extension exercise, the icons can be cut out and shared out among the students. They can then be used as cue cards in role plays. Students should be encouraged to use the correct articles and endings.

Answers
1 Mein Haus hat einen Garten.
2 Unsere Wohnung hat eine Zentralheizung.
3 Es gibt sechs Etagen in dem Hochhaus.
4 Ich wohne in einem Wohnblock. Wir haben einen Balkon.
5 Franziska wohnt in einem Wohnblock. Es gibt da eine Garage.
6 Familie Rodrigez wohnt in einem Wohnblock. Es gibt drei Etagen und einen Garten.
7 Ich wohne in einem Haus. Es gibt eine Garage und einen Balkon.
8 Unser Haus hat eine Zentralheizung und zwei Etagen.

S p r a c h t i p p

Dativ (2)
This item introduces the dative adjectival ending with the indefinite article.

8 Lies was! Wer wohnt hier?

Answers
A) Hier wohnt Frau Hoppe.
B) Hier wohnt Emma.
C) Hier wohnt Frau Pötters.
D) Hier wohnt Justus.
E) Hier wohnt Herr Kazim.

9 Sag was! Beschreib ein Haus

This item encourages the students to describe one of the pictures. No answer is given as many are possible, depending on the ability of the student.

10 Hör zu! Wo wohnen sie?

This exercise in the book should only be attempted by the more able students although all students should be able to listen to the descriptions and look at the pictures in the book. Weaker students should be encouraged to listen out for key words e.g. **modern**, **Garten**. As an alternative, weaker students could attempt PCM 5.4 which uses the same transcript.

Transcript

Narrator: Wo wohnen Yasemin, Laura, Matthias und Pierre?

Yasemin: Hallo! Hier ist Yasemin. Wo ich wohne? Ich wohne in einem neuen Haus. Das Haus ist auch sehr modern. Es gibt einen Garten . . . ja, einen großen Garten, und eine Garage . . . für Vaters Auto. Wir wohnen am Stadtrand von Mainz, also etwa 30 Minuten vom Zentrum weg.

Laura: Hi! Hier spricht Laura. Ich wohne sehr zentral – direkt in der Stadtmitte. Wir haben eine Wohnung in einem Hochhaus. Das Hochhaus ist leider gar nicht schön – echt hässlich! Und in der Stadtmitte ist es oft sehr laut.

Matthias: Servus! Hier ist der Matthias. Ja, wo wohne ich? Also meine Eltern haben einen Bauernhof in Tirol. Das ist ganz auf dem Land. Das Haus ist schon sehr alt . . . über hundert Jahre. Es ist wirklich gemütlich. Ich bin gern da. Ich finde unseren Balkon am schönsten. Mutter hat immer Blumen auf dem Balkon. Bei uns auf dem Land ist es sehr ruhig.

Pierre: Salut! Hier spricht Pierre. In Frankreich wohne ich auf dem Dorf. Wir haben eine kleine Wohnung in einem sehr alten Haus. Das Haus hat drei Etagen. Unsere Wohnung ist in der dritten Etage.

Answers

a)	modernen	i)	Land
b)	Garten	j)	alt
c)	Garage	k)	Balkon
d)	Stadtrand	l)	ruhig
e)	Stadtmitte	m)	Dorf
f)	Wohnung	n)	Haus
g)	Hochhaus	o)	Etagen
h)	laut		

PCM 5.3   Sag was! Beschreibe die Häuser. Was gibt es?   E

For this item students are required to form full sentences with the vocabulary practised above. They will also practise **es gibt**. Students should be encouraged to use the correct articles and accusative case endings. They should be reminded about word order / position of verb.

Answers

Im Reihenhaus Wilhelmstraße gibt es eine Zentralheizung, eine Garage und einen Balkon.

Im Haus Sonnenschein gibt es einen Garten, eine Zentralheizung und drei Etagen.

Im Hubertushof gibt es einen Garten, eine Garage und einen Balkon.

In der Villa Wohngut gibt es einen Garten, eine Zentralheizung und zwei Etagen.

PCM 5.4   Hör zu! Wo wohnen sie?   A

Replay the dialogue from Ex. 10, **Hör zu! Wo wohnen sie?** This is a simple matching exercise. Students have to listen out for the key phrases describing where exactly people live and find the matching pictures. This item is given as an alternative to Ex. 10 for weaker students.

Answers

1 Laura
2 Yasemin
3 Pierre
4 Matthias

Sprachtipp

Dativ (3)

This item introduces the dative of the definite article.

Übung: dem, der, oder den? Füll die Lücken aus!

Answers

1 Ich wohne auf <u>dem</u> Land.
2 Petra wohnt in <u>der</u> Stadt.
3 Wir wohnen auf <u>dem</u> Dorf.
4 In <u>dem</u> Haus wohnt Anna.
5 Wer wohnt in <u>der</u> Wohnung?
6 Sie wohnen in <u>den</u> Häusern in der Dorfstraße.
7 In <u>dem</u> Wohnblock wohnt meine Tante.
8 Meine Eltern wohnen auf <u>dem</u> Land.

---

11 Lies den Cartoon und hör zu! Der Umzug

Matthias, David and Heinz are helping Anna and Florian move into a new flat. The boys are keen to help the beautiful Anna, but leave Florian to sort out his furniture himself.

Transcript

Narrator: Florian und Anna haben eine neue Wohnung. Sie ziehen um. Matthias, Heinz und David helfen.

David: Wo ist eure Wohnung?

Anna: Oben, im dritten Stock. Der Schrank ist für das Schlafzimmer. Der Tisch ist für die Küche.

Heinz: Wo ist die Küche?

Anna: Vorne, rechts.

Heinz: Alles klar? Ist das Annas Bett?

Florian: Nein, das ist mein Bett. Die Stühle gehören Anna.

Heinz: Hier, David. Die Stühle sind für Annas Zimmer.

David: Deine Möbel sind alle oben in der Wohnung, Anna!

Anna: Tschüs! Vielen Dank, Jungs!

Florian: Und meine Möbel . . . ???!!

Kulturtipp Wohnen in Deutschland

This item gives some cultural information about German-speaking countries. If your school exchanges letters with a school in a German-speaking country, they may wish to exchange photos or handwritten plans of their houses and compare them.

Vokabeltipp Die Zimmer im Haus

This item brings in the main vocabulary for listing rooms within a house and saying where they are situated.

12 Hör zu! Wo sind ihre Zimmer?

This item explains how to describe which floor your room is on.

Transcript
Ich heiße Yussuf. Ich habe einen Bruder, Mohammed und eine Schwester. Sie heißt Laila. Wir wohnen in einem großen Haus. Mein Zimmer ist ganz oben unter dem Dach. Also im zweiten Stock. Lailas Zimmer ist unten im Erdgeschoss. Also im Erdgeschoss ist Lailas Zimmer. Mohammeds Zimmer ist im ersten Stock – ja, im ersten Stock wohnt Mohammed.

Answers
Yussuf – 2nd floor
Laila – ground floor
Mohammed – 1st floor

Sprachtipp

Dativ (4)
This item introduces adjectival endings with the dative of the definite article.

Übung: dem, der, oder den? Füll die Lücken aus!
This item practises the endings introduced in the **Sprachtipp** above.

Answers
1 Anja wohnt in der kleinen Stadt.
2 Wer wohnt in der schönen Wohnung?
3 Sie wohnen in den kleinen Häusern in der Dorfstraße.
4 In dem modernen Wohnblock wohnt meine Schwester.
5 Meine Eltern wohnen in dem alten Haus.

13 Schreib was! Sag was! Wo wohnen die Familien?

This item encourages the students to write full sentences about where these people live.

Answers
Familie Meier wohnt im Erdgeschoss.

Herr Schuster wohnt im Erdgeschoss.
Familie Nadini wohnt im ersten Stock.
Familie Lehrer wohnt im ersten Stock.
Familie Ergül wohnt im zweiten Stock.
Herr Pauli und Frau Nord wohnen im zweiten Stock.
Frau Glaser wohnt im dritten Stock.
Herr Anatoli wohnt im dritten Stock.

PCM 5.5 Hör zu! Ein komisches Haus A

A simple listening exercise on rooms and floors. Students could discuss why this is an odd house. As an extension activity, more able students could make up descriptions of their own "odd house" and let a partner guess where the rooms are.

Transcript
Boy: Das ist mein Haus. Es gibt einen Keller, ein Erdgeschoss, den ersten und den zweiten Stock.
Girl: Was gibt es im Keller?
Boy: Im Keller gibt es das Badezimmer und das Esszimmer.
Girl: Das Badezimmer und das Esszimmer sind im Keller? Aha! Und was gibt es im Erdgeschoss?
Boy: Im Erdgeschoss gibt es ein Büro und das Elternschlafzimmer.
Girl: Ein Büro und ein Schlafzimmer im Erdgeschoss? Das ist aber komisch. Was gibt es denn im ersten Stock?
Boy: Im ersten Stock ist die Toilette und das Wohnzimmer.
Girl: Die Toilette und das Wohnzimmer sind im ersten Stock? Was gibt es im zweiten Stock?
Boy: Im zweiten Stock gibt es mein Schlafzimmer und die Küche.
Girl: Dein Zimmer und die Küche sind im zweiten Stock, unter dem Dach? Das ist aber ein komisches Haus!
Boy: Ja!!!

Answers
Cellar:	A, G
Ground floor:	H, D
First floor:	F, B
Second floor:	C, E

14 Schreib was! Zimmer im Haus

This item further consolidates the position of the rooms and encourages students to correct false sentences.

Answers
1 F – Die Küche ist im Erdgeschoss.
2 R
3 F – Die Toilette ist im ersten Stock.
4 F – Das Wohnzimmer ist im Erdgeschoss.
5 R
6 F – Es gibt ein Badezimmer im ersten und zweiten Stock.
7 R
8 F – Es gibt ein Büro im Keller.

15 Sag was! Was für Zimmer gibt es? **E**

This item further consolidates the position of the rooms, this time in speech.

Vokabeltipp **Wo ist das Zimmer?**

This item gives more vocabulary so that the students can say exactly where rooms are.

Sprachtipp

Adjectives standing alone **E**
In case the students want to make up adverts or write lists, the endings of the adjectives standing alone are given here.

16 Hör zu! Unser Haus

This item gives a description of Achim's house and consolidates the vocabulary introduced in the **Vokabeltipp**.

Transcript
A: Sag, mal, Achim. Wo wohnst du? Kannst du uns dein Haus beschreiben?
B: Ja klar! Ich wohne bei meinen Eltern. Wir wohnen in einem modernen Reihenhaus. Es gibt zwei Etagen und einen Keller.
Im Erdgeschoss ist der Flur, eine Toilette, die Küche, das Esszimmer und das Wohnzimmer. Vorne im Erdgeschoss ist der Flur. Links vom Flur ist eine kleine Toilette. Ganz links vorne ist die Küche.
A: Also Moment mal; die Küche ist links vorne. Der Flur ist rechts vorne und die Toilette in der Mitte?
B: Richtig. Die Toilette ist zwischen der Küche und dem Flur. Das Esszimmer ist in der Mitte, gegenüber der Treppe und das Wohnzimmer ist hinten.
A: Das Wohnzimmer ist ganz hinten?
B: Ja, genau. Es ist ziemlich groß.
A: Und was ist oben?
B: Oben in der ersten Etage ist mein Zimmer, das Zimmer von meinem Bruder Karlo, das Badezimmer, das Elternschlafzimmer und das Büro.
A: Wo ist dein Zimmer?
B: Mein Zimmer ist vorne. Das Zimmer von meinem Bruder Karlo ist auch vorne. Mein Zimmer ist rechts und Karlos ist links.
A: Dein Zimmer ist vorne rechts und Karlos vorne links, aha! Und was ist hinten?
B: Hinten links ist das Büro und hinten rechts das Elternschlafzimmer.
A: Und wo ist das Badezimmer?
B: Das Badezimmer ist in der Mitte.
A: Was ist den ganz unten?

B: Ganz unten im Haus sind der Keller und die Garage. Der große Keller ist hinten und die Garage ist vorne.
A: Die Garage ist im Keller? Interessant!

Answers

Flur	1	Wohnzimmer	5	Badezimmer	10
Toilette	2	Achims Zimmer	8	Büro	11
Esszimmer	4	Karlos Zimmer	9	Keller	6
Küche	3	Elternschlafzimmer	12	Garage	7

17 Schreib was! Mein Haus

This item consolidates the previous items. If you have a link with a German-speaking school you may wish to encourage the students to send their descriptions to the school.

18 Lies was! Zu vermieten!

This item encourages students to spot the deliberate mistakes and to not take everything at face value.

Answers
1 R
2 F – Das Haus ist alt.
3 R
4 F – Der Garten ist nicht schön.
5 F – Es gibt keine Garage.
6 R
7 R

19 Schreib was! Beschreib das Haus jetzt richtig

This item encourages the students to give a free description of what the house is really like. As an extension activity, students could cut out pictures in tourist brochures and decide how the holiday villa might look in reality (a type of "Holidays from Hell" exercise!). They could be encouraged to write an "under the counter" description of the real villa!

20 Hör zu und sing mit: Der Wohn-Rap

This rap song consolidates the words learned in this unit. Students should be encouraged to sing along. There is an instrumental version on the tape after the full Rap. More able students could be encouraged to make up their own verses changing small details in the song.

Transcript

Boy	Girl
Wo wohnst du?	Ich wohne in einem Haus.
Sag mir, wo wohnst du?	Das Haus ist auf dem Land.
Wo wohnst du?	Es ist groß und alt,
Sag mir, wo wohnst du?	hat einen Garten und Balkon.

Wo ist dein Zimmer?	Mein Zimmer ist im dritten
Sag mir, wo ist dein Zimmer?	Stock,
Wo ist dein Zimmer?	im dritten Stock, im dritten
Sag mir, wo ist dein Zimmer?	Stock.
	Mein Zimmer ist im dritten
	Stock,
	oben unterm Dach.

Girl	Boy
Wo wohnst du?	Ich wohne in einer
Sag mir, wo wohnst du?	Wohnung,
Wo wohnst du?	Sie ist in der Innenstadt.
Sag mir, wo wohnst du?	Das Haus ist neu und laut.
	Aber meine Freunde wohnen
	da!

Wo ist dein Zimmer?	Mein Zimmer ist im
Sag mir, wo ist dein Zimmer?	Erdgeschoss,
Wo ist dein Zimmer?	im Erdgeschoss, im
Sag mir, wo ist dein Zimmer?	Erdgeschoss.
	Mein Zimmer ist im
	Erdgeschoss,
	unten im Erdgeschoss!

21 Schreib was! Wie wohnen sie?

As soon as the students are familiar with the words of the song they should be able to write in a table which words refer to which house.

Answers

Mädchen	Junge
Haus	Wohnung
auf dem Land	in der Innenstadt
alt, groß	laut, neu
Garten / Balkon	Freunde
im dritten Stock	Zimmer im Erdgeschoss
unter dem Dach	unten

22 Gruppenarbeit: Mach selber einen Wohn-Rap.

Students should be encouraged to make up their own verses for the rap tune.

23 Hör zu und sing mit! Mein Haus – dein Haus **E**

This item further consolidates the vocabulary. The vocabulary this time is more complicated. There is

an instrumental version on the tape after the full Rap. More able students could be encouraged to make up their own verses changing small details in the song.

Transcript

1
Ich bau mir ein Haus,
das steht mitten in der Stadt.
Es hat 'nen Fußballplatz im Garten
und 'nen Swimmingpool im Bad.

Refrain 1
Dein Haus, dein Haus,
wie sieht dein Haus aus?

2
Mein Zimmer ist ganz oben,
ganz oben unter'm Dach.
Dort spiele ich Gitarre
und mache ganz viel Krach.

Refrain 1

3
Ich bau dir ein Haus,
das steht weit weg auf dem Land.
Ein Pferd steht da auf dem Balkon.
Es gibt Blumen an der Wand.

Refrain 2
Mein Haus, mein Haus,
so sieht mein Haus aus?

4
Dein Zimmer ist im Erdgeschoss
und es ist violett.
Da gibt es 20 Katzen
und ein Himmelbett.

Refrain 2
Refrain 1

24 Was passt zum ersten Haus / zum zweiten Haus?

An activity which encourages students to listen out for details in the song.

Answers

Haus 1	Haus 2
in der Stadt	Pferd
Zimmer unter dem Dach	Zimmer im Erdgeschoss
Fußballplatz	Himmelbett
lautes Zimmer	Blumen
Swimmingpool	violettes Zimmer
	Balkon
	Katzen
	auf dem Land

25 Mal ein Bild von den Häusern im Lied

An activity for all abilities – again encouraging students to build on the detail in the song.

 Häuser und Wohnungen

These websites give typical advertisements for houses in Germany. You could download some of the advertisements and use them in class.

Students could be encouraged to read some of the advertisements and:

- draw a picture of the house and copy the description for wall display.
- write a longer description of the house, based on the advertisement.
- choose their favourite house and say why they like it.
- Use the pictures for a game where one partner chooses a house and the other has to guess which one has been chosen.

Einheit B   Mein Zimmer

Unit 5 B will introduce how to:
- *describe a bedroom*
- *describe furniture*
- *give opinions about rooms and furniture*

PCMs 5.6 – 5.16 accompany this section.

1   Schreib was! Florians Möbel

This item is really a **Vokabeltipp** in disguise! The intention is that the students associate the words with the pictures. The words are purposefully numbered in the order Masculine, Feminine, Neuter so that the students will see them arranged in the **Vokabeltipp** in a colour coded manner. The picture can be exploited orally in a variety of ways depending on the ability range of the students. At a simple level questions can be asked such as:

„Was ist das?" – to elicit responses such as:
„Das ist ein Fernseher."

Slightly more difficult is the question in the book eliciting the accusative case:

„Was für Möbel gibt es in deinem Zimmer?"
„Es gibt einen Sessel."

More able students may be able to cope with:

„Was für Möbel gibt es in deinem Zimmer?"
„Es gibt ein rotes Sofa."

Answers
1. Fernseher – tv set
2. Kleiderschrank – wardrobe
3. Schrank – cupboard
4. Schreibtisch – desk
5. Sessel – armchair
6. Tisch – table
7. Stuhl – chair
8. Teppich – rug, carpet
9. CD-Spieler – cd player
10. Computer – computer
11. Videorecorder – video recorder
12. Lampe – lamp
13. Tür – door
14. Wand – wall
15. Bett – bed
16. Bild – picture
17. Fenster – window
18. Poster – poster
19. Regal – shelf
20. Sofa – sofa, settee

PCM 5.6   Gruppenarbeit: Hilf Florian!

This item relates back to the cartoon story in Unit 5A, when Florian is left with all his furniture but the boys have helped Anna! Tell your students that Florian has got someone to help him carry in the furniture but unfortunately not all the items are in the right place. It is a simple exercise which practises the vocabulary relating to furniture.

Answers

This is an open exercise and there are no particular "right" answers. Students decide which pieces belong in which room – some items might fit in more than one room, as in the example. Here are a few possible answers:

Der Herd ist für die Küche.
Die Stereoanlage ist für das Wohnzimmer oder Florians Zimmer.
Die Lampe ist für Florians Zimmer.
Das Bett ist für Florians Zimmer.
Die Waschmaschine ist für das Badezimmer oder die Küche.

PCM 5.7   Sag was! Wo bin ich?

This item further consolidates the vocabulary for items of furniture introduced in Kapitel 5 and makes use of the picture in PCM 5.6. Students will need to change **der**, **die**, **das** to **ein**, **eine**, **ein**. They will describe items in one of the rooms in such a way that their partner will be able to guess where they are. As they will be using **es gibt** they will need to revise the accusative case, particularly with **der** words, e.g. „Es gibt hier einen Herd, …"

For this exercise it is important that students know the gender of the noun. They should always be encouraged to note down the gender with each new word they learn.

They will also need to know **im** and **in der** in order to ask which room their partner is in, e.g. „Bist du in der Küche?"

PCM 5.8   Lies was! Zu verkaufen!

Students have to recognise the words for the furniture items and need to colour the pictures in correctly. This fun activity is suitable for all levels and allows for a creative outlet. As an extension activity, students could be encouraged to write their own ads and to draw pictures. This would be an opportunity to practise DTP / art package skills!

Answers

1D – orange and yellow   3B – grey and blue
2A – purple   4C – dark green and red

2   Sag was! Was gibt es in Florians Zimmer?

Here students have to identify which items of furniture are actually in Florian's room. They must take care to ensure they have the correct gender for those items.

Answers

In meinem Zimmer gibt es:

einen Kleiderschrank	eine Tür
einen Schreibtisch	eine Wand
einen Tisch	ein Bett
einen Stuhl	ein Fenster
einen Teppich	ein Poster
einen CD-Spieler	ein Regal
einen Computer	ein Sofa
eine Lampe	

PCM 5.9   Sag was: In meinem Zimmer gibt es . . .

This exercise practises the vocabulary for the furniture items by using visual cues. It is a preliminary exercise for more complex work on furniture and rooms. Students should be reminded to use the correct accusative forms of the articles after **es gibt**.

Answers

In meinem Zimmer gibt es:
1   einen Kleiderschrank und ein Bett.
2   einen Tisch, einen Stuhl und ein Regal.
3   einen Sessel und ein Sofa.
4   eine Lampe und einen Schreibtisch.
5   einen Fernseher und einen Computer.
6   einen Schreibtisch und ein Bild.

3   Hör zu! Heinz' Möbel

Following on from the pictures of the previous exercises, this item now requires students to identify the same vocabulary in a listening item. The fact that Heinz has no computer and does no homework may be possible items for discussion!

Transcript

Woman: Was für Möbel gibt es in deinem Zimmer, Heinz?
Heinz: Hm, es gibt da einen Fernseher und einen DVD-Spieler.
Woman: Einen Fernseher und einen DVD-Spieler? Hast du auch einen Computer?
Heinz: Nein, leider habe ich keinen Computer.
Woman: Und was gibt es da noch?
Heinz: Äh . . . es gibt in meinem Zimmer einen Sessel und einen Schrank.
Woman: Einen Sessel und einen Schrank . . . ist das alles? Hast du kein Bett?
Heinz: Ach so, ja klar! Es gibt auch ein Bett.

Woman:	Es gibt doch auch einen Schreibtisch und einen Stuhl, oder?
Heinz:	Einen Schreibtisch? Einen Stuhl? Nein, das gibt es in meinem Zimmer nicht!
Woman:	Wo machst du denn die Hausaufgaben?
Heinz:	Ich mache keine Hausaufgaben!
Woman:	Oh!

Answer: **1, 3, 6, 7, 8**

S p r a c h t i p p

Was für?

This item explains the very important expression **Was für?**

Dativ (5) **E**

This item further consolidates the dative endings, this time for the possessive adjectives.

Übung: -em oder -er? Füll die Lücken aus!

This item consolidates the **Sprachtipp** above.

Answers

1 Was für Möbel gibt es in dein**em** Zimmer?
2 In mein**em** Haus gibt es drei Schlafzimmer.
3 In unser**er** Wohnung wohnen meine Eltern und ich.
4 In mein**em** Dorf gibt es keine Schule.
5 In mein**er** Stadt wohnen viele Leute.
6 Es gibt sechs Wohungen in unser**em** Wohnblock.
7 Wie viele Etagen gibt es in dein**em** Hochhaus?
8 Was für Zimmer gibt es in eur**er** Wohnung?

≣ Wörterbuch **Finde den Plural**

This item encourages correct use of dictionaries.

Answers

der Stuhl (¨e)	der Computer (-)	das Bild (-er)
der Tisch (e)	die Lampe (-n)	die Wand (¨e)
die Tür (-en)	das Bett (-en)	das Sofa (-s)
die Regel (-n)	der Sessel (-)	der Schrank (¨e)

4 Schreib was! Was gibt es in deinem Traumzimmer?

This item gives students, who do not like their own room, a chance to describe what they would like in their room – those who do not like drawing might be encouraged to cut out items from old catalogues or brochures. Weaker students may just prefer to label the items of furniture while more able students can write sentences e.g. „In meinem Traumzimmer gibt es ein Bett."

The more adventurous may be able to try:

„In meinem Traumzimmer gibt einen kleinen Fernseher."

PCM 5.10 Meine Laune **A**

This is a lighthearted exercise based on the type of cards which can be hung on bedroom doors. Students can be encouraged to make up their own card, either using the expressions given or inventing new ones.

Answers

1 C, **2** D, **3** A, **4** B, **5** G, **6** F, **7** H, **8** E

Vokabeltipp **Möbel beschreiben**

This item introduces the key adjectives for describing furniture. As the ability to give full descriptions is a requirement at GCSE, it is important for students to start practising early!

Die Farben

This item introduces a selection of colours. More able students should be encouraged to use the terms **hell** and **dunkel** with the colours.

S p r a c h t i p p

Er, sie, es, sie

This item reminds students that **er**, **sie** and **es** can all mean "it", and that **sie** can be used for "they" in all genders.

PCM 5.11 Schreib was! Er, sie oder es?

Reinforcement activity for the **Sprachtipp** on the words for "it". It may be necessary to remind students that a noun is still masculine, feminine, neuter or plural even if it does not have the words **der**, **die**, or **das** written in front of it.

Answers

1	Es	3	Sie	5	Er	7	Er	9	Er
2	Sie	4	Sie	6	Er	8	Es	10	Sie

5 Schreib was! Ein Möbelkatalog

This item consolidates the use of adjectives already introduced and shows how catalogue descriptions may be used in class.

Answers

There are many possible answers here. These are some suggestions:

der Schrank:	groß, alt, häßlich, braun.
der Tisch:	klein, modern, rosa, neu.
die Lampe:	hübsch, klein, modern, blau und gelb.
das Sofa:	groß, violett, bequem.
der Stuhl:	orange, unbequem.
das Bett:	alt, bequem, groß.

6 Sag was! Anna beschreibt die Möbel

This item further consolidates descriptions by encouraging students to describe items of furniture. Again this can be done at a basic level (without using adjectival endings) or at a more advanced level:

e.g. „Der Schrank ist groß und alt." „Es gibt einen großen alten Schrank."

7 Hör zu! Der Sessel (1)

In this item Anna and Florian are discussing furniture and expressing opinions about the furniture. The item makes full use of adjectival endings and expressions of opinion.

Transcript

Anna: Florian, ich habe einen alten, blauen Sessel. Wie gefällt er dir?

Florian: Alt und blau? Er gefällt mir sehr gut. Er ist sehr gemütlich. Und dir?

Anna: Mir gefällt der Sessel nicht. Ich mag blau nicht.

Florian: Ich habe einen neuen, grünen Sessel.

Anna: Ach, mir gefällt der grüne Sessel nicht so gut. Er ist zu unbequem und zu modern!

Florian: Okay.

Anna: Aber du hast einen roten, modernen Sessel. Er ist schön bequem!

Florian: Jaaa! Der rote Sessel gefällt mir sehr gut.

Anna: Na prima! Mir auch!

Answers: **1** a, **2** c, **3** b

8 Hör zu! Der Sessel (2)

Please replay the song from Ex. 7, **Hör zu! Der Sessel (1)**.

Answer: 3

9 Lies den Cartoon und hör zu! Florians Sofa

The cartoon continues the story of the **Partykeller** and consolidates adjectives of description.

Transcript

Heinz: Dein Zimmer ist hell und modern.

Florian: Danke.

Heinz: Aber dein Sofa ist alt und häßlich!
Hoppla! Jetzt ist dein Sofa dreckig!
Schau mal! Das Sofa ist schön und modern. Und gar nicht teuer.

Florian: Ich weiß nicht . . .

Heinz: Anna gefällt rot gut!

Florian: Hmmmm . . .

Heinz: Kann ich dann dein altes Sofa haben?! Für den Partykeller? (sound effect of book hitting head)

Heinz: auwa!!!!

10 Schreib was! Richtig oder falsch?

1 F – Florians Sofa ist alt.

2 R

3 F – Anna gefällt rot.

4 R

Lerntipp Dingsbums

A short item which may cause some hilarity but which has nothing to do with "bums".

Sprachtipp

Präpositionen mit dem Dativ

This item introduces prepositions which take the dative. Prepositions which take both accusative and dative will be dealt with in a later chapter.

Übung: Füll die Lücken aus!

Answers

1 Ich habe einen Plan von <u>meiner</u> Wohnung.

2 Wir wohnen auf <u>dem</u> Lande.

3 Sie wohnt in <u>einem</u> Haus in Bremen.

4 Heinz spielt mit <u>der</u> Band.

5 Mein Zimmer ist unter <u>dem</u> Dach.

6 Das Badezimmer ist zwischen <u>den</u> Schlafzimmern.

7 Die Wohnung liegt <u>am</u> Stadtrand.

8 Das Hochhaus steht <u>im</u> Stadtzentrum.

Vokabeltipp Richtungen

This item gives further vocabulary to assist in room descriptions, including prepositions.

PCM 5.12 Schreib was! Wo sind die Tiere?

A simple gap-filling exercise for all levels which practises the most frequent prepositions of place with the dative case. Here the dative is given, the students just have to insert the preposition.

Answers

1 Der Hund ist <u>auf</u> dem Sofa.

2 Das Pferd ist <u>hinter</u> dem Sofa.

3 Die Katze ist <u>unter</u> dem Tisch.

4 Der Vogel ist <u>im</u> Schrank.

5 Die Maus ist <u>neben</u> dem Sofa.

6 Die Schlange ist <u>vor</u> dem Sessel.

PCM 5.13   Schreib was! Bello hat sich versteckt (1)

A simple gap filling exercise practising the correct use of the dative definite articles with the prepositions. This time students will have to insert the article in the correct form, therefore they may need to check the genders of the furniture items from the **Vokabeltipp**. Encourage students to find the dog hidden (under the bed) in the picture and to answer the questions with yes / no constructions.

Answers
1   Ist Bello hinter <u>dem</u> Schrank?
2   Ist Bello zwischen <u>dem</u> Sessel und <u>dem</u> Sofa?
3   Ist Bello in <u>dem</u> Schrank?
4   Ist Bello vor <u>der</u> Tür?
5   Ist Bello neben <u>den</u> Stühlen?
6   Ist Bello unter <u>dem</u> Bett?

PCM 5.14   Sag was! Bello hat sich versteckt (2)

A pair exercise following on from Bello 1 to consolidate the prepositions with the dative. Students hide Bello in the picture and ask each other yes / no questions to find the dog.

PCM 5.15   Hör zu! Wo ist das Buch?

A creative task where students have to understand very simple directions. It could be used as a preparatory exercise before Exercise 13 in the Pupil's Book.

Transcript
Eins:
Boy: Wo ist dein Buch? Ist dein Buch auf dem Stuhl?
Girl: Nein, mein Buch ist unter dem Stuhl.
Boy: Ach so, unter dem Stuhl!
Zwei:
Girl: Wo ist deine Tasche? Ist sie auf dem Stuhl?
Boy: Ja, genau. Meine Tasche ist auf dem Stuhl.
Drei:
Girl: Wo ist deine Katze? Ist sie unter dem Tisch?
Boy: Nein, meine Katze ist rechts neben dem Tisch.
Girl: Rechts neben dem Tisch? Ach so!
Vier:
Boy: Wo ist das Bild?
Girl: Das Bild ist an der Wand über dem Bett.
Fünf:
Boy: Wo ist dein Hund?
Girl: Mein Hund?
Boy: Ja, ist er auf dem Sofa?
Girl: Nein, mein Hund ist hinter dem Sofa.

Answers
1   The book is under the chair.
2   The bag is on the chair.
3   The cat is next to the table on the right.
4   The picture is above the bed.
5   The dog is behind the sofa.

11   Hör zu! Pia hat ihre Schultasche vergessen

A short item to practise the prepositions with the dative case as well as the vocabulary to do with rooms.

Transcript
Pia: Hallo, hier ist Pia!
Markus: Hallo, was gibt's?
Pia: Markus, gut, dass du noch da bist. Ich habe meine Schultasche vergessen. Kannst du sie suchen?
Markus: Klar. Wo ist deine Tasche?
Pia: In meinem Zimmer.
Markus: Okay. Mensch, wie sieht's denn hier aus! Chaos pur!!!
Pia: Ist doch jetzt egal! Links an der Wand ist ein Stuhl. Ist die Tasche auf dem Stuhl?
Markus: Nein. Hier sind nur deine Klamotten.
Pia: Und neben dem Stuhl?
Markus: Schuhe.
Pia: Was ist auf dem Schrank?
Markus: Da steht dein Fernseher . . . und jede Menge Müll.
Pia: Auf dem Bett?
Markus: Da liegt dein Squash-Schläger.
Pia: Ist die Tasche unter dem Bett?
Markus: Nein, unter dem Bett sind nur ein paar Bücher.
Pia: Oh Mann! Was mach ich denn jetzt. Meine Tasche ist weg!
Markus: Aha! Ich hab sie gefunden!
Pia: Wo ist sie denn?
Markus: Hinter deiner Gitarre an der rechten Wand
Pia: Hinter der Gitarre? Ach ja!!! Danke, Markus.
Markus: Ich bring dir die Tasche in die Schule.

Answer
The bag is next to the guitar.

Beantworte die Fragen auf Deutsch!

Further questions may be asked orally here to practise the prepositions.

Answers
1   Wo sind Pias Klamotten?   auf dem Stuhl.
2   Wo sind Pias Schuhe?   neben dem Stuhl.
3   Was ist auf dem Schrank?   der Fernseher und Müll.
4   Wo ist der Squashschläger?   auf dem Bett.
5   Was ist unter dem Bett?   Bücher.
6   Wo ist die Gitarre?   rechts an der Wand.

12   Lies was! Julias Zimmer

This Reading practice item includes the same sort of vocabulary the students have just practised as a Listening activity.

Answers

A			B		
1	der Schreibtisch	4	**1**	two windows	
2	das Aquarium	5	**2**	2 goldfish	
3	das Bett	1	**3**	hardly any books	
4	der Kleiderschrank	2	**4**	a CD-player	
5	das Regal	3			

13 Schreib was! Wie sieht dein Zimmer aus?

This item sums up what they have learned in this unit and uses the items learned in Julia's letter. It is good practise for GCSE-type questions later!

14 Lied: So richtig nett ist's nur im Bett

Students should be encouraged to listen out for the words they have learned in the unit and to sing along if they wish.

Transcript

Zuhaus' gibt's viele Möbel:
ein Sofa und 'ne Bank.
Ich hab auch einen Schreibtisch,
vier Stühle und 'nen Schrank.

Doch . . . .
So richtig nett
ist's nur im Bett!
Den ganzen Tag
in meinem Bett.

Mein Bett ist urgemütlich.
Mein Bett ist riesengroß.
Mein Bett ist ruhig und friedlich.
Ich find' es ganz famos!

Denn . . .
So richtig nett
ist's nur im Bett!
Den ganzen Tag
in meinem Bett.

Vorne ist das Video
Oben das TV.
Rechts ist der Computer.
Das Radio ist blau.

Ja . . .
(2x)
So richtig nett
ist's nur im Bett!
Den ganzen Tag
in meinem Bett.

15 Hör zu und beantworte die Fragen

This item encourages students to listen carefully to the song in order to be able to identify the words required in the answers. Please replay the song from Ex. 14, **So richtig nett ist's nur im Bett**. Question 4 allows for an open answer.

Answers

1 ein Sofa, eine Bank, ein Schreibtisch, Stühle, ein Schrank, ein Bett, ein Video, ein Computer, ein Radio (any 3)

2 a) gemütlich b) groß c) ruhig

3 Was ist vorne? das Video, der Videorecorder
Was ist oben? das TV, der Fernseher
Was ist rechts? der Computer
Was ist blau? das Radio

4 Wie findest du dein Bett? open answer

 **Möbel**

The websites give descriptions of furniture in German and could be used by students to describe their own or their dream bedrooms. Weaker students could copy descriptions. More able students could write a description of the furniture using adjectives and expressions of opinion.

PCM 5.16   Lies was! „Endlich mal Möbel die Fun bringen."   **E**

This item is an advertisement from a manufacturer of furniture – in this case specifically for young people. It is a more difficult exercise but should encourage the more able to identify key words in unfamiliar text and provides valuable practice in reading unfamiliar texts.

Answers

1 Lieblingsmusik
2 meine beste Freundin
3 wenn wir Gitarre üben!
4 Sie sehen total gut aus!

1 have fun / listen to her favourite music / read books / watch television / hang around / jump around playing guitar.
2 guitar
3 she thinks they look great
4 tips about the home / young people's rooms

 Leseseite

The Leseseite gives the type of activity students might find later at GCSE level and includes unfamiliar vocabulary in authentic advertisements.

Answers

1. D	2. A	3. E	4. C	5. B

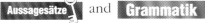 **Aussagesätze** and **Grammatik**

These pages are useful quick references for students working alone or in pairs – on a classwork or homework assignment. They are also useful for revision purposes, as they sum up the important grammar and vocabulary of the chapter.

Kapitel 6 **Mein Tag**

Einheit A   Was machst du?

Unit 6A will introduce:
- *daily routine*
- *travelling to work / school*

PCMs 6.1 – 6.11 accompany this section.

1   Ein toller Morgen

This cartoon introduces the key words for daily routine while David dreams of stardom. This cartoon brings in two useful exclamations: **Aua!** (used if you hurt yourself) and **Hoppla!** (used if you have dropped something, or if you bump into someone accidentally).

Transcript

Narrator:	Freitag, nach der Schule.
Pia:	Heinz, David spielt Keyboard!
Heinz:	Klasse! Komm morgen zur Bandprobe.
Pia:	Ich hol dich um 10 Uhr ab.
Narrator:	David, der Popstar.
David:	11 Uhr – Ich wache auf. Es gibt Frühstück im Bett. Ich sehe fern.
	12 Uhr – Ich stehe auf. Ich trinke Tee und bade – cool! Ich höre Musik.
	14 Uhr – Ich ziehe meine Klamotten an. Ich fahre ins Studio.
Narrator:	Samstag, 10 Uhr.
Pia:	Es ist 10 Uhr. Gleich ist Bandprobe. Was macht David?
Mrs. Miller:	David schläft.
Narrator:	Samstag, 10.30 Uhr
David:	Aua!
Pia:	Hoppla! Was machst du da?
David:	Skateboard fahren!
Narrator:	11 Uhr, in Heinz' Probekeller.
Heinz:	Hallo! Da seid ihr ja!
Yasemin :	Wo ist dein Keyboard, David?
David:	Oh . . . zu Hause!

PCM 6.1   Lies was! FUNSTICKER

The purpose of this item is to revise the calendar. Copy the calendar page up to 12 times for each student so that they can plan all or part of their year. You could encourage them to colour in "special" days (good or bad!) and to start writing simple comments in German e.g. **Super Tag!**

2   Schreib was! David, der Popstar (1)

This item draws the students' attention to the key phrases for this topic, expressions which they will have to use themselves later.

Answers

Ich wache auf.
Ich esse Frühstück.
Ich sehe fern.
Ich stehe auf.
Ich trinke Tee.
Ich bade.
Ich höre Musik.
Ich ziehe meine Klamotten an.
Ich fahre ins Studio.

Vokabeltipp   Was machst du?

This item reinforces the vocabulary and gives the English for those items found in the story and a few more besides.

Sprachtipp

Schwache und starke Verben

This item revises the endings of weak verbs and introduces some common strong verbs. You should emphasise the fact that strong verbs only act differently in the **du** and **er**, **sie**, **es** parts of the verb – the other parts are quite regular.

3   Schreib was!   **E**

This item consolidates the work on the present tense of common verbs.

Answers
1 wohnen
David <u>wohnt</u> jetzt in Deutschland.
Ich <u>wohne</u> in der Nähe von London.
Wo <u>wohnst</u> du?

2 arbeiten
Mein Vater <u>arbeitet</u> in einem Büro.
Wir <u>arbeiten</u> in den Sommerferien.

3 haben
Er <u>hat</u> keine Geschwister.
Sie <u>hat</u> einen Hund.

4 sein
Ich <u>bin</u> ein Popstar.
Ihr <u>seid</u> im Wohnzimmer.

5 fahren

Meine Eltern <u>fahren</u> nach Hause.

Wie <u>fährst</u> du dahin?

6 essen

Was <u>isst</u> du gern?

Wir <u>essen</u> Frühstück.

PCM 6.2 Schreib was! Verben

This is an additional exercise to practise simple verb endings in the present tense.

Answers

1 Peter <u>findet</u> seine Schultasche nicht.

2 Wir <u>wachen</u> jeden Morgen um 7 Uhr auf.

3 Wann <u>stehst</u> du morgens auf, Christina?

4 Jan und Emil <u>ziehen</u> sich gerade an.

5 Frau Thom <u>geht</u> um halb sieben zur Arbeit.

6 Was <u>machst</u> du da, Martina?

7 Ich <u>höre</u> eine CD von der neuen Band.

8 Wir <u>lernen</u> dienstags Deutsch.

PCM 6.3 Schreib was! Starke Verben

This is an additional exercise to practise strong verbs.

Answers

1 Wann <u>schläfst</u> du?

2 <u>Essen</u> wir bald Mittagessen? Ich habe Hunger!

3 Frau Kasparow <u>fährt</u> mit dem Auto zur Arbeit.

4 Ich <u>sehe</u> nicht gern fern.

5 Janina <u>isst</u> morgens Cornflakes.

6 Ich <u>fahre</u> gern Skateboard.

7 Du <u>siehst</u> doch auch gern 'Freunde' im Fernsehen, oder nicht?

PCM 6.4 Schreib was! Haben und sein

This is an additional exercise to practise the important verbs haben and sein.

Answers

1 Wir <u>haben</u> einen MiniDisk-Spieler.

2 <u>Bist</u> du Engländer?

3 Ihr <u>habt</u> beide rote Haare!

4 Tom <u>ist</u> mein Freund.

5 <u>Seid</u> ihr Geschwister?

6 Katja <u>hat</u> ihre Hausaufgaben nicht.

7 Da sind Rebecca und Florian. Sie <u>haben</u> ein Eis!

8 Ich <u>habe</u> eine Katze und einen Hund.

9 <u>Hast</u> du Haustiere?

10 Wir <u>sind</u> Zwillinge.

11 Ich <u>bin</u> 12 Jahre alt.

12 Frau Heinrichs, <u>sind</u> Sie müde?

PCM 6.5 Schreib was! Übersetze

This item consolidates the idea that there is only one form of the present tense in German i.e. "do" or " . . . . . . ing" are never translated.

Answers

1 Ich wohne in einer Wohnung.

2 Wo wohnst du?

3 Er wohnt in London.

4 Was machst du?

5 Ich schlafe.

6 Ich schlafe um 11 Uhr.

7 Schläfst du um 8 Uhr?

8 Wir gehen zur Schule.

9 Geht Tim zur Schule?

10 Geht ihr jetzt zur Schule?

4 Schreib was! Was machst du, Beate?

A further item to consolidate the basic vocabulary for Daily Routine and to allow the students to practise the **ich** form of some common verbs associated with this topic.

Answers

1 Ich stehe auf.

2 Ich gehe zur Schule.

3 Ich mache meine Hausaufgaben.

4 Ich gehe ins Bett.

5 Ich sehe fern.

6 Ich gehe nach Hause.

7 Ich esse Mittagessen.

8 Ich ziehe meine Klamotten an.

9 Ich lerne Chemie.

10 Ich schlafe.

5 Sag was! Beates Tag

This item consolidates the new vocabulary and allows the students to practise their own dialogues.

S p r a c h t i p p

Trennbare Verben

This item consolidates the use of the separable verbs which have been used in this unit.
Weaker students would need assistance to complete this task.

6 Schreib was!

Answers

1 Beate wacht um halb sieben auf.

2 Ich stehe schnell auf.

3 Nach dem Frühstück sieht sie eine halbe Stunde fern.
4 David zieht seine neue Jacke an.
5 Ich ziehe meinen alten Mantel aus.

PCM 6.6   Schreib was! Separable verbs   E

This is an additional exercise to practise separable verbs. Students can cut the words out and form sentences. There are several possible solutions.

 Kulturtipp **Der Schultag**

This item could lead to a discussion about school times in various countries and what sort of school day the students prefer.

7   Hör zu! Rennfahrer Rudi Raser: Mein Morgen

This item focuses on the racing driver Rudi Raser and what he enjoys doing in the day. Students should be encouraged to listen while looking at the pictures in the book.

Transcript

Tanja:	Guten Tag. Mein Name ist Tanja Schröder. Ich mache ein Interview mit Rudi Raser, dem berühmten Rennfahrer. Herr Raser, was machen Sie morgens?
Rudi:	Ich stehe um 4 Uhr auf, Tanja. Ich esse um 4.30 Uhr Frühstück.
Tanja:	Sie stehen um 4 Uhr auf, Herr Raser? Das ist aber früh. Und was machen Sie dann?
Rudi:	Ich gehe um 5 Uhr zum Training.
Tanja:	Sie gehen um 5 Uhr zum Training, aha. Und wann trainieren Sie?
Rudi:	Ich trainiere von 6 Uhr bis 9 Uhr.
Tanja:	Von 6 bis 9? Und was machen Sie dann?
Rudi:	Ich trinke um 9 Uhr Kaffee.
Tanja:	Sie trinken um 9 Uhr Kaffee? Und dann?
Rudi:	Ich trainiere von 9.30 Uhr bis 12 Uhr.
Tanja:	Sie trainieren also bis 12 Uhr mittags. Und was machen Sie dann?
Rudi:	Ich ziehe meinen Helm aus.
Tanja:	Ja, und wann essen Sie zu Mittag?
Rudi:	Ich gehe um 12.30 Uhr zum Mittagessen.

Answers

4 Uhr	Bild 5
4.30 Uhr	Bild 4
5 Uhr	Bild 6
von 6 Uhr bis 9 Uhr	Bild 2
9 Uhr	Bild 3
von 9.30 bis 12 Uhr	Bild 2
12.00 Uhr	Bild 7
12.30 Uhr	Bild 1

8   Schreib was! David, der Popstar (2)

This item encourages the students to review the cartoon and the key vocabulary for this unit by writing out what David does at certain times of day.

Answers

1	11 Uhr	Ich wache um 11 Uhr auf.
2	12 Uhr	Ich stehe um 12 Uhr auf.
3	14 Uhr	Ich ziehe um 14 Uhr meine Klamotten an.

PCM 6.7   Partnerarbeit. Was machst du?

This provides a more hands-on activity to consolidate describing daily routine. Students will need coloured pencils and scissors. The cards can be re-used as cue cards or for pelmanism games.

9   Lies was! Didi Disko (1)

A reading item to practise the **er** form of the verbs relating to daily routine. The true / false exercise encourages students to think carefully about what they are reading.

Answers

1 R
2 F – Didi geht nicht zur Schule.
3 R
4 R
5 F – Didi macht um 21 Uhr Pause.
6 F – Didi geht um 4 Uhr nach Hause.
7 F – Didi isst sein Abendessen in der Disko.
8 F – Didi schläft um 6 Uhr.

10   Didis Kalender

Answers

Freitag	Samstag
14 Uhr	**3 Uhr**
Didi schläft.	Didi arbeitet.
Didi steht auf.	**4 Uhr**
Didi frühstückt.	Didi geht nach Hause.
Didi sieht fern.	**5 Uhr**
18 Uhr	Didi ist zu Hause.
Didi fährt zur Arbeit.	Didi isst.
Didi macht Musik.	Didi geht ins Bett.
21 Uhr	**6 Uhr**
Didi macht Pause.	Didi schläft.
Didi isst sein Abendessen.	
22 Uhr	
Didi arbeitet.	

Vokabeltipp **Der Arbeitstag**

This item consolidates the vocabulary in **Didis Tag.**

Vokabeltipp **Reflexive Verben**

This item gives a number of key reflexive verbs prior to the **Sprachtipp** which introduces how they work grammatically.

11 Sag was! Didi Disko (2)

Pupils will need to work with a partner – one partner should take the part of Didi and the other a journalist doing an interview. The reporter just needs to change the times, Didi has to refer to the short Reading item.

Reporter: Was machst du <u>um 14 Uhr</u>, Didi?
Didi: <u>Ich stehe</u> um 14 Uhr <u>auf</u>.

S p r a c h t i p p

Reflexive Verben
This item gives the full paradigm of a reflexive verb and explains how the reflexive pronouns work.

Übung
This item practises the reflexive verbs given in the **Sprachtipp**.

Answers
1 Ich wasche <u>mich</u> im Badezimmer.
2 Du duschst <u>dich</u> um 8 Uhr.
3 Er trocknet <u>sich</u> schnell.
4 Sie kämmt <u>sich</u> vor dem Spiegel.
5 Meine Schwester und ich schminken <u>uns</u>.
6 Wann zieht ihr <u>euch</u> an?
7 Nach der Schule ziehen sie <u>sich</u> um.

Vokabeltipp **Was ziehst du an?**

This item helps the students to see how to use the verb **anziehen** with items of clothing.

12 Hör zu! Was ziehen sie an?

This item consolidates the vocabulary for items of clothing.

Transcript
Man: Was ziehst du im Sommer an?
Girl: Im Sommer ziehe ich mir mein T-Shirt und meine Hose an.
Man: Und was ziehst du im Winter an?
Girl: Im Winter ziehe ich mir einen warmen Pullover und eine Jacke an.
Man: Was ziehst du in der Disko an?
Girl: In der Disko ziehe ich einen Rock an.

Answers
A) Im Sommer 4, 2   B) Im Winter 1, 3   C) In der Disko 6

PCM 6.8   Schreib was! Reflexive verbs

Additional practise for reflexive verbs. Students can cut words out and form sentences on the table.

Answers
Ich wasche mich.
Du duschst dich.
Ihr fönt / rasiert euch.
Pedro fönt / rasiert sich.
Sie kämmen / schminken sich.
Wir kämmen / schminken uns.

PCM 6.9   Spiel: Was ziehen sie an?

A light-hearted dice game, practising the words for the most common items of clothing. The preparation phase gives students the opportunity to be creative (colouring and cutting). Best played in groups of 2–4 players. Players can decide whether they want to play with one or two figures. All clothes go in the middle.

Students should be encouraged to speak German during the game.

Useful phrases:
Wer ist dran?   Whose turn is it?
Du bist dran!   It's your turn.
Wer hat den Würfel?   Who's got the dice?
Ich habe eine 4.   I've got a 4.
Ich habe die Schuhe.   I have the shoes.
Ich brauche ein T-Shirt.   I need a t-shirt.
Das habe ich schon.   I've got that already.
Das brauche ich nicht.   I don't need that.
Ich bin fertig.   I've finished.
Ich habe gewonnen.   I've won!

13 Hör zu und lies! Susi Schön und Fritz Faul (1)

This item consolidates the use of the reflexive verbs, in particular the **er** and **sie** forms.

Transcript
Susi Schön und Fritz Faul wollen in die Disko.
Es ist 19 Uhr. Susi duscht sich. Fritz isst Pommes auf dem Sofa. Fauler Fritz!
Um zwanzig vor acht fönt sich Susi. Fritz sieht fern.
Susi schminkt sich um 20 Uhr. Schöne Susi! Fritz schminkt sich nicht. Fritz zieht sich die Jacke an.
Es ist viertel nach acht. Fritz geht zu Susi. Susi zieht sich an.
Es ist halb neun. Fritz trifft Susi. Susi ist schön, aber Fritz war zu faul. Fritz ist nicht schön. Susi ist wütend. Sie sagt:

Wie siehst du denn aus, Fritz?!!! Geh nach Hause! Wasch dich! Rasier' dich! Kämm' dich! Zieh dich um!

Answers

Zeit	Susi	Fritz
19 Uhr	Susi duscht sich.	Fritz isst Pommes.
19.40 Uhr	Susi fönt sich.	Fritz sieht fern.
20 Uhr	Susi schminkt sich.	Fritz zieht sich die Jacke an.
20.15	Uhr Susi zieht sich an.	Fritz geht zu Susi.

14 Sag was! Susi Schön und Fritz Faul (2)

This item encourages the students to manipulate language – changing **er / sie** to **ich**.

Beispiel: Susi: *Ich dusche mich um* 19 Uhr.

15 Schreib was! Susi Schön und Fritz Faul (3)

This item encourages more manipulation of verbs – this time from the imperative to the present tense

Answers

1 Wasch dich!   Er wäscht sich.
2 Rasier dich!   Er rasiert sich.
3 Kämm dich!   Er kämmt sich.
4 Zieh dich um!   Er zieht sich um.

Sprachtipp

Imperative

This grammar item revises the use of the imperative, first introduced in Chapter 4, and introduces the imperative of separable and reflexive verbs.

Übung: Was ist richtig?

Answers

1 Guten Morgen, Herr Prange. Essen Sie Ihr Mittagessen.
2 Guten Tag, Hans. Komm nach Hause!
3 Peter und Thomas! Es ist schon neun Uhr! Steht schnell auf.
4 Guten Morgen, Frau Schmidt. Kommen Sie herein.
5 Sonja, morgen in der ersten Stunde hast du Deutsch. Mach deine Hausaufgaben!
6 Yasemin, du bist in der Küche. Iss dein Frühstück.

16 Lied: Der Guten Morgen Rap (1)

This song practises weak verbs, reflexive verbs, the imperative and the topic of daily routine.

Transcript
Aufsteh'n! Aufsteh'n!
Los jetzt, los jetzt! Aufsteh'n!
Duschen, waschen, Haare kämmen.
Zieh dich an und dann geht's los!
Ich steh auf! Du stehst auf!
Er, sie, es steht auf!

Wir steh'n auf, ihr steht auf,
sie stehen alle auf!
Aufsteh'n! Aufsteh'n!
Los jetzt, los jetzt! Aufsteh'n!
Frühstück essen, Kaffee trinken.
Zieh dich an und dann geht's los!
Ich zieh' mich an, du ziehst dich an
Anette zieht sich an.
Wir zieh'n uns an, ihr zieht euch an,
sie zieh'n sich alle an!
Losfahr'n! Losfahr'n!
Wir müssen alle losfahr'n.
Zur Schule geh'n, zur Schule fahr'n,
Um 8 Uhr geht es los!!
. . . Guten Morgen!

Sprachtipp

Imperativ

This item widens the students' knowledge of the language by exposing them to colloquial use of the imperative.

17 Der Guten Morgen Rap (2)

Replay **Der Guten Morgen Rap** from Ex. 16. After listening, students should practise the forms of weak and reflexive verbs.

Answers

aufstehen	sich anziehen
ich stehe auf	Ich ziehe mich an
du stehst auf	du ziehst dich an
er, sie, es steht auf	er, sie, es zieht sich an
wir stehen auf	wir ziehen uns an
ihr steht auf	ihr zieht euch an
sie stehen auf	sie ziehen sich an

PCM 6.10   Hör zu: Der Guten Morgen Rap (3)

Students should listen closely and critically to **Der Guten Morgen Rap** in order to decide what is <u>not</u> mentioned (replay Ex. 16).

Answers

The following are not mentioned in the song: 1, 2, 4, 8

PCM 6.11   Gruppenarbeit: Der Guten Morgen Rap (4)

This item encourages students to write their own lyrics. The chorus is simply formed by conjugating verbs. There is an instrumental version on the tape after the full Rap. Students could be encouraged to add more verses or to write a version about what they do in the morning.

Einheit B   Hilfst du mit?

Unit 6B will introduce:
- *how to say what students do to help at home.*

PCMs 6.12 – 6.18 accompany this section.

1   Das Handy

This item introduces the useful vocabulary for texting friends in Germany.

Transcript

Pia:	Tschüs Mama. Ich gehe in die Stadt.
Mother:	Nimm dein Handy mit!
Pia:	Okay.
mobile 1	Piep, piep, piep!
Text message on mobile 1:	HI MEINE SCHÖNE! WAS MACHST DU?
mobile 1:	Piep, piep, piep!
Text message on mobile 1:	:-) FRÜHSTÜCKE JETZT. UND DU???
mobile 1:	Piep, piep, piep!
Text message on mobile 1:	<3 FAHRE IN DIE STADT. DU AUCH?
mobile 1:	Piep, piep, piep!
Text message on mobile 1:	WARTE IM CAFÉ. WO BIST DU? X X X
mobile 2 – Mother's message:	WER BIST DU?
Text message on mobile 1:	PIERRE<3
Pia:	Hallo, Mama. Ich habe das falsche Handy.
Mother:	Ach so! Das hier ist **dein Handy**! Ach, Pia . . . Wer ist **Pierre**?!

Kulturtipp Text messages

Text messages are frequently used by young people as cheaper alternatives to telephoning – it might be worthwhile spending some time on texting – comparisons could be made.

:-)	lustig, glücklich	>:-<	schlechte Laune
:D	lachen	<3	Herz, Liebe (heart)
:-(	traurig	X	Kuss (kiss)
:'-(	weinen	( )	Umarmung (hug)

 **SMS**

The website gives you lots more ideas for texting messages including more "smileys" and abbreviations. They could be compared with English text messages.

2   Sag was! Was macht Pierre?

This item allows the students to expand the text messages into full sentences.

Answers

A Was sagt Pierre? Mache Sätze.

Ich frühstücke jetzt.

Ich fahre in die Stadt.

Ich warte im Café.

B Wann macht Pierre das?

Er frühstückt um 11.05 Uhr.

Er fährt um 11.25 Uhr in die Stadt.

Er wartet um 11.40 Uhr im Café.

Vokabeltipp Helfen

This item gives the useful vocabulary for helping around the home.

3   Hör zu! Was passiert hier?

This item helps to make more use of the new vocabulary by asking the students to match pictures with expressions.

Transcript

Eins:	*sound of a TV*
Zwei:	*sound of snoring*
Drei:	*sound of washing the dishes*
Vier:	*sound of vacuum*
Fünf:	*sound of shower*
Sechs:	*sound of lawnmower*

Answers

1	fernsehen	4	Staub saugen
2	schlafen	5	sich duschen
3	abspülen	6	den Rasen mähen

4   Sag was! Wer hilft zu Hause?

The question is sufficiently vague to allow for various "family" combinations. The last column allows students to include other family members. Once the students have ticked their preferred columns, they should then attempt to make up sentences.

Answers

These are sample answers only. There are obviously various combinations.

Ich räume auf.

Meine Tante spült ab.

Meine Schwester kauft ein.

Mein Vater kocht.

Meine Schwester saugt Staub.

Mein Bruder mäht den Rasen.

5 Schreib was! Was machen Pia und ihre Mutter?

This item encourages the students to look back at the cartoon and to manipulate the verbs.

A Was machen sie?

10:35 Uhr: Pia geht in die Stadt.

10:50 Uhr: Pias Mutter spült ab.

11.05 Uhr: Pias Mutter saugt Staub.

11.25 Uhr: Pias Mutter kauft ein.

11.40 Uhr: Pias Mutter kocht.

11.55 Uhr: Pias Mutter kommt nach Hause.

B Was sagen sie?

Pia: Ich gehe um 10.35 Uhr in die Stadt.

Pias Mutter: Ich spüle um 10.50 Uhr ab.

Ich sauge um 11.05 Uhr Staub.

Ich kaufe um 11.25 Uhr ein.

Ich koche um 11.40 Uhr.

Ich komme um 11.55 Uhr nach Hause.

6 Sag was! Wie oft hilfst du mit?

Here the onus has been placed on the independent learner. Useful vocabulary is given in the **Vokabeltipp: Wann?**

These are sample answers only. There are obviously various combinations.

Answers

Ich räume oft auf.

Meine Schwester kauft nie ein.

Mein Vater kocht ab und zu . . .

PCM 6.12 Schreib was! Helfen

This is an additional exercise to practise separable verbs and verbs associated with helping round the house. Students need to be able to differentiate between separable and non-separable verbs.

Answers

1 Meine Mutter kocht das Essen.

2 Mein Bruder spült ab.

3 Du trocknest ab!

4 Wir räumen unser Zimmer auf.

5 Meine Eltern mähen den Rasen.

6 Ich sauge Staub.

7 Hör zu! Was hilft Marius? Was hilft Franziska? (1)

This item practises again the separable verbs and expressions of time.

Transcript

Franziska:	Hilfst du im Haushalt, Marius?
Marius:	Ja, klar! Ich räume zum Beispiel meistens mein Zimmer auf.
Franziska:	Ist das alles?
Marius:	Nein, das ist nicht alles. Ich mähe auch jede Woche den Rasen.
Franziska:	Spülst du auch ab?
Marius:	Nein, ich spüle nicht ab. Wir haben eine Spülmaschine. Und was machst du zu Hause?
Franziska:	Ich spüle ab und zu ab, aber ich trockne nie ab. Das macht meine Schwester.
Marius:	Was machst du sonst noch?
Franziska:	Ich sauge manchmal Staub.
Marius:	Aha.

Answers

Marius:	aufräumen, den Rasen mähen
Franziska:	abspülen, staubsaugen

PCM 6.13 Hör zu: Was hilft Marius? Was hilft Franziska? (2)

This item requires students to listen to the recording from the book again, but this time more critically.

Answers

1 R, 2 R, 3 F, 4 F, 5 R, 6 F, 7 R, 8 F

Vokabeltipp Wann? Wie oft?

This item gives the useful time expressions for frequency and times of day.

Sprachtipp

Verb second!

This item introduces the basic word-order rules.

Übung: Schreib den Satz mit den unterstrichenen Wörtern am Anfang.

Answers

1 Meistens essen wir in der Küche.

2 Oft fährt mein Vater in die Stadt.

3 Immer schenkt mir meine Oma Geld zum Geburtstag.

4 Jeden Abend muss ich meine Hausaufgaben machen.

5 Jeden Tag sieht meine Schwester wenigstens vier Stunden fern.

6 Nie helfe ich zu Hause.

7 Morgens steht mein Bruder immer sehr spät auf.

8 Morgen Abend gehen wir in die Disco.

PCM 6.14 Schreib was! Verb second

This is an additional exercise to practise the position of verbs. Students need to practise the "verb second" rule.

Answers

1 Morgens gehe ich in die Schule.
2 Am Nachmittag kauft Mutter ein.
3 Mein Bruder räumt nie sein Zimmer auf.
4 Abends kocht Vater das Essen.
5 Im Winter ziehen wir einen Mantel an.
6 Wie oft hilfst du im Haushalt?
7 Meine Schwester kocht ab und zu das Abendessen.
8 Jeden Tag ziehst du das selbe T-Shirt an.

8 Meinungsumfrage (1): Wie sieht dein Morgen aus?

This item is a questionnaire which you may prefer to do orally.

Sprachtipp

nicht

This item reminds the students of the importance and proper use of **nicht**.

9 Sag was! Meinungsumfrage (2) E

This item requires the students to be able to use the **ich** and the **er**, **sie**, **es** forms of the verb.

Vokabeltipp Wie kommst du zur Schule?

This item gives the key methods of transport students use to get to school.

PCM 6.15 Hör zu! Wie kommen sie zur Schule?

A simple listening exercise practising the expressions for getting to school. After the matching, students should be encouraged to form sentences.

Transcript

Narrator:	Petra	sound of car
Narrator:	Anatole	sound of walking feet
Narrator:	Miriam	sound of bicycle bell
Narrator:	Jakob	sound of skateboard
Narrator:	Vina	sound of bus

Answers

Petra fährt mit dem Auto – 3
Anatole geht zu Fuß – 4
Miriam fährt mit dem Fahrrad – 2
Jakob fährt mit dem Skateboard – 5
Vina fährt mit dem Bus – 1

PCM 6.16 Sag was! Wie kommst du zur Schule?

This is an additional exercise to practise expressions of transport in order that students can say how they come to school. The final **Ich gehe** . . . needs to be highlighted as this is not a method of transport!

Answers

1 Ich fahre mit dem Skateboard zur Schule.
2 Ich fahre mit dem Bus zur Schule.
3 Ich fahre mit dem Fahrrad zur Schule.
4 Ich fahre mit dem Auto zur Schule.
5 Ich fahre mit dem Zug zur Schule.
6 Ich gehe zu Fuß zur Schule.

10 Meinungsumfrage: Wie kommst du zur Schule?

Students should be encouraged to ask questions in German.

PCM 6.17 Hör zu! Mein Wochenende (1)

This item is a matching exercise and allows students to practise listening for gist.

Transcript

Eins: Am Wochenende schlafe ich gern lange. Ich bleibe morgens gern bis 11 Uhr im Bett.
Zwei: Für mich fängt das Wochenende erst am Samstagmittag an. Samstags habe ich immer viel Arbeit. Samstagvormittag muss ich immer Hausaufgaben machen. Manchmal muss ich 3 Stunden lang für die Schule arbeiten.
Drei: Bei uns ist Samstags Putztag. Da müssen alle mithelfen. Wir saugen Staub und mähen den Rasen und räumen auf – wir machen alle Hausarbeiten.
Vier: Sonntag ist bei uns zu Hause ein richtiger Fernsehtag! Wir machen den Fernseher schon Sonntagmorgens an und sehen den ganzen Tag Filme und Videos an. Ich finde das so richtig gemütlich.

Answers

1 G, 2 C, 3 F, 4 B

PCM 6.18 Hör zu! Mein Wochenende (2)

Students should listen to the short descriptions again, this time with more attention to the detail in order to decide if the item is true or false.

Answers

1	F	5	R
2	R	6	R
3	R	7	F
4	F	8	F

S p r a c h t i p p

Präpositionen mit dem Akkusativ.

This item and the exercise below practise the prepositions with the accusative case.

Übung: Füll die Lücken aus!

Answers
1 Gehen Sie um <u>den</u> Platz herum.
2 Er geht durch <u>die</u> Stadtmitte.
3 Ich spiele gegen <u>meinen</u> Freund.
4 Sie gehen ohne <u>meine</u> Schwester ins Kino.
5 Wir sitzen um <u>den</u> Tisch.
6 Sie laufen <u>den</u> Fluss entlang.

11 Lies was! Ich bin ein Schlüsselkind

This item gives some more complex reading practise and a useful model for letter writing. The students may wish to discuss how they feel about "latch key kids".

Answers
1 R, 2 F, 3 F, 4 R, 5 R

12 Schreib was! Jonas, das Schlüsselkind

This item practices word order and in particular the "verb second" rule. It also practises the third person singular form of the verb.

Answers
1 Morgens geht Jonas zur Schule.
2 Um viertel nach acht beginnt die Schule.
3 Um halb neun fängt Mutters Arbeit an.
4 Um ein Uhr hört die Schule auf.
5 Mittags isst Jonas Butterbrot.
6 Manchmal macht er Spaghetti.
7 Nachmittags macht er Hausaufgaben.
8 Manchmal spült er ab oder saugt staub.
9 Um halb fünf kommt Mama nach Hause.
10 Ab und zu geht er mit seiner Mutter einkaufen.
11 Manchmal essen Jonas und seine Mutter Pommes.

13 Schreib was! Beantworte Jonas' Brief

This type of Writing task is similar to ones which the student will encounter in examinations.

Aussprache • • • • • • • • • • • • • • • • • • •

VW

Students often like learning tongue twisters – in this case trying out the tongue twister ensures you practise the sounds!

Transcript
W Wer will den Wagen waschen?
V Es ist vormittags um viertel vor vier.
Kannst du das sagen?
Vetter Willfried, wie viel Vögel wohnen bei Vater Wolfgang?

Wilma und Willi Vormann, Waltraut und Veith Vogel fahren zu viert VW. Willi und Wilma fahren vorne und Familie Vogel will nach hinten.

Zzzzz . . . zett und S

Z and **S** frequently cause problems of pronunciation. This pronunciation exercise practises both sounds.

Transcript
Z: Zimmer, zwei, Zwillinge
S: Sessel, sieben, Sohn
Zimmer
sieben
zwei
zwanzig
Sessel
Zentralheizung
Sofa
zwischen
Sohn
Zwillinge
Süden

14 Spiel: Pantomime

Miming is an enjoyable activity for students. They will have to practise the question words and the vocabulary from this unit in order to ascertain what the mime artist is trying to say!

15 Lied: Fleißige Leute

A new song based on a traditional German tune (originally *Wer will die lustigen Waschfrauen seh'n?*) to sum up the words learned this chapter. The transcript below also indicates when you should do certain actions.

Transcript
Wer will fleißige Leute seh'n?
Der muss zu uns nach Mainz geh'n.
Wir lernen, wir lernen, wir lernen jeden Tag. *(pretend to read a book)*
Wir lernen, wir lernen, wir lernen jeden Tag.

Wer will fleißige Leute seh'n?
Der muss zu uns nach Mainz geh'n.
Wir kochen, wir kochen, wir kochen jeden Tag (2x) *(pretend to stir a pot)*

Wer will fleißige Leute seh'n?
Der muss zu uns nach Mainz geh'n.
Wir spülen, wir spülen, wir spülen immer ab. (2x) *(pretend to do the dishes)*

Wer will fleißige Leute seh'n?
Der muss zu uns nach Mainz geh'n.
Wir räumen, wir räumen, wir räumen immer auf. (2x)
(pretend to pick up things from the floor)

Wer will fleißige Leute seh'n?
Der muss zu uns nach Mainz geh'n.
Wir saugen, wir saugen, wir saugen immer Staub (2x)
(pretend to vacuum)

Leseseite

A novel way of introducing daily routine – that of the football manager. You could invite those who have played the popular computer game "Football Manager" to explain the game a little to others in the class who have not heard of it!

Answers

1 Breakfast with the Chairman.
2 Speaks to the new trainer.
3 That the trainer will stay.
4 He is given the sack at 15.00.
5 The computer game Football Manager.

Fülle die Lücken in den Sätzen aus

This item gives further practice with verbs:

1 Der Fussballmanager <u>frühstückt</u> um 8.00 Uhr.
2 Um 10:00 Uhr <u>spricht</u> er mit dem neuen Trainer.
3 Er sagt auf der Pressekonferenz: Der Trainer <u>bleibt</u>.
4 Nach der Pressekonferenz <u>macht</u> er Mittagspause.
5 Um 15 Uhr <u>geht</u> der Trainer <u>weg</u>.

Lerntipp Use your new words!

Learning strategies can be shared – different students will find different methods suit them best.

 and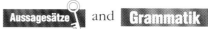

These pages are useful quick references for students working alone or in pairs – on a classwork or homework assignment. They are also useful for revision purposes, as they sum up the important grammar and vocabulary of the chapter.

Kapitel 7 Freizeit und Hobbys

Einheit A   Mein Hobby

Unit 7A will introduce how to:
- *describe hobbies*
- *arrange to meet someone*

PCMs 7.1 – 7.8 accompany this section.

1   Ein Super-Date – Teil 1

This cartoon introduces some basic words for arranging a meeting and describing hobbies. Laura and Bettina both like Matthias and are vying for his attention. The exercises encourage the students to find the key phrases and expressions.

Transcript

Laura:	Hoppla!
Matthias:	Hallo Laura! Warte! Ich helf dir! Internet! Ist das dein Hobby?
Laura:	Ja, Mein Hobby ist das Internet.
Matthias:	Ich surfe auch gern im Internet.
Laura:	Danke, Matthias. Das war echt nett.
Matthias:	Was machst du heute Abend? Sollen wir uns treffen?
Laura:	Ja, total gerne! Wann?
Matthias:	Um 5 Uhr vor dem Kino!
Matthias:	Hallo Bettina! Kann ich dir helfen?
Bettina:	Oh, Matthias! Ja, bitte!
Bettina:	Mein Hobby ist Fahrrad fahren. Was ist dein Hobby?
Matthias:	Das ist auch mein Hobby!
Bettina:	Danke, du bist ein Schatz! Möchtest du heute Abend mit mir ins Kino gehen?
Matthias:	Ja, warum nicht. Um 5 Uhr?

2   Lies den Cartoon!

Answers

A Wie sagt man das auf Deutsch?
1 Ist das dein Hobby?
2 Mein Hobby ist das Internet.
3 Mein Hobby ist Fahrrad fahren.
4 Was ist dein Hobby?

B Beantworte die Fragen auf Deutsch!
This item can be answered in full sentences, or, if you prefer, with short answers.
1 Laura und Matthias (surfen gern im Internet).
2 Heute Abend um 5 Uhr.
3 Vor dem Kino.
4 (Ihr Hobby ist) Fahrrad fahren.

Vokabeltipp Mein Hobby

This item reinforces the vocabulary and gives the English for those items found in the story and for the most common phrases and verbs relating to hobbies which the students may be interested in.

3   Lies was! Stars und ihre Hobbys

An opportunity here to talk about Claudia Schiffer and the Schumacher brothers as well as to practise the verbs relating to the topic of freetime. Further details about these famous people could be found on the Internet. e.g. More information on Michael Schuhmacher can be found on:

www.michael-schumacher.de
www.michael-schumacher.com

Answers

Claudia Schiffer:	4 (Sport treiben), 5 (malen), 7 (lesen)
Michael Schumacher:	1 (Tennis spielen), 2 (schwimmen), 3 (Fußball spielen), 6 (Ski fahren).

4   Sag was! Meine Hobbys

An opportunity for the students to practise with a partner the vocabulary they have learned. Survey results could be displayed on the classroom walls with appropriate visual illustrations / graphs.

Vokabeltipp Was machst du gern?

In examinations students will be expected to give descriptions and opinions. This item practises describing how much you like something. Students should be encouraged to express their preferences.

Sprachtipp

Was machst du lieber? Was machst du am liebsten?
The **Sprachtipp** consolidates the **Vokabeltipp** above and encourages active use of the vocabulary for expressing preferences. Students should be encouraged to express their opinions in German.

Übung: Was macht sie gern?
Questions 1-3 require the students to answer in the 3rd person singular form, while question

4 requires them to return to the first person singular.

Answers

1 Thomas hört gern Musik. Thomas schwimmt lieber. Thomas spielt am liebsten Fußball.

2 Anja liest gern Comics. Anja zeichnet lieber. Anja geht am liebsten aus.

3 David geht gern ins Theater. David geht lieber ins Museum. David bleibt am liebsten zu Hause.

4 open answers – students should use the correct verb form (1st person singular).

Kulturtipp Wer darf in die Disko?

This **Kulturtipp** could lead to discussion about what students can and cannot do at what age in England, Scotland, Wales or Northern Ireland. Different terms for different age groups: e.g. child, adolescent, teenager, young person, adult could be discussed and compared with the German terms given in the textbook.

---

5 Persönlichkeitstest. Was für ein Freizeittyp bin ich? **E**

This is quite a difficult exercise, but the format is based on similar articles in teenage magazines with which many students will be familiar. All students will need help from the teacher to understand the questions then to look at the answers and decide what sort of a **Freizeittyp** they are. They should be encouraged to discuss the definitions and try to work out what they say before comparing their findings with their friends.

---

6 Hör zu! Unsere Lieblingshobbys (1)

This item encourages the students to listen for detail and further consolidates the material on freetime activities.

Transcript

Laura: Was machst du gern, Matthias?

Matthias: Ich mag Sport.

Laura: Sport? Ich mag auch Sport. Was für Sport machst du denn gern?

Matthias: Ich fahre gern Rad und ich fahre Ski.

Laura: Fahrrad fahren und Ski fahren – was machst du denn lieber?

Matthias: Lieber? Ach, am liebsten fahre ich Fahrrad, glaube ich. Das ist mein Lieblingssport.

Laura: Ach, Fahrrad fahren interessiert mich auch. Aber ich fahre nicht so gern Ski.

Matthias: Du magst Ski fahren nicht? Oh. Was sind denn deine Hobbys, Laura?

Laura: Ich spiele gern Squash und ich liebe das Internet.

Matthias: Ist das Internet dein Lieblingshobby?

Laura: Ja, das Internet. Das Internet finde ich am besten. Das ist mein Lieblingshobby.

Matthias: Ich interessiere mich auch für das Internet!

Laura: Echt?

Matthias: Ja, ich finde das Internet interessant. Aber Squash ist nichts für mich. Das spiele ich nicht so gern.

Laura: Schade. Naja, sollen wie dann zusammen Fahrrad fahren?

Matthias: Oh ja, prima Idee!

Answers

	nicht gern	gern	Lieblingshobby
Laura	Ski fahren	Fahrrad fahren, Squash	Internet
Matthias	Squash	Ski fahren, Internet	Fahrrad fahren

---

7 Schreib was! Unsere Lieblingshobbys (2) **E**

This item encourages students to write full sentences about what they have just heard.

PCM 7.1 Hör zu: Mein Hobby

This item practises some key vocabulary for hobbies.

Transcript

Narrator: Julia	*sound of horse riding*
Narrator: Lars	*sound of computer game*
Narrator: Jennifer	*sound of people playing tennis*
Narrator: Alexeij	*sound of swimming*
Narrator: Cheng	*sound of friends in a café*
Narrator: Timo	*sound of someone practising the piano*

Answers

Julia: B
Lars: F
Jennifer: A
Alexeij: C
Cheng: E
Timo: D

Julias Hobby ist Reiten.
Lars' Hobby ist der Computer.
Jennifers Hobby ist Tennis.
Alexeijs Hobby ist Schwimmen.
Chengs Hobby ist Freunde treffen.
Timos Hobby ist Klavier spielen.

PCM 7.2 Schreib was! Sag was! Andere Interessen

A simple cued role play where students practise talking about their preferred hobbies and use the expression **lieber**. Students need to change the infinitive construction in the question to a statement in the present tense.

Answers

1 – Interessierst du dich für Reiten?
  – Nein, ich fahre lieber Fahrrad!
2 – Interessierst du dich für Klavier spielen?
  – Nein, ich spiele lieber Fußball!
3 – Interessierst du dich für Schwimmen?
  – Nein, ich fahre lieber Ski!
4 – Interessierst du dich für Computer?
  – Nein, ich spiele lieber Tennis!
5 – Interessierst du dich für Fotografieren?
  – Nein, ich male lieber!

PCM 7.3   Spiel: Hobbys raten   **E**

This game gives students the opportunity to practise talking about hobbies and to use constructions with **gern**. You could bring equipment needed for various hobbies into the classroom or ask students to bring in something to do with their hobbies, e.g. tubes of paint (**malen**), a packet of seeds (**im Garten arbeiten**), a tutu (**Ballett**).

Students could look at the items and guess the hobby or pick them out of a bag.

Yes / No – type guessing games are another option. („Ist mein Hobby . . . ?" „Spiele ich gern . . . ?")

PCM 7.4   Spiel: Hobby – Memory   **A**

Together with the picture cards for the Game **Hobbys raten** these cards make up a set of Pelmanism cards. Mix both sets and lay out in a grid face down. Each player can turn over two cards in an attempt to find a matching set (word and picture).

Vokabeltipp   Bist du in einem Verein?

This item encourages the use of expressions of time.

Additionally you could introduce:

nachmittags, morgens vor der Schule, einmal / dreimal pro Woche

8   Lies was! Vereine

This item encourages students to cope with vocabulary items which they are not always

familiar with and revises the days of the week. (N.B. This item will appear later in the final test, with different questions!)

Answers

1 On Tuesdays and Thursdays.
2 Saturday and Sunday. You have to ring to find out which age groups play when.
3 On Tuesdays, Thursdays and Fridays.
4 On a Tuesday.

PCM 7.5   Hör zu: Mein Verein

A simple matching exercise in which the vocabulary for **Vereine** is practised.

Transcript

Irina: Ich heiße Irina. Ich sammle Teddybären. Meine Teddysammlung ist schon ziemlich groß.
Martin: Ich heiße Martin. Mein Hobby ist Fotografieren. Ich bin in einem Foto-Club.
Bettina: Ich heiße Bettina. Mein Hobby ist singen. Ich singe im Jazz -Chor. Da singen wir Jazz, Blues und auch Gospellieder.
Robert: Hallo! Ich bin der Robert. Ich sammle Briefmarken aus aller Welt. Am interessantesten finde ich die Briefmarken aus Afrika und Asien.

Answers

Irina: E
Martin: F
Bettina: B
Robert: A

PCM 7.6   Hör zu! Vereinstermine

A simple listening exercise. Students need to listen out for expressions of time.

Transcript

Boy: Anke, sag mal, spielst du eigentlich immer noch so gern Tennis?
Girl: Ja, ich liebe Tennis! Ich spiele jetzt im Verein.
Boy: Ja, im Verein? Toll! Wie oft trainierst du denn?
Girl: Ich trainiere dreimal pro Woche.
Boy: Dreimal pro Woche? Und wann?
Girl: Ich gehe montags, mittwochs und samstags in den Verein.
Boy: Am Samstag auch? Um wie viel Uhr denn?
Girl: Samstags spiele ich vormittags Tennis. Das Training ist um 10 Uhr morgens.

Answers

1 Sie spielt dreimal pro Woche.
2 Sie spielt montags, mittwochs und samstags Tennis.
3 Sie spielt um 10 Uhr (vormittags) Tennis.

Sprachtipp

Modalverben

This item introduces the six modal verbs which are very commonly used in German and explains their use.

können (to be able to, "can")

müssen (to have to, "must")

wollen (to want to)

sollen (to be supposed to, to be meant to, to be due to)

dürfen (to be allowed to, "may")

mögen (to like)

Übung

This item gives the students practice in the formation of 3 of the commonest modal verbs.

Answers

Was kann man machen?

1 Ich kann Fotos machen.

2 Du kannst Fußball spielen.

3 Er kann Tennis spielen.

4 Wir können im Chor singen.

Was muss man machen?

5 Ich muss meine Hausaufgaben machen.

6 Ihr müsst Briefe schreiben.

7 Wir müssen unsere Großeltern besuchen.

8 Sie müssen einkaufen gehen.

Was darf man / darf man nicht machen?

9 Ich darf nicht in eine Gaststätte gehen.

10 Du darfst Bier trinken.

11 Er darf keine Zigaretten rauchen.

12 Wir dürfen in die Disko gehen.

man

Students should be encouraged to use **man** whenever it is appropriate for them to do so. They need to be aware that it is very common in German.

9 Sag was! Bist du im Verein?

This item further consolidates the days of the week in the **montags, dienstags** etc. form and also adds **morgens, abends** etc. Students should be encouraged to work in pairs to practise the dialogues.

10 Quiz: Sport

1 Wie viele Spieler pro Mannschaft gibt es bei diesen Sportarten?

A short item to revise numbers and to consolidate the freetime expressions.

Answers

Fußball	11	Eishockey	6
Handball	7	Beach-Volleyball	2
Volleyball	6	Basketball	5
Squash	1	Feldhockey	11

11 Sportarten und Länder

This item gives a little cultural information on some popular sports. Students could be encouraged to look up the words necessary to describe their favourite sport.

This item allows students to use the information they have just noted down and to make up complete sentences in German.

 **Sport**

Students could be encouraged to look at these sites and to try and get the gist of what they read. They could also be encouraged to note down vocabulary they learn, or even to create a project in German about their favourite sports.

Kulturtipp Sport in deutschsprachigen Ländern

Here we have some cultural information about freetime activities in German-speaking countries.

PCM 7.7 Jugend und Sport in der Schweiz

An item from another German-speaking country! In order to avoid confusing students the **Neue Rechtschreibung** has been used in this exercise.

Answers

1 von Vereinen aller Art

2 landauf, landab

3 Sprecht miteinander

4 Du weißt was du gern tun willst!

5 Burschen und Mädchen

Beantworte auf Englisch!

1 Youth Clubs / Theatre Clubs / Film clubs.

2 swimming, ballet, gymnastics, tennis, cross-country skiing, surfing, mountaineering, sailing, athletics, football, walking, diving etc.

3 14–22.

4 about 300.

5 Squash is very popular with young people; it's fun; you run around a lot.

6 Skiing.

7 Cycling.

12 Lied: Der Freizeit Rap (1)

Students could be encouraged to sing along with the tune. The more adventurous could attempt to add further verses, or even make up their own version of the Freizeit Rap, using the instrumental version on the tape.

Transcript

Was ist dein Hobby?
Was machst du gern?
Alle machen etwas.
Siehst du auch gern fern?

Heinz hat viele Hobbys,
Computer und TV
Er spielt gern Gitarre,
Fußball und auch Squash.

Was ist dein Hobby?
Was machst du gern?
Alle machen etwas.
Siehst du auch gern fern?

Pia schwimmt und schläft gern.
Sie liebt ihr Telefon.
Sie liest und schreibt gern Briefe.
Am liebsten spielt sie Bass.

Was ist dein Hobby?
Was machst du gern?
Alle machen etwas.
Siehst du auch gern fern?

Yasemin mag Karate.
Sie findet lesen gut.
Am liebsten spielt sie Schlagzeug.
Das Internet ist gut.

Was ist dein Hobby?
Was machst du gern?
Alle machen etwas.
Siehst du auch gern fern?

13 Lied: Der Freizeit Rap (2)

Here students should be encouraged to identify those items which are not required by members of the band. It tests the skill of identifying details in a listening text. Please replay the rap from Ex. 12, **Der Freizeit Rap**.

Answers

1 Heinz does not need the books and the bike.
2 Pia needs everything in the picture.
3 Yasemin does not need the ballet shoes and the camera.

PCM 7.8 Lied: Der Freizeit Rap (3)

An extension activity for the rap song which encourages students to listen to the words more closely. Please replay the rap from Ex. 12, **Der Freizeit Rap**.

Answers

1 Yasemin
2 Pia
3 Pia
4 Heinz
5 Yasemin
6 Pia
7 Heinz
8 Pia

Einheit B   Einladungen

Unit 7B will introduce how to:
- *make an arrangement to meet someone*

PCMs 7.9 – 7.19 accompany this section.

1   Ein Super-Date – Teil 2

This cartoon takes the story a little further. Matthias has arranged to meet Laura and Bettina at the same time and the same place, but opts to go to football instead. Heinz rushes over to meet both girls but they are unimpressed by his suggestions and decide to go home.

Transcript

Matthias:	Hallo Heinz! Wie geht's?
Heinz:	Prima. Sag mal, hast du ein Date mit Bettina? Toll!!!
Matthias:	Ich treffe mich um 5 Uhr mit Bettina und mit Laura.
Heinz:	Mit Laura auch? Wow!
Matthias:	Oh je! Ich hab' um 5 Uhr ja gar keine Zeit. Ich hab' ein Fußballturnier!!!
Laura:	Hallo Bettina. Was machst du denn hier?
Bettina:	Ich habe ein Date mit einem ganz süßen Typen.
Laura:	Ich auch, aber er kommt zu spät.
Heinz:	Hallo Girls! Sorry, Matthias hat leider keine Zeit. Sollen wir zu mir gehen? Ich hab eine tolle DVD-Sammlung!
Heinz:	Terminator 3 ist gut! Ein prima Action-Film!
Bettina:	Oh! Ich muss heute Abend babysitten!
Laura:	Ich glaube, ich habe meine Hausaufgaben vergessen!

2   Lies was! Wie sagt man das auf Deutsch?

This item encourages the students to look back over the cartoon in Einheit A in order to find the expressions listed.

Answers
1   Was machst du heute Abend?
2   Sollen wir uns treffen?
3   Möchtest du heute Abend mit mir ins Kino gehen?
4   zu spät
5   keine Zeit
6   Sollen wir zu mir gehen?

3   Beantworte die Fragen   **E**

This item encourages good comprehension skills and an ability to manipulate language.

Answers
1   Er hat ein Fußballturnier.
    Er spielt Fußball.
2   Er will DVDs sehen.
    Filme sehen / fernsehen.
3   Bettina muss babysitten.
4   Laura muss Hausaufgaben machen.

Vokabeltipp   Einladungen

This item gives the most useful phrases for making arrangements to meet someone and can be used for role plays to practise arranging a meeting.

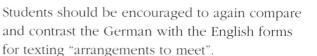

zu
This item introduces the use of the word **zu** with verbs. This could be contrasted with the earlier item on modal verbs, which do not require **zu**.

4   Schreib was! SMS – Nachrichten (1)   **A**

Students should be encouraged to again compare and contrast the German with the English forms for texting "arrangements to meet".

As an extension exercise students could be encouraged to write out some text messages and see if their partner can understand what they have written. For further text message formats, refer to **Kapitel 6, Einheit B, Kulturtipp** and of course the Internet site: www.smszone.de.

Answers
Möchtest du in der Pause in die Stadt? Hast du Lust? Dirk
Hallo! Hast du Lust, morgen ins Kino zu gehen? Lena
Hast du nach der Schule Zeit? Willst du ins Café? Jan

Vokabeltipp   Wann und wo?

This item gives students further useful phrases they will need to know in order to prepare for a role play about arranging a meeting in German.

5   Sag was! Nach der Schule

This item practises making arrangements in speech. This follows nicely on from the text messaging item. As an extension exercise students could be encouraged to make up their own dialogues based on the text messages they have produced.

Präpositionen mit dem Dativ? oder mit dem Akkusativ?

This item practises some of the prepositions which can take the accusative or the dative. Weaker students will probably need assistance in order to decide which case to use.

Übung: Füll die Lücken aus!

Answers

1 Das Brot ist auf <u>dem</u> Tisch.
2 Ich gehe in <u>die</u> Küche.
3 Ich koche in <u>der</u> Küche.
4 Wir wohnen auf <u>dem</u> Land.
5 Die Jungen gehen über <u>die</u> Brücke.
6 Der Hund schläft unter <u>dem</u> Stuhl.
7 Wir treffen uns vor <u>der</u> Schule.
8 Ich gehe <u>ins</u> Bett.

PCM 7.9   Schreib was! Contracted Prepositions

This item offers more practice on the **Sprachtipp** item.

Answers

1 Wir wohnen im Osten von Berlin.
2 Ich stehe am Fenster.
3 Oma kommt ins Wohnzimmer.
4 Ich gehe ans Fenster.
5 Die Katze geht aufs Dach.

PCM 7.10   Schreib was! Dativ oder Akkusativ ? (1)

This item offers a further simple exercise on the dative and accusative.

Answers

1	Das Bild hängt an der Wand.	D
2	Hänge das Bild an die Wand.	A
3	Setz dich auf den Stuhl!	A
4	Ich sitze auf dem Stuhl.	D
5	Ich wohne in der Stadt.	D
6	Ich fahre in die Stadt.	A
7	Der Hund liegt unter dem Tisch.	D
8	Der Hund geht unter den Tisch.	A
9	Parke das Auto vor das Haus.	A
10	Das Auto steht vor dem Haus.	D

PCM 7.11   Schreib was! Dativ oder Akkusativ? (2)

This item offers a further practice on dative and accusative prepositions.

Answers

1 Das Bett ist neben dem Tisch.
2 Ich gehe in die Stadt.
3 Ich gehe ins Bett.
4 Ich wohne in einer Wohnung.
5 Das Auto ist vor der Garage.
6 Ich gehe unter die Brücke.

6   Hör zu! Eine Verabredung

This item encourages students to listen out for key elements in what they hear.

Transcript

Heinz: Hallo Pia! Was machst du heute Nachmittag? Hast du Zeit?
Pia: Ja, ich hab' Zeit. Was sollen wir machen?
Heinz: Florian hat ein neues Computerspiel. Das ist voll gut! Möchtest du mitspielen?
Pia: Oh ja, gerne! Wann treffen wir uns?
Heinz: Um 2 Uhr? Geht das?
Pia: Das ist zu früh. Ich hab heute echt viele Hausaufgaben. Ist 4 Uhr in Ordnung?
Heinz: Ja, 4 Uhr ist gut.
Pia: Prima! Ich bin um 4 Uhr bei dir.
Heinz: Nein, nicht bei mir. Das Spiel ist bei Florian.
Pia: Gut. Dann bin ich heute Nachmittag bei Florian. Tschüs!

Answers

C 4 o'clock
H Florian's place

7   Logikrätsel: Wer trifft wen?

A logic puzzle like those students often enjoy doing in English. Weaker students will need help here. The item could be worked out in a group, with a small prize for the students who come up with the correct answers first. Students should be encouraged to look at the information given, both in the written sentences and in the pictures of the boys: e.g. 4. says „Ahmet trifft sich um 7 Uhr", so the second boy must be <u>Ahmet</u>. 5. says „Lutz wartet am kino", so the first boy must be <u>Lutz</u>. By process of elimination the third boy must be Peter and he is meeting . . . etc.

Answers

Ayse trifft sich mit Peter um 5 Uhr im Schwimmbad.
Maria trifft sich mit Lutz um 8 Uhr im Kino.
Babsi trifft sich mit Ahmet um 7 Uhr zu Hause.

Lerntipp **gehen, machen, spielen, fahren**

This item gives the student vocabulary for use with these important verbs, which are most necessary for the topic area.

8 and PCM 7.12 Schreib was! Mein Terminkalender

An activity to encourage students to write freely and use practical German for an everyday task.

For this item you will need to use the PCM 7.12.

PCM 7.13 Rollenspiel: Verabrede dich

A guided role play practising simple routines for arranging a meeting.

9 Sag was! Verabrede dich

This item encourages the students to use in practice the phrases which they have been learning. The role play makes active use of the vocabulary introduced.

PCM 7.14 Hör zu! Einladungen (1) [A]

Three simple listening exercises where students learn to accept and decline invitations.

Transcript

Boy:	Hallo Klara! Was machst du heute Nachmittag?
Klara:	Warum?
Boy:	Hast du Lust, ins Café zu gehen?
Klara:	Ach nein, ich habe leider keine Zeit. Ich muss Hausaufgaben machen.
Boy:	Hallo Benjamin, hast du Zeit?
Benjamin:	Hallo! Ja, ich habe Zeit. Warum? Was hast du vor?
Boy:	Sollen wir ins Kino gehen?
Benjamin:	Ins Kino? Nein, es tut mir Leid. Ich habe keine Lust.
Boy:	Maja, hey, Maja!
Maja:	Hi! Wie geht's?
Boy:	Gut, danke. Was machst du gerade? Möchtest du schwimmen gehen?
Maja:	Schwimmen? Gute Idee! Ja, gerne!
Boy:	Prima!

Answers

	Ja	Nein
Klara		X
Benjamin		X
Maja	X	

PCM 7.15 Hör zu! Einladungen (2) [A]

An extension activity in which students need to listen out for details of the arrangements. Please replay the dialogue from PCM 7.14, **Hör zu! Einladungen**.

Answers

1 Was will der Junge mit Klara machen?
  Er will ins Café gehen. E
2 Was will der Junge mit Benjamin machen?
  Er will ins Kino gehen. D
3 Was will der Junge mit Maja machen?
  Er will schwimmen gehen. C

PCM 7.16 Lies was! FAHRRAD-VERLEIH

This item is based on a genuine flier from an Austrian bicycle hire shop, practising expressions of time and numbers.

Answers

1 S 60,—
2 S 150,—
3 S100,—
4 S 200,—
5 Ja. / 40% Kinderermässigung

1 Ja.
2 Nein.
3 Nein.

Vokabeltipp Film und Fernsehen

This item provides the important expressions so that students will be able to give descriptions of television programmes or films.

10 Hör zu! Was für ein Film ist das?

An item to practise the new vocabulary relating to descriptions of films. Able students should be encouraged to write their answers in full sentences.

Transcript

Kino eins:	*excerpt from a musical*
Kino zwei:	*romantic music*
	Man: Ich liebe dich, Rebecca!!! Ich werde dich immer lieben!
Kino drei:	*horror film sounds*
Kino vier:	*action film sounds*
Kino fünf:	*Western style music*
	Man: Hallo, Cowboy!
Kino sechs:	*sound of laughter*

Answers

Kino 1 – D	In Kino 1 läuft ein Musical.
Kino 2 – B	In Kino 2 läuft ein Liebesfilm.
Kino 3 – F	In Kino 3 läuft ein Horrorfilm.
Kino 4 – A	In Kino 4 läuft ein Actionfilm.
Kino 5 – C	In Kino 5 läuft ein Western.
Kino 6 – E	In Kino 6 läuft eine Komödie.

11 Hör zu! Mein Lieblingsfilm (1)

Students are encouraged to listen out for detail.

Transcript

Interviewerin:	Guten Tag. Ich mache ein Interview für das Filmmagazin. Wie heißen Sie?
Drakula:	Ich heiße Graf Drakula.
Interviewerin:	Oh! Und was für Filme gefallen Ihnen, Graf Drakula? Sind Sie ein Fan von Horrorfilmen?
Drakula:	Oh nein!!! Ich sehe am liebsten Liebesfilme mit schönen Frauen!
Interviewerin:	Liebesfilme? Wie interessant! Und du heißt . . . ?
Rotkäppchen:	Rotkäppchen. Mein Name ist Rotkäppchen.
Interviewerin:	Was gefällt dir denn im Kino?
Rotkäppchen:	Ich sehe am liebsten Horrorfilme.
Interviewerin:	Horrorfilme? Bist du dafür nicht ein bisschen zu jung?
Rotkäppchen:	Ach was!
Interviewerin:	Und darf ich fragen, wie Sie heißen?
Bond:	Ich heiße Bond, James Bond.
Interviewerin:	Herr Bond, was für Filme sehen Sie gern?
Bond:	Ich liebe Sportsendungen. Sport interessiert mich sehr.
Interviewerin:	Danke. Und wer bist du?
Heidi:	Ich bin die Heidi.
Interviewerin:	Ach ja, die Heidi aus der Schweiz, richtig. Magst du nicht Tierfilme?
Bond:	Nein, Tierfilme finde ich langweilig. Ich sehe am liebsten Actionfilme.
Interviewerin:	Actionfilme? Vielen Dank.

Answers

Name	Lieblingsfilm
Graf Drakula	Liebesfilme
Rotkäppchen	Horrorfilme
James Bond	Sportsendungen
Heidi	Actionfilme

12 Sag was! Mein Lieblingsfilm (2)

This item consolidates the information collected in the previous exercise and encourages students to conjugate verbs.

 www. **Was möchtest du heute Abend machen?**

Students should be encouraged to find these internet sites, but care should be taken that students do not <u>actually</u> purchase tickets through some of these sites, as it is very easy to do so!

13 Wann siehst du fern?

Students need to read carefully to sift through the details in order to get the right piece of information!

Answers

1	Antonia	3	Tom
2	Tina	4	David

PCM 7.17 Lies was! Was gibt es im Fernsehen? (1)

An exercise practising the vocabulary for discussing TV programmes. This item encourages students to write full sentences in answer to the questions.

Answers

1 Auf ZDF kann man Fußball sehen.
2 Auf Kabel 1 kann man einen Western sehen.
3 Auf Pro 7 kann man eine Komödie sehen.
4 Auf RTL kann man eine Talkshow sehen.
5 Auf Sat 1 kann man eine Krimiserie sehen.

PCM 7.18 Lies was! Was gibt es im Fernsehen? (2)

This additional activity encourages closer reading of the text.

Answers

1 Sendung 1 heißt Siska.
2 Sendung 2 heißt Ilona Christen.
3 Sendung 3 heißt Manchester United gegen Lazio Rom.
4 Sendung 4 heißt Micky's fröhlicher Valentinstag.
5 Sendung 5 heißt Dennis.

PCM 7.19 Sag was! Was gibt es im Fernsehen?

This role play is a cue card exercise in disguise. Students practise the vocabulary for television programmes.

Spiel: Richtig oder falsch?

Enlarge and cut out the cue cards for films.

Hold up a card and say for example : „Heute Abend gibt es einen Horrorfilm."

Students have to stand up if this statement is correct (you are showing the correct cue card). If the statement is wrong they remain seated. Those who get the answer wrong are out. After a while students can take over the role of caller.

This game can also be played with cue cards for other topics (colours, activities, hobbies etc.).

Kulturtipp Verwandte Sprachen

Students can see that the roots of the German language are quite close to the roots of the English language.

Aussprache Rrrrr! ● ● ● ● ● ● ● ● ● ● ● ● ● ● ● ●

This item practises the German **r** sound.

Transcript
Rechts ist ein richtig ruhiges Restaurant.
Ritas rote Ratte rasiert sich.

14 Lied: TV-Total

Students should be encouraged to sing along or to identify those vocabulary items which they have learned in this chapter:

Transcript
Ich steh auf und mach die Glotze an.
Frühstücksfernsehen ist voll gut.
Ohne TV läuft hier gar nichts.
Dann geht's mir gar nicht gut.

Fernsehen, fernsehen,
ich liebe nur mein Fernsehen.
Fernsehen, fernsehen,
was läuft denn jetzt im Fernsehen?

Vormittags gibt's 'ne Gameshow,
und Fernsehserien pur.
Am Mittag kommt 'ne Talkshow,
Kinderfilme um drei Uhr.

Fernsehen, fernsehen,
ich liebe nur mein Fernsehen.
Fernsehen, fernsehen,
was läuft denn jetzt im Fernsehen?

Am Nachmittag gibt's'n Western,
die Nachrichten um sechs.
Am Abend kommt ein Horrorfilm,
und der Actionfilm *Mad Max*.

Fernsehen, fernsehen,
ich liebe nur mein Fernsehen.
Fernsehen, fernsehen,
was läuft denn jetzt im Fernsehen?

Ob Musical, ob Drama,
für Kinder oder Sport,
ich seh mir einfach alles an.
Das Fernsehen ist mein Freund.

Fernsehen, fernsehen,
ich liebe nur mein Fernsehen.
Fernsehen, fernsehen,
mein liebes, liebes Fernsehen!

Answers
1 He switches the telly on.
2 Game shows, soaps, talk shows, children's programs, westerns, news, horror movies, action movies, musicals, dramas, sports programs.
3 He loves TV. He is a TV addict.
4 open answer

15 Sag was! Meine Freizeit

Here again the students get a chance to practise what they have learned to say about their own freetime activities.

 Leseseite ···

The Leseseite gives the type of activity students might find later in examinations and includes unfamiliar vocabulary in authentic messages.

Answers
Finde im Text:
1 im Internet surfen
2 Im Sommer gehe ich (eigentlich) jeden Tag ins Freibad.
3 Ich freue mich auf Montag.
4 Obwohl ich fast jede Woche was zu tun hab

Schreib Bettina, Christina, Daniel oder Klaus.
1 Bettina
2 Daniel
3 Klaus
4 Christina
5 Bettina
6 Christina

 Aussagesätze and Grammatik

These pages are useful quick references for students working alone or in pairs – on a classwork or homework assignment. They are also useful for revision purposes, as they sum up the important grammar and vocabulary of the chapter.

Kapitel 8 Essen und Trinken

Unit 8A will introduce how to:
- *talk about food and drink*

PCMs 8.1 – 8.7 accompany this section.

1 Liebe geht durch den Magen – Teil 1

This cartoon introduces some basic words for food. Laura and Yasemin have decided to make a dinner for Matthias' birthday. Laura is keen to impress Matthias, so wants to cook something typically German – although Matthias is in fact Austrian. After trying the comprehension questions in English students may be encouraged to speculate as to whether Laura and Yasemin's friends might really like sausage and sauerkraut.

Transcript

Narrator: Matthias hat Geburtstag. Laura und Yasemin kochen ein Essen.
Laura: Was ist ein typisch deutsches Essen?
Yasemin: Ich weiß nicht. Zu Hause kochen wir türkisch.
Laura: Sauerkraut . . . Würstchen . . . Kartoffeln . . .
Yasemin: Mag Matthias Sauerkraut?
Laura: Bestimmt!!! Alle Deutschen mögen das!
Yasemin: Und Österreicher?
Laura: Wie viel Salz brauchen wir für die Kartoffeln?
Yasemin: Ich weiß nicht. Viel!
Und, wie schmeckt das Sauerkraut?
Laura: Uuuh! Viel zu sauer!
Yasemin: Wir brauchen Zucker! . . .
Ich decke den Tisch.
Laura: Ich koche die Würstchen. (sound of doorbell) Oh! Es klingelt! Die Gäste sind schon da!

2 Sag was! Fragen zum Cartoon

Answers
1 It is Matthias' birthday and they have invited some friends around.
2 Sauerkraut, sausages and potatoes.
3 Laura thinks it is a typical German meal.
4 They don't seem to be very good at cooking – the potatoes might be too salty.

Vokabeltipp Hast du Hunger?

This item introduces the basic vocabulary for food. Students could be encouraged to draw and label some of the items for classroom display in order to consolidate the vocabulary. Alternatively you may choose to use some of their drawings as flashcards. They could also create small Bingo cards with items of food instead of numbers. When you show the flashcard or call out the name of the food / drink, they can cover their picture, just as in the game of number bingo.

Pass auf!

This item is to inform the students that **Marmelade** is a false friend and that to say marmalade you have to say **Orangenmarmelade**.

Vokabeltipp Hast du Durst?

This item introduces the basic vocabulary for drinks.

Lerntipp Deutsches Essen und Trinken

Students should be encouraged to look in their local supermarket for German food or food with German names. German-owned retailers in Great Britain often carry a wide range of German products. Aldi and Lidl products often include German labelling. Students could do some research to find out if there is a German retailer in their town.

PCM 8.1 Hör zu! Was essen sie zum Mittagessen?

This item practises identification of single vocabulary items, in this case – food items.

Transcript

Paul: Was isst du zum Mittagessen, Irene?
Irene: Ich esse zum Mittagessen Nudeln. Nudeln sind mein Lieblingsessen.
Paul: Ist das alles?
Irene: Nein, zum Nachtisch esse ich noch ein Eis.
Paul: Hm, lecker, ein Eis! Und was trinkst du?
Irene: Ich trinke Limonade. Ein großes Glas Limonade! Was isst du zum Mittagessen, Paul?
Paul: Ich esse zum Mittagessen Reis mit Hähnchen.
Irene: Reis mit Hähnchen? Lecker!
Paul: Und ich trinke einen Apfelsaft. Ich liebe Apfelsaft!
Irene: Hast du auch einen Nachtisch?
Paul: Ja, ich esse eine Banane.

Answers

Irene isst: C, D   Irene trinkt: E
Paul isst: H, I, A   Paul trinkt: F

PCM 8.2   Spiel: Mittagessen

A lighthearted game in which students can practise the names of food items.

Students can first colour in and cut out the game
cards.

Cards are then mixed and put face down in a stack.

It is the aim of the game to fill your card with the
5 required food items.

Players draw a card from the top of the stack
when it is their turn. They say aloud what food
item they have drawn:

Ich esse . . .
Ich trinke . . .
Ich habe . . .

They will need to be reminded to use the accusative case after these verbs!

If they still need a card for that category, they put
it on the appropriate space on their board. If that
category has already got a card on it, they can
choose which card they prefer:

Ich esse / trinke lieber . . . .

The unwanted cards are put aside and reshuffled.

The game continues until the first player has a
complete meal.

The game cards can also be used as mini-
flashcards.

Spiel: Der Vielfraß (the greedy guts)   [A]

Sit in a circle. The first player begins by saying:
„Ich esse . . ." + one food item.

The next player repeats the phrase and adds
another food item (or drink). Make sure students
say „ich trinke" if they add a drink rather than a
food item.

As you go round the circle you keep repeating the
food items the previous players have named and
adding to the chain.

As a variation, players can add actions to the food
items they name (which might or might not be
helpful). These actions also have to be repeated.
Students need to see how long they can make the
chain before the first player makes a mistake.

3   Sag was! Was isst die Familie Gruber?

This item practises the writing of simple sentences
on the topic of food and drink. Prior to this exercise you may need to revise the accusative case
(Pupil's Book, Chapter X page xx), for masculine
items like:

„Frau Gruber isst zum Frühstück einen Apfel /
einen Salat / einen Joghurt."

You may also wish to point out that although
English says "a cup of coffee" or "a glass of
orange juice" in German these items become **eine
Tasse Kaffee / ein Glas Orangensaft** i.e. no "of"
is needed.

As **mit** is used here without an article there
should be no need to remind them of the dative
case endings.

Zum is given to them, so should not cause a
problem – obviously you may wish to remind able
students that this is in fact a contraction of
zu + dem.

Answers

Herr Gruber isst zum Frühstück drei Brötchen und ein Ei.
Er trinkt zum Frühstück eine Tasse Kaffee.
Er isst zum Mittagessen Hühnchen, Möhren und Kartoffeln, und
ein Stück Torte.
Er trinkt zum Mittagessen Bier.
Er isst zum Abendessen 3 Würstchen mit Senf und Brot, Käse
und Tomaten.

Frau Gruber isst zum Frühstück einen Apfel und eine Banane.
Sie trinkt zum Frühstück ein Glas Milch.
Sie isst zum Mittagessen einen Salat, ein Brötchen und
Erdbeeren.
Sie trinkt ein Glas Mineralwasser.
Sie isst zum Abendessen eine Suppe und einen Joghurt.
Sie trinkt ein Glas Orangensaft.

Marianne isst zum Frühstück Cornflakes, ein Brot mit Honig und
eine Orange (Apfelsine).
Sie trinkt zum Frühstück eine Tasse Tee.
Sie isst zum Mittagessen eine Pizza, einen Apfel und ein Eis.
Sie trinkt zum Mittagessen eine Limonade.
Sie isst zum Abendessen Nudeln mit Soße, Käse und einen Salat
und etwas Schokolade.

4   Sag was! Was isst du?

This item should build nicely on the previous
exercise although here the students will need the
forms **ich esse** and **ich trinke**. It may be worth
pointing out here that **trinken** is in fact a weak
verb, but **essen** is a strong verb and therefore
irregular in its **du** and **er, sie, es** forms.

Lerntipp **isst oder ist?**

This item brings the similarity between certain forms of the two verbs **essen** and **sein** to the students' attention.

Additional Activity   E

For classes that may appreciate the play on words you could try asking them in spoken German how many meanings they can find for the following e.g.

Man isst was man isst / Man ist was man ist / Man ist was man isst.

You eat what you eat / You are what you are / You are what you eat.

5   Lied: Wir haben Hunger!

A good song to sing along to – hopefully the students will appreciate the humour. You could ask whether they have heard of / seen anyone eating flies (perhaps on a survival-type programme) or snails (perhaps on a food or holiday programme).

Transcript
Wir haben Hunger, Hunger, Hunger,
haben Hunger, Hunger, Hunger,
haben Hunger, Hunger, Hunger,
haben Durst!

Wenn wir nichts kriegen, kriegen, kriegen,
essen wir Fliegen, Fliegen, Fliegen,
essen wir Fliegen, Fliegen, Fliegen
von der Wand.

Wenn die nicht schmecken, schmecken, schmecken,
essen wir Schnecken, Schnecken, Schnecken,
essen wir Schnecken, Schnecken, Schnecken,
und werden krank.

Vokabeltipp **Was magst du?**

This item gives the useful questions and answers for expressing preferences about food. Students could be encouraged to talk about their own food and drink preferences and any food allergies / intolerances. The personal pronoun **Sprachtipp** gives the dative form of the pronouns students may need with **schmecken**.

 **Essen und Trinken**

Students should be encouraged to look at the websites listed and also to do their own searches

for specialities in German-speaking countries. If you have a link with a school in a German-speaking country, you could ask the German students to send you pictures of their favourite meals.

Sprachtipp

Personal Pronouns
The table is given to help the students decide which pronoun to use. It is important that the students remember that there are 3 ways of saying "you" in German – and each one has its own accusative and dative forms. In addition they should be reminded that **er, sie** and **es** can all mean "it" depending on whether the "thing" in question is masculine, feminine or neuter.

The accompanying exercise practises various forms of the pronouns. Students will probably need assistance with this exercise.

Übung: Ersetze die unterstrichenen Wörter mit einem   E **Pronomen!**

Answers
1   <u>Er</u> gibt eine Party.
2   <u>Sie</u> spricht mit <u>ihm</u>.
3   Sie sagen <u>ihm</u>, was sie essen möchten.
4   <u>Sie</u> rufen <u>ihn</u> an.
5   <u>Wir</u> fahren mit <u>ihnen</u> in die Stadt.
6   Ich kaufe <u>es</u> für <u>ihn</u>.

PCM 8.3   Hör zu! Es schmeckt uns nicht!

A simple listening exercise practising the adjectives describing food.

Transcript
Kellner:	Schmeckt es Ihnen?
Mann:	Nein, es schmeckt uns gar nicht!
Kellner:	Oh! Was ist denn nicht in Ordnung?
Mann:	Meine Suppe ist zu kalt, viel zu kalt!
Kellner:	Die Suppe ist kalt? Oh, das tut mir Leid.
Frau:	Und meine Bratwurst ist viel zu scharf! Das kann man ja nicht essen!
Kellner:	Ihre Wurst ist zu scharf? Entschuldigung! Ist denn bei den Kindern alles in Ordnung?
Junge:	Nein, meine Nudeln sind viel zu salzig. Da ist mindestens ein Kilo Salz drin – Bah!
Kellner:	Tut mir Leid. Ich bringe gleich neue Nudeln. Und was ist bei dir nicht in Ordnung?
Mädchen:	Bei mir ist alles in Ordnung. Mein Eis schmeckt priiiima! Aber es ist viel zu klein. Kann ich bitte noch ein Eis haben, Mama?

Answers
1 c, 2 a, 3 d, 4 b

PCM 8.4 Schreib was! Personalpronomen im Nominativ

This item revises personal pronouns in the nominative case.

Answers

1 <u>Wir</u> essen immer um 7 Uhr zu Abend.
2 Maria mag keinen Kuchen und <u>sie</u> isst kein Eis.
3 Es ist schon 9 Uhr. <u>Sie</u> sind zu spät!
4 Otto kommt heute zu mir. <u>Er</u> isst mit uns zu Mittag.
5 Um wie viel Uhr wollt <u>ihr</u> kommen?
6 Wie spät ist <u>es</u>?
7 Was magst <u>du</u> lieber, Tee oder Kaffee?
8 Haben <u>Sie</u> Lust, mit in die Stadt zu kommen, Herr Fazal?

PCM 8.5 Schreib was! Personalpronomen im Akkusativ

This item revises personal pronouns in the accusative case.

Answers

1 Hallo Ali und Naila, ich sehe <u>euch</u>!
2 Das ist mein Kaninchen, Pucki. Ich finde <u>es</u> ganz süß!
3 Sprich lauter! Ich kann <u>dich</u> nicht hören.
4 Wir sind alte Freunde. Wir kennen <u>uns</u> schon seit 40 Jahren.
5 Da ist Kai. Seine Mutter fährt <u>ihn</u> mit dem Auto zur Schule.
6 Wo sind Tom und Walter. Ich kann <u>sie</u> nicht sehen?
7 Sagen Sie mal, Frau Jansen, sehen <u>Sie</u> meine Tasche irgendwo?
8 Ich bin hier! Kannst du <u>mich</u> sehen?

PCM 8.6 Schreib was! Personalpronomen im Dativ

This item revises personal pronouns in the dative case.

Answers

1 Schmeckt es <u>dir</u> Dana?
2 Wie geht es Paula? Gefällt <u>ihr</u> die neue Schule?
3 Ich will das haben! Gib es <u>mir</u>!
4 Gehst du heute zu Peter? Dann sage <u>ihm</u> bitte, er soll zur Party kommen.
5 Tobias und Jonas lieben das Essen in Italien. Es schmeckt <u>ihnen</u> ganz toll!
6 Wir finden den Kuchen lecker. Er schmeckt <u>uns</u> wirklich gut!
7 Das ist mein Meerschweinchen. Ich gebe <u>ihm</u> jeden Tag frische Möhren.
8 Hallo, Franziska und Julia. Ich habe <u>euch</u> einen Brief geschrieben.

PCM 8.7 Gruppenarbeit: Gemischte Pronomen

This item revises a selection of personal pronouns and should only be attempted by the more able, possibly with assistance from the teacher.

Answers

Many different solutions possible. Some of the possibilities are:

Das Essen	schmeckt	mir.	
Er	liebt	sie.	
Ich	mag	dich.	
Das T-Shirt	gefällt	uns.	
Wir	rufen	euch	an.
Es	geht	ihm	gut.
Du	kennst	ihn	nicht.
Ich	finde	mich	schön.

6 Hör zu! Mein Lieblingsessen (1)

This item encourages the students to pick out the key words from a conversation about food.

Transcript

Yasemin: Hallo, Leute, sagt mal, was esst ihr eigentlich gerne? Habt ihr ein Lieblingsessen?
Also ich hab schon ein Lieblingsessen. Ich liebe nämlich Eis. Schokoladeneis und Erdbeereis mag ich am allerliebsten. Bei uns in Mainz gibt's ein paar echt gute Eiscafés!

Matthias: Ich liebe Spätzle mit Käsesoße. Das sind so eine Art Nudeln. Diese Nudeln sind typisch für Süddeutschland und Österreich. Und am besten schmecken Spätzle eben mit einer Käsesoße.

Laura: Mir schmeckt der deutsche Kuchen so gut. Hier gibt es wirklich ganz viele verschiedene Sorten Kuchen und Torten. Am liebsten esse ich Sachertorte. Mmmh! Lecker!

Heinz: Ich mag Pommes Frites am liebsten. Ja, mein Lieblingsessen sind Pommes mit Ketchup.

Pia: Mein Lieblingsessen ist Obst. Ich mag Obst gerne: Äpfel, Bananen, Weintrauben, Orangen . . . Und ich esse gern Salate. Ja, Obst und Salate esse ich am liebsten.

Answers

Yasemin: E
Matthias: B
Laura: A
Heinz: C
Pia: D

7 Hör zu! Mein Lieblingsessen   **E**

The previous exercise merely required students to pick out individual words. This exercise builds on the previous one and encourages the students to write full sentences.

Answers

Yasemin isst am liebsten Eis.
Matthias isst am liebsten Nudeln (mit Käsesoße).
Laura isst am liebsten Kuchen.
Heinz isst am liebsten Pommes mit Ketchup.
Pia isst am liebsten Obst und Salate.

8 Sag was! Mein Lieblingsessen (3)

This item builds on the previous items and encourages the students to give their own individual preferences. More able students can also use the following **Vokabeltipp** to give reasons why they do / do not like certain items of food.

Vokabeltipp Wie schmeckt das?

This item introduces more vocabulary for describing preferences.

9 Schreib was! Wie schmeckt das?

This item encourages students to think of the items listed in terms of taste and to attribute to them a particular taste.

Answers

süß	sauer	salzig	scharf	bitter	fettig	mild
Schokolade	Zitrone	Schinken	Chilli	Kaffee	Pommes	Reis

Wie schmeckt das?   A

As an additional activity you could play a "tasting game" – provided you ensure you are aware of any food intolerances the students may suffer from!

Bring in a selection of food (e.g. chocolate, lemon, ham, coffee, tea, sugar, rice, tomato, cake, biscuit etc) and a blindfold.

Choose three students to be the "blindfolded panel" or divide the students into groups, where one is blindfolded.

The blindfolded volunteer must say what the item tastes like and see if they can name the item.

The rest might give helpful (or unhelpful) clues where necessary.

Kulturtipp Spezialitäten

This item introduces some specialities from German-speaking countries. The item can be extended by using the Internet. Partner schools can be encouraged to send details of local specialities.

10 Lies was! Das darf ich nicht essen (1)

Some students may suffer from allergies, others will probably know someone who has a food intolerance so this item is important in order that the students will be able to express such intolerances.

11 Schreib was! Wer darf was nicht essen? Es gibt mehrere Möglichkeiten.

Students may not always come up with the same answers as some will be stricter or better informed about the contents of some food items. It could for instance be argued that chocolate cannot be eaten by someone who has a milk allergy as some chocolate contains milk. Some vegetarians may also not eat chocolate for similar reasons.

Answers

Kemal G.:	4, 7, 10, 11
Anne W.:	2, 3, 11
Martin H.:	1, 2, 3, 5, 6, 8, 11, 12
Ljuba M.:	1, 4, 5, 7, 9, 10, 11

Additional activity

As an additional activity students could be encouraged to prepare a card for someone in the class / school who has an allergy. You should tell the students that this person is travelling to a German-speaking country and needs to take a card with them to show in hotels / restaurants. Students can use „Das darf ich nicht essen" and the vocabulary in this unit to assist them.

Sprachtipp

Doch

Doch is an important, frequently used word and students need to be aware of when to use it. To sum up:

When you <u>disagree</u> with a negative question or statement, you have to say **Doch!**

Doch can also be used as a fill-in word if you want to disagree.

12 Partnerarbeit. Das darf ich nicht essen (2)

This item consolidates the „Das darf ich nicht essen" exercise and the **Sprachtipp** above, by getting students to respond using **doch**.

Einheit B   Ich möchte etwas bestellen!

Unit 8B will introduce how to:
- *order a meal and express preferences*

PCMs 8.8 – 8.13 accompany this section.

1   Liebe geht durch den Magen – Teil 2

This cartoon continues the story line from the cartoon in unit A. Laura and Yasemin have cooked a dinner for Matthias' birthday. Laura was keen to impress Matthias, so has cooked something typically German, but unfortunately her cooking skills leave a little to be desired! Pia's elder brother Markus, who is wheelchair bound, has difficulties getting up the stairs.

Students could be encouraged to look for the English equivalent to: „Liebe geht durch den Magen" – The way to a man's heart is through his stomach.

Transcript

Laura:	Herzlichen Glückwunsch zum Geburtstag!
David:	Wer sitzt hier?
Pia:	Mein Bruder Markus. Er ist zu spät.
Markus:	Hallo Pia! Ich kann nicht rein. Hier ist eine Treppe!
Pia:	Oh je! Das tut mir Leid!
Florian:	Wartest du schon lange?
Markus:	Nein.
Laura:	Möchtest du etwas Sauerkraut?
David:	Oh! Die Bockwurst ist ja kalt!
Heinz:	Igitt! Die Kartoffeln sind viel zu salzig!
Pia:	Und das Sauerkraut schmeckt süß! Oh je!
Matthias:	Das macht doch nichts. Ich esse keine Würstchen. Ich bin Vegetarier. Sollen wir Pommes Frites bestellen?
Heinz:	Oh ja! Mein Lieblingsessen!

2   Schreib was!

Answers

1 Er ist Pias Bruder.
2 Es gibt eine Treppe.
3 Sie sind zu salzig.
4 Sie ist kalt.
5 Es ist zu süß.
6 Er isst kein Fleisch.
7 Sie wollen alle Pommes.

Vokabeltipp Essen bestellen

This **Vokabeltipp** gives useful vocabulary and phrases for ordering food in a restaurant.

3   Hör zu und schreib was! Im Restaurant

This item makes full use of the expressions given in the **Vokabeltipp** in a restaurant situation.

Transcript

Kellner:	Möchten Sie einen Tisch für vier?
Vater:	Ja, bitte.
Kellner:	Was möchten Sie trinken?
Vater:	Für mich eine Cola bitte.
Mutter:	Und die Speisekarte, bitte.
Kellner:	Wer hat den Saft?
Sohn:	Der Saft ist für mich, danke.
Kellner:	Was möchten Sie essen?
Tochter:	Ich möchte eine Tagessuppe, bitte.
Mutter:	Was möchtest du essen, Patrick?

Answers
The following answers show which utterances go with which picture.

1:	waiter – f	father – j			
2:	waiter – a	father – g	mother – i	
3:	waiter – b	boy – h			
4:	waiter – c	girl – d	mother – e	

Kulturtipp Konditoreien

This item gives cultural information about the terms: **Konditorei / Eiscafé / Eisdiele**.
You could talk about your own experiences when eating in these establishments or ask a partner school to send photos of their local cafés, if possible showing typical cakes or ice cream.

Sprachtipp

ich möchte
Obviously, the students would not get far in Germany without the exprerssion: **ich möchte** and it is important that they understand when to use it and how useful it is!

4   Schreib was! Was bestellen Sie?

This item allows the students to study a menu and decide what each dish contains. It is also important to point out the key headings on a menu:

Vorspeisen, Hauptgerichte, Beilagen, Nachtisch, warme / kalte Getränke

Once they have studied the menu and know what each dish consists of, they can then look at the characters and decide what Frau Berta

Bickerbecker, Herr Jürgen Ernst, Sabinchen and Dr Klaus van Gemmern might want to eat. Finally they could decide what they themselves would like from such a menu and order the items using **ich möchte.**

There are no set answers to this exercise – the students are free to choose what they think the characters may like!

Vokabeltipp **Bezahlen**

This **Vokabeltipp** brings in the key phrases for paying the bill in a restaurant or café.

PCM 8.8   Rollenspiel: In der Konditorei

This gives students the opportunity to practise ordering in a café.

PCM 8.9   Sag was! Wie sagt man das auf Deutsch?

This item revises restaurant phrases.

Answers
- Ober! / Bedienung!
- Die Speisekarte, bitte.
- Ich möchte bitte einen Hamburger mit Pommes (Frites).
- Das ist zu kalt.
- Die Rechnung, bitte.
  Ich möchte bezahlen.
- Wo sind die Toiletten, bitte?

PCM 8.10   Hör zu! Was passt?

This item revises phrases for use at the dinner table.

Transcript
Eins:

Frau 1:	Prost!
Mann 1:	Ja, zum Wohl!

Zwei:

Frau 2:	Herr Ober, die Speisekarte bitte.
Kellner:	Kommt sofort.

Drei:

Mutter:	Möchtest du noch etwas Suppe, Robert?
Sohn:	Nein, danke, Mama. Ich bin schon satt.

Vier:

Mann:	Bedienung! Die Rechnung bitte. Ich möchte bezahlen.
Kellnerin:	Die Rechnung kommt sofort.

Fünf:

Frau:	Guten Appetit, Klaus.
Mann:	Guten Appetit.

Answers
1 C, 2 A, 3 E, 4 B, 5 D

---

5   Hör zu! Stimmt das?

This item revises numbers and most specifically prices and also explains how to complain about a bill. It refers back to the menu on page 152.

Transcript
Gast 1

Frau:	Herr Ober, die Rechnung bitte.
Kellner:	Ja, einen Moment. Was hatten Sie zu Essen?
Frau:	Ich hatte eine Tagessuppe und ein Grillhühnchen.
Kellner:	Tagessuppe und Hühnchen. Ja. . . . Hatten Sie auch ein Dessert?
Frau:	Nein, ich hatte kein Dessert.
Kellner:	Und Getränke?
Frau:	Ich hatte eine Tasse Kaffee.
Kellner:	. . . Und einen Kaffee. Das macht . . . Fünf Euro zwanzig.
Frau:	Vielen Dank.
Kellner:	Auf Wiedersehen.

Gast 2

Kellner:	Möchten Sie noch einen Kaffee?
Mann:	Nein danke. Ich möchte bitte bezahlen.
Kellner:	Sofort! Was hatten Sie zu Essen?
Mann:	Ich hatte das Steak und einen kleinen Salat.
Kellner:	Steak und Salat . . .
Mann:	Und zum Nachtisch hatte ich ein Eis mit Sahne.
Kellner:	Was für Getränke hatten Sie?
Mann:	Einen Apfelsaft und ein Mineralwasser.
Kellner:	Mineralwasser . . . Das macht zusammen siebzehn Euro und zwanzig Cent.
Mann:	Danke, ich möchte bitte mit Kreditkarte bezahlen.
Kellner:	Natürlich. Dankeschön.

Answers

Gast 1		Gast 2	
1 × Tagessuppe	1,50	1 × Rindersteak	9,80
1 × Grillhähnchen	4,20	1 × kleiner Salat	1,00
1 Kaffee	1,20	1 Eis mit Sahne	1,50
	6,90	1 Apfelsaft	1,20
		1 Mineralwasser	0,70
			14,20

---

6   Sag was! Im Restaurant

This item requires the students to look back to Exercise 4 and to create a role play based on this item in order to further practise the vocabulary in the unit.

Kulturtipp **WC**

It is obviously important to be able to ask where the toilet is! It is worth noting here that in some older establishments e.g. youth hostels, the toilets may still be indicated by 00 on the door.

7 Hör zu! Frühstück bei Familie Schuh

This gap-filling activity encourages students to listen out for detail. The Listening item also encourages students to think about what they have for breakfast and to compare this with what Heinz and David like to eat. It also practises expressions which can be used at table and should be particularly useful for students planning to go on exchange visits.

Students should be encouraged to take note of cultural differences such as tea with lemon, bread rolls (Brötchen) and meat for breakfast, but also the absence of some familiar food items such as 'Marmite' and 'Ribena' or similar cordials. Teachers could also point out that Germans don't always have cereal for breakfast and that not all British brands of cereal might be available. Marmelade and toast are also unusual as is the traditional British cooked breakfast. Instead, students will encounter a large variety of breads and meats.

Transcript

Narrator:	Heinz hat David zum Sonntagsfrühstück einge-laden.
Frau Schuh:	Guten Morgen, David. Setz dich!
David:	Guten Morgen! Danke.
Frau Schuh:	Möchtest du einen Kaffee?
David:	Nein danke, Kaffee mag ich nicht so gern. Darf ich einen Tee haben?
Frau Schuh:	Natürlich, David. Tee mit Zitrone?
David:	Nein, lieber mit Milch und Zucker, bitte.
Heinz:	Hallo David! Morgen, Mama, Morgen Papa. Guten Appetit!
Herr Schuh:	Danke gleichfalls, Heinz.
Heinz:	Was gibt es zum Frühstück?
Herr Schuh:	Es gibt Brötchen, gekochte Eier, Käse und Wurst. Was möchtest du?
Heinz:	Kannst du mir bitte die Brötchen reichen?
Herr Schuh:	Hier, bitte.
David:	Darf ich auch ein Brötchen haben?
Herr Schuh:	Natürlich, David. Greif zu!
Frau Schuh:	Möchtest du noch etwas Tee, David?
David:	Nein, danke, ich habe noch Tee. Der Tee ist sehr lecker, Frau Schuh!
Frau Schuh:	Oh, danke David!
David:	Haben Sie auch Marmite?
Heinz:	Marmite? Was ist das denn?
David:	Och, ich glaube, das gibt es nur in Großbritannien.

Answers

1 d
2 b
3 e
4 c
5 a
6 f

 **Am Tisch**

This **Vokabeltipp** introduces the key phrases and expressions for eating at someone's house.

Kulturtipp Guten Appetit!

This item gives cultural information about German etiquette and is particularly useful if you are intending to take your students on an exchange visit to Germany.

8 Sag was! Wie sagt man das?

This item encourages students to look back over the unit and find the useful expressions.

Answers

1 Guten Appetit!
2 Was gibt es zum Abendessen?
3 Greif zu!
4 Ich bin satt.
5 Darf ich bitte noch etwas Brot haben?
6 Gibst du mir bitte das Salz?
7 Prost!

9 Rollenspiel

Students should be able to make up their own role play based on the expressions they have just found and by looking back through the chapter.

10 Hör zu! Eine Telefonbestellung

Many German (and British) people enjoy Italian food. This is a typical conversation between someone ordering a pizza and an Italian waiter. It gives useful vocabulary for ordering by telephone.

Transcript

Man:	Marcos italienischer Imbiss, guten Abend.
Petra:	Guten Abend. Ich möchte gern etwas bestellen.
Man:	Ja, bitte. Wie ist ihr Name?
Petra:	Petra Albrecht.
Man:	Und Ihre Telefonnummer?
Petra:	55 06 31.
Man:	Was möchten Sie bestellen, signora?
Petra:	Eine kleine Pizza mit Käse und Tomaten.
Man:	Eine kleine Pizza Käse / Tomaten, ja. Sonst noch etwas?
Petra:	Ja, und eine Portion Pommes, bitte.
Man:	Eine kleine oder große Portion Pommes?
Petra:	Eine große Portion bitte. Und einen gemischten Salat.
Man:	Einen gemischten Salat. In Ordnung.
Petra:	Das ist alles.

Man:	Gut. Holen Sie das ab oder sollen wir es mit dem Pizza-Taxi bringen?
Petra:	Wir holen das ab. Wie lange dauert das?
Man:	Das ist in einer halben Stunde fertig.
Petra:	In 30 Minuten also?
Man:	Ja, genau.
Petra:	Danke, tschüs.
Man:	Buona sera, signora!

Answers

1. (Er kommt) aus Italien.
2. (Sie möchte) eine kleine Pizza mit Käse und Tomaten.
3. (Sie will) eine große Portion Pommes.
4. (Sie bestellt) einen gemischten Salat.
5. Nein, (Frau Albrecht holt das Essen ab.)
6. (Sie muss) 30 Minuten (warten).

 ### *Kulturtipp* Der Imbiss

Imbiss, **Schnellimbiss**, **Schnellrestaurant** and **Imbissstube** are all important words for students interested in eating in German-speaking countries. Students could be encouraged to talk about where they like to eat.

PCM 8.11   Keldorado

This item encourages students to identify the words they know in more unfamiliar text.

Answers

1 Richtig.
2 Keldorado hat große Panoramafenster zum Schwimmbad.
3 Keldorado hat eine Sonnenterasse.
4 Keldorado bietet italienische Spezialitäten.
5 Keldorado bietet Fisch- und Fleischgerichte.
6 Richtig.
7 Keldorado bietet Riesenpizzas.
8 Richtig.

PCM 8.12   Lies was! Träume in Eis

Another item which encourages students to identify the words they know among more unfamiliar text, this time about ice cream – so a menu some may be more familiar with!

Answers

1 Eisbiene.
2 Eisschokolade.
3 Heiße Himbeeren mit Vanilleeis und Sahne.
4 Eiskaffee.
5 Joghurttraum / Coppa Tutti Frutti.
6 Bananensplit.
7 Walnussbecher.
8 Pinocchio.

PCM 8.13   Lies was! VEGETARIERREPORTAGE   **E**

A more difficult text requiring more careful reading and containing new vocabulary.

Answers

Finde im Text

1 Meine Freunde sagen, dass ich spinne
2 ich sehe es ganz anders.
3 ich kann nicht sagen
4 Tiere sind doch auch Lebewesen

Beantworte auf Englisch!

1 Many years
2 They think she is mad
3 Because she saw a TV programme about the transport of animals.
4 Her mother
5 Definitely not.
6 That they are living creatures too, just like humans.

Einheit C Ostern

Unit 8C will introduce:
- *Easter*
- *special occasions*

PCMs 8.14 – 8.20 accompany this section.

1 Sag was! Osterbilder

This item should be introduced with the **Kulturtipp**.

Answers

Osternest mit Ostereiern, Osterhase, Osterfeuer, Osterkuchen.

Kulturtipp Ostern

This item gives useful background information about Easter celebrations in Germany. Obviously, this is a sensitive issue in a class containing people from different religions or cultures, but it is an important celebration in German-speaking countries and therefore a valid discussion item.

2 Lies was! Ein Brief (1)

The letter prepares students for reading examination-type questions.

Answers
1 To her grandmother's.
2 The whole family (uncles, aunts, cousins)
3 She will be colouring eggs.
4 Easter eggs.
5 To church.
6 On Easter Monday.

As a follow-up activity more able students could write their own letter based on the letter, or respond to the questions set in the letter. Another exercise is given in PCM 8.15, so that students may have their own copy of the text as a "model" letter.

 Ostern

These sites give useful additional information about Easter.

PCM 8.14 Lies was! Ein Brief (2)

This reading item should be attempted after **Ein Brief (1)** in the Pupil's Book. Students need to

read the text more closely and reply in German. (Answers can be lifted straight from the text).

Answers
1 Auf die Osterferien.
2 Auf dem Land.
3 Am Ostersamstag.
4 In Omas Garten.
5 Schokoladenostereier.
6 Osterbrötchen.
7 Am Abend.
8 Nach Linz (nach Hause).

PCM 8.15 Schreib was! Ein Brief (3)

This exercise encourages students to use the vocabulary learnt in this unit as freely as they can, allowing more able students some scope for expansion. It prepares students for the kinds of tasks faced in examinations and set as course-work.

PCM 8.16 Lies was! Das Osterhasenmuseum

This item allows students to identify times and prices for visits to museums.

Answers
Beantworte die Fragen auf Englisch!
1 every day: 10-18 (10 – 6 o'clock).
2 250m
3 Isartorplatz
4 € 8,00
5 € 7,50
6 € 15,00

PCM 8.17 Quiz: Aus welchen Ländern kommt dieses Essen?

This is a quiz. Students should be encouraged to write the name of the country. More able students should be able to manage the full sentence with **kommt aus**, but may need reminding about feminine countries.

Answers
Baguette kommt aus Frankreich.
Emmenthaler Käse kommt aus der Schweiz.
Haggis kommt aus Schottland.
Paella kommt aus Spanien.
Hamburger kommt aus Amerika.
Frankfurter kommt aus Deutschland.
Pommes und Fisch kommt aus England / Großbritannien.
Tortilla kommt aus Mexiko.
Edamer Käse kommt aus den Niederlanden.
Pizza kommt aus Italien.
Schwarzwälder Torte kommt aus Deutschland.

Kaviar kommt aus Russland.
Chop Suey kommt aus China.
Curry kommt aus Indien.
Sachertorte kommt aus Österreich.
Döner Kebab kommt aus der Türkei.
Couscous kommt aus Afrika.

PCM 8.18   Lies was! Ostereier färben   E

Students may have painted Easter eggs like this in their primary schools and may have stories to tell about this. The vocabulary is quite difficult but the concept is one which should be easily grasped.

Answers

brown – onion skins – a	red – beetroot – d
yellow – saffron – b	blue – blueberries – e
green – spinach – c	yellow – turmeric – f

PCM 8.19   Gruppenarbeit: Entwirf ein Osterei   A

Students could be encouraged to colour in an actual egg or a paper picture and then to write simple descriptions of their eggs.

PCM 8.20   Lies was! Der Osterhase aus Hefe   E

This item is included as an additional activity – although the vocabulary is difficult it might be possible for the students to try to make an **Osterhase** at home, provided the teacher gives some advice beforehand!

3   Hör zu! Ostern mit der Band

Pia is delighted that the band has a gig on Easter Saturday. She is telling Matthias and she asks him to be a Roady for them. The activity revises expressions for arranging a meeting.

Transcript

Matthias:	Hallo Pia!
Pia:	Hallo Matthias! Wie geht's?
Matthias:	Prima. Sag mal, habt ihr jetzt auch Osterferien?
Pia:	Ja, wir haben Ferien, aber es gibt viel zu tun!
Matthias:	Warum? Was machst du denn Ostern?
Pia:	Weißt du das noch nicht?
Matthias:	Nein! Sag schon, was ist los?
Pia:	Mensch, Matthias!!! Die Band hat einen Auftritt!
Matthias:	Einen Auftritt? Wo?
Pia:	Die Band spielt im Jugendzentrum an der Frankfurter Straße.
Matthias:	Im Jugendzentrum? Das ist ja klasse! Wann spielt ihr denn?

Pia:	Wir werden am Ostersamstag spielen. Da gibt es eine Osterdisko. Stell dir vor, eine Osterdisko mit unserer Band, der Anstoß-Band!!!
Matthias:	Mensch, Pia! Das ist toll! Herzlichen Glückwunsch!
Pia:	Was machst du denn am Ostersamstag? Hast du Lust, zu kommen?
Matthias:	Ostersamstag? Klar, kein Problem. Da hab ich den ganzen Tag Zeit.
Pia:	Oh, prima. Hast du Lust, unser Roady zu sein?
Matthias:	Roady? Das macht bestimmt Spass. Wann soll ich kommen?
Pia:	Wir treffen uns am Samstagnachmittag um 4 Uhr bei Heinz.
Matthias:	Samstagnachmittag um 4 Uhr bei Heinz! Voll gut! Ich werde da sein!!!

Answers

1 c, **2** b, **3** d, **4** a, **5** d

Wörterbuch   und *Aussprache*   Betonung

This item explains where the "stress" comes in a German word. The stressed syllable is usually marked by a little hyphen before the stressed part or by a dot underneath, or it is underlined. Encourage the students to look for the stress when they look up words in a dictionary.

Transcript

Apfel, Apfel
Apfelsine, Apfelsine
Kartoffeln, Kartoffeln
Schokolade, Schokolade
Bratwurst, Bratwurst
Mineralwasser, Mineralwasser
Vorspeise, Vorspeise
Getränke, Getränke
Mittagessen, Mittagessen
Käsekuchen, Käsekuchen

S p r a c h t i p p

Inseparable verbs

This **Sprachtipp** helps the students to understand inseparable verbs.

4   Der Wettbewerb

In this, the final cartoon story for Book 1 Pia, Heinz and David are in the practice cellar with instruments, but not playing yet. Heinz is hungry and not paying attention to what the others are saying. Pia and David decide to give him a nickname. Yasemin comes in with a newspaper cutting advertising a competition. The first prize is a trip to Berlin. The story will be continued in Book 2.

Transcript

Pia:	Heinz aus Mainz . . . was für ein blöder Name! Gar nicht cool.
David:	Wir müssen ihm einen Spitznamen geben!
Heinz:	Ich habe Hunger!
Pia:	Einen Spitznamen . . . hm . . . also Heinz hat rote Haare . . . Red?
David:	Zu Englisch. Was Deutsches gefällt mir besser.
Heinz:	Ach, so eine leckere Pommes mit Ketchup . . .
Pia:	Das ist es – Ketchup! Rote Haare, wie Ketchup.
David:	Pommes mit Ketchup! Heinz' Lieblingsessen! Wir nennen ihn „Pommes"!
Yasemin:	Hallo Pia! Hallo David! Hallo Heinz! . . .
Heinz:	Pommes! Mein neuer Spitzname ist Pommes!
Yasemin:	Das müsst ihr lesen! Sollen wir da mitmachen?!!
Pommes:	Zeig uns die Zeitung mal!
Yasemin:	Wettbewerb! Ein Lied für Berlin. Seid ihr unter 18 Jahren? Habt ihr eine Band? Dann schreibt ein Lied über eure Band und schickt es uns (auf Cassette, CD oder MiniDisk). Erster Preis: Eine Reise nach Berlin für die ganze Band!

5 Beantworte die Fragen auf Englisch!

Answers

1 His name is not cool / trendy enough.
2 He needs a nickname.
3 He is hungry and not paying attention to what they are saying.
4 Pommes because he loves chips.
5 It's a competition for bands.
6 They have to write a song about themselves.
7 The first prize is a trip to Berlin.
8 *open answer*

6 Beantworte die Fragen auf Deutsch!

Answers

1 Pia und David müssen Heinz einen Spitznamen geben.
2 Was Deutsches gefällt David besser.
3 Sie nennen ihn Pommes.
4 Yasemin zeigt der Band einen Wettbewerb.

7 Lied: Der Anstoß-Rap (Ein Lied für Berlin)

The song is a lighthearted revision exercise of vocabulary learned in the book. This is the band's entry to the **Ein Lied für Berlin** competition and the students can speculate whether or not the band will win the trip. They will have to wait until Book 2 to find out what actually happens. An instrumental version is available on the tape. Once students have learnt to sing along to the tape they could pretend to be the Anstoß-Band and perform the song with the instrumental. They could even dress up as characters from the book.

Transcript

Anstoß! – Hier ist was los!
Wir sind die Anstoß Band:
Pia – David – Heinz – Yasemin!
Wir tanzen, lachen
und wir machen
alle gern Musik.

Pia hat den Groove
auf ihrem scharfen Bass.
Sie ist ein bisschen ausgeflippt.
Sie will jede Menge Spaß!

Refrain: Anstoß! – . . .

David hat den Tastensound
an Keyboard und Klavier.
Er kommt aus Balerno, Schottland,
doch jetzt wohnt er hier.

Refrain: Anstoß! – . . .

Heinz hat rote Haare
wie Ketchup auf Pommes Frites.
Er singt und spielt Gitarre.
Das wird bestimmt ein Hit!

Refrain: Anstoß! – . . .

Yasemin spielt bei uns die Drums.
Sie gibt den Rhythmus an.
Sie macht Karate, ist gut drauf,
kommt bei uns voll gut an!

Anstoß! – Hier ist was los!
Hier ist was los!
Hier ist was los!
Anstoß!

Leseseite

This item revises the topic of food by giving the students another menu to work with. They could also practise role play activities or write out short sketches based on the text given.

Answers

1 Two filled rolls and a cup of coffee.
2 Every day.
3 a € 1,28   c € 1,02
  b € 1,53   d € 0,77

Aussagesätze and Grammatik

These pages are useful quick references for students working alone or in pairs – on a class-work or homework assignment. They are also useful for revision purposes, as they sum up the important grammar and vocabulary of the chapter.

Test 2

Test 2 provides you with Speaking, Listening, Reading and Writing material based on the topics the students have studied in *Anstoß 1*.

I Sprechen – Rollenspiele

This item gives you a choice of two role plays and a selection of questions to conduct a short oral examination with your students.

IIA Lies was! Eine neue Wohnung

This item revises descriptions of houses.

Answers
1 Weingarten
2 88250
3 86m^2
4 11th September
5 1st floor
6 Yes, a garage
7 3
8 Quiet, central location
9 The balcony faces South
10 by e-mail on meier@weingarten.de

IIB Lies was! Mani Privat

This item revises personal identification, food, drink and hobbies.

Answers
1 Fürstenfeldbruck bei München
2 13.6.82
3 Zwillinge
4 1,80m
5 Pizza mit Schinken, Salami, Peperoni und Champignons
6 Eisgekühlte Sprite-Limonade
7 Surfen, Basketball, Volley- und Fußball

IIC Lies was! Vereine   **E**

Students are encouraged to read critically and to correct the mistakes. The use of modal verbs and **nicht** is also practised.

Answers
1 Ja, der HTC Uhlenhorst möchte neue Hockeyspieler.
2 Ja, Jugendliche können dienstags und donnerstags Hockey spielen.
3 Nein, Mädchen dürfen beim HSV Dümpten nicht Fußball spielen. Sie dürfen Handball spielen.
4 Nein, man kann im Stadion Blötterweg nicht kegeln. Man kann Fußball spielen.
5 Ja, im Kegelverein sollen Männer und Frauen anrufen.
6 Nein, man kann nicht einmal pro Woche kegeln. Man kann einmal pro Monat kegeln.
7 Ja, man kann nur am Wochenende Fußball spielen.
8 Nein, man kann morgens nicht Handball spielen. Man kann abends Handball spielen.

III Hör zu! Meine Freizeit

This listening exercise should be attempted before students conduct a survey themselves. It will provide them with model answers for their own survey.

Transcript

1 Was sind deine Hobbys?	Meine Hobbys sind Kino und Tennis.
2 Bist du in einem Verein?	Ja, ich bin im Tennisclub.
3 Siehst du gern fern?	Ja, ich sehe gern fern.
4 Hast du einen eigenen Fernseher?	Nein, ich habe keinen eigenen Fernseher.
5 Wie oft siehst du pro Tag fern?	Ich sehe zwei Stunden pro Tag fern.
6 Was für Sendungen siehst du gern?	Ich sehe gern Fernsehserien und Krimis.
7 Wie heißt deine Lieblingssendung?	Meine Lieblingssendung heißt *Marienhof*.
8 Welche Sendung findest du doof?	Ich finde Talkshows doof.
9 Wie heißt dein Lieblingsschauspieler?	Mein Lieblingsschauspieler heißt Freddy Prinze Junior.
10 Wie heißt deine Lieblingsschauspielerin?	Meine Lieblingsschauspielerin heißt Cameron Diaz.

Answers
1 Meine Hobbys sind Kino und Tennis.
2 Ja, ich bin im Tennisclub.
3 Ja, ich sehe gern fern.
4 Nein, ich habe keinen eigenen Fernseher.
5 Ich sehe zwei Stunden pro Tag fern.
6 Ich sehe gern Fernsehserien und Krimis.
7 Meine Lieblingssendung heißt Marienhof.
8 Ich finde Talkshows doof.
9 Mein Lieblingsschauspieler heißt Freddy Prinze Junior.
10 Meine Lieblingsschauspielerin heißt Cameron Diaz.

IV Schreib was!

Open answers.

Action Plans, Profiles and Student Certificates

Action Plan Masters should be completed by the students after each assessment to show where they need to improve (e.g. to highlight vocabulary they still need to learn / grammar they need to master) and how they intend to progress.

The Student Profile Masters show the objectives of each chapter and include columns for the student and the teacher to record assessment.

The Certificate Master lists items covered in the textbook. It is intended for the school's internal use only – to promote a positive attitude to language learning – a feeling that the students have achieved something. The certificate does not relate to an examination grade.

| Name: _____ | Klasse: _____ | Datum: _____ |

Steckbrief

Vorname: *Heinz (Pommes)*	Nachname: *Schuh*
Adresse:	Telefonnummer:
	Nationalität:
	Alter:
	Geburtstag:

Aussehen:
Charakter:
Familie: Mutter: Vater: Geschwister:
Haustiere:
Schule: Lieblingsfächer: Sonstiges:
Haus/Wohnung: Zimmer:
Hobbys:
Lieblingsessen:
Rolle in der Band:
Sonstiges:

Vorname: *Yasemin*	Nachname: *Akbar*
Adresse:	Telefonnummer:
	Nationalität:
	Alter:
	Geburtstag:

Aussehen:
Charakter:
Familie: Mutter: Vater: Geschwister:
Haustiere:
Schule: *Gesamtschule Stadtmitte* Lieblingsfächer: Mag nicht: Sonstiges:
Haus/Wohnung: Zimmer:
Hobbys:
Lieblingsessen:
Rolle in der Band:
Sonstiges:

Name: _____	Klasse: _____	Datum: _____

Steckbrief

Vorname: *Pia*	Nachname: *Klein*
Adresse:	Telefonnummer:
	Nationalität:
	Alter:
	Geburtstag:

Aussehen:
Charakter:
Familie: Mutter: Vater: Geschwister:
Haustiere:
Schule: Lieblingsfächer: Mag nicht: Sonstiges:
Haus/Wohnung: Zimmer:
Hobbys:
Lieblingsessen:
Rolle in der Band:
Sonstiges:

Vorname: *David*	Nachname: *Miller*
Adresse:	Telefonnummer:
	Nationalität:
	Alter:
	Geburtstag:

Aussehen:
Charakter:
Familie: Mutter: Vater: Geschwister:
Haustiere:
Schule: *Gesamtschule Stadtmitte* Lieblingsfächer: Mag nicht: Sonstiges:
Haus/Wohnung: Zimmer:
Hobbys:
Lieblingsessen:
Rolle in der Band:
Sonstiges:

Steckbrief

Vorname: *Laura*	Nachname: *Miller*
Adresse:	Telefonnummer: Handy:
	Nationalität:
	Alter:
	Geburtstag:
Aussehen:	
Charakter:	
Familie: **Mutter:** **Vater:** **Geschwister:**	
Haustiere:	
Schule: **Lieblingsfächer:** **Mag nicht:** **Sonstiges:**	
Haus/Wohnung: **Zimmer:**	
Hobbys:	
Lieblingsessen:	
Rolle in der Band:	
Sonstiges:	

Vorname: *Matthias*	Nachname: *Hasler*
Adresse:	Telefonnummer:
	Nationalität:
	Alter:
	Geburtstag:
Aussehen:	
Charakter:	
Familie: **Mutter:** **Vater:** **Geschwister:**	
Haustiere:	
Schule: *Mozart-Gymnasium* **Lieblingsfächer:** **Mag nicht:** **Sonstiges:**	
Haus/Wohnung: **Zu Hause:** **Zimmer:**	
Hobbys:	
Lieblingsessen:	
Rolle in der Band:	
Sonstiges:	

Steckbrief

	Vorname:	Nachname:
	Adresse:	Telefonnummer:
		Nationalität:
		Alter:
		Geburtstag:

Aussehen:
Charakter:

Familie:
Mutter:
Vater:
Geschwister:

Haustiere:

Schule:
Lieblingsfächer:
Mag nicht:
Sonstiges:

Haus/Wohnung:
Zimmer:

Hobbys:

Lieblingsessen:

Rolle in der Band:

Sonstiges:

1.1 Sieh dir die Bilder an. Sag was!

Look at the pictures. Say something! Which greeting should you use?

1
2
3

4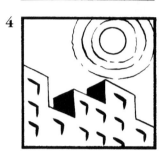
5
6

1.2 Hör zu! Begrüßungen

Schreib den Buchstaben ins Kästchen.
Write the correct letter in the box.

A
B
C

D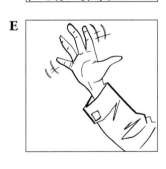
E

1 Frau Karstens [E] 4 Maja [ ]

2 Ben [ ] 5 Tatjana und Olaf [ ]

3 Herr Gruber [ ]

1.3 Wie heißt du?

Say the names of the characters and then introduce yourself.

Wie heißt du?

Ich _____ Heinz

Ich bin _____

Wer ist das?

Das ist Matthias.

Und wie heißt du?

1.4 Hör zu! Wer hat gute Laune?

Welcher Name passt zu welchem Bild?
Which name goes with which picture?

Beispiel: 1   Ling   *D*

2   Pablo

3   Anke

4   Mark

5   Katrin

A

B

C

D

E

1.5 Das Alphabet

Male die Bilder!
*Draw or colour in
the pictures!*

G

der Garten

M

die Mutter

T

die Tür

A

das Auto

H

das Haus

N

die Nase

U

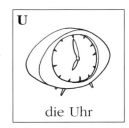

die Uhr

B

das Boot

I

der Igel

O

das Ohr

V

die Vase

C

der Camper

J

die Jacke

P

das Pferd

W

die Waage

D

das Dach

K

die Katze

Q

der Quirl

X

das Xylophon

E

das Ei

L

der Lehrer

R

das Radio

Y

das Joghurt

F

das Fenster

S

die Sonne

Z

der Zauberer

1.6 Im Klassenzimmer

Here are some of the instructions you will hear your teacher use quite often and may see in the book:

Auf Deutsch	In German
Auf Englisch	In English
Beantworte die Fragen.	Answer the questions.
Beispiel	Example
Beschreib	Describe
Beschrifte	Label
Ergänze	Complete
Finde	Find
Frag die anderen in der Klasse.	Ask the others in the class.
Füll . . . aus	Fill . . . in
Gib die Informationen in den Computer ein.	Key in the information in the computer.
Gruppenarbeit	Group work
Hier ist/ sind . . .	Here is/are . . .
Hör zu	Listen
Hör zu und lies mit	Listen and read
Lern	Learn
Lest . . . zusammen vor.	Read . . . out loud together.
Lies	Read
Mach das Buch zu.	Close your book.
Macht andere Dialoge.	Make up other dialogues.
Mal . . . an	Colour in . . .
Nenn . . .	Name . . .
Partnerarbeit	Pair work
Richtig oder falsch?	True or false?
Sag was!	Say something!
Schau mal . . . an	Look at . . .
Schlag . . . im Wörterbuch nach.	Look . . . up in the dictionary.
Schreib was!	Write something!
Sieh . . . an.	Look at . . .
Stellt Fragen.	Ask each other questions.
Such . . .	Look for . . .
Trag . . . ein	Fill . . . in
Unterstreiche . . .	Underline . . .
Wähle . . . aus	Choose . . .
Was ist das?	What is that?
Was ist die richtige Reihenfolge?	What is the correct order?
Was paßt zusammen?	What goes together?
Was zu lesen!	Something to read!
Was zu zeichnen!	Something to draw!
Was zum lernen!	Something to learn!
Was zum lesen!	Something to read!

 **Partnerarbeit: Sag was! Mach ein Interview!**

Partner B should interview Partner A in order to be able to fill out the blank cards with the relevant details.

Partner A

Vorname: *Carlo*	Vorname: *Catherine*
Nachname: *Karamba*	Nachname: *Robert*
Wohnort: *München*	Wohnort: *Paris*
Nationalität: *Spanier*	Nationalität: *Französin*

Vorname: *Paolo*	Vorname: *Steffi*
Nachname: *Rossi*	Nachname: *Kohl*
Wohnort: *Rom*	Wohnort: *Wien*
Nationalität: *Italiener*	Nationalität: *Österreicherin*

Partner B

Vorname:	Vorname: ....
Nachname:	Nachname: ....
Wohnort:	Wohnort: ....
Nationalität:	Nationalität: ....

Vorname:	Vorname: ....
Nachname:	Nachname: ....
Wohnort:	Wohnort: ....
Nationalität:	Nationalität: ....

1.8 Europa

Photocopiable map of Europe, with names in German.

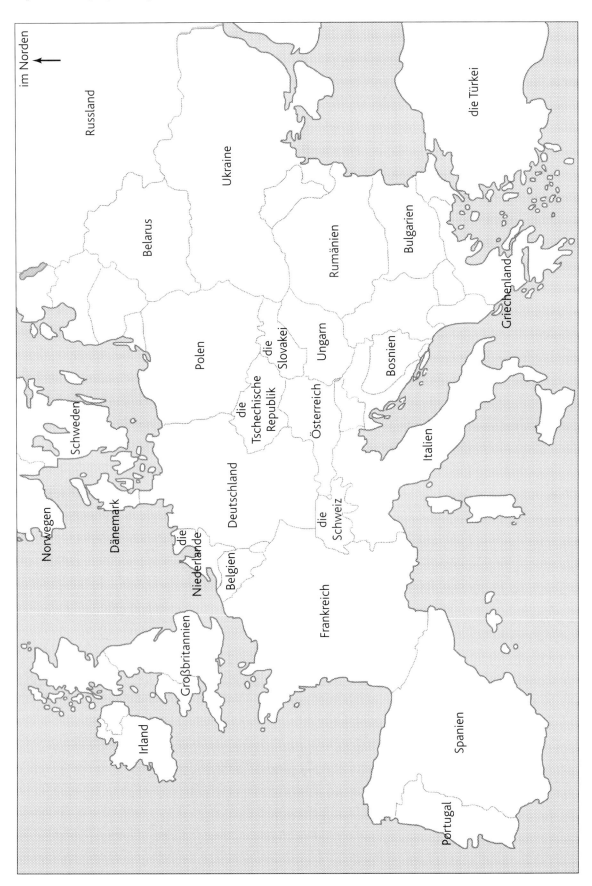

1.9 Hör zu! Wo wohnen sie?

Was passt zusammen? Finde den Namen, den Wohnort und das Land.

Match up the name, the city and the country.

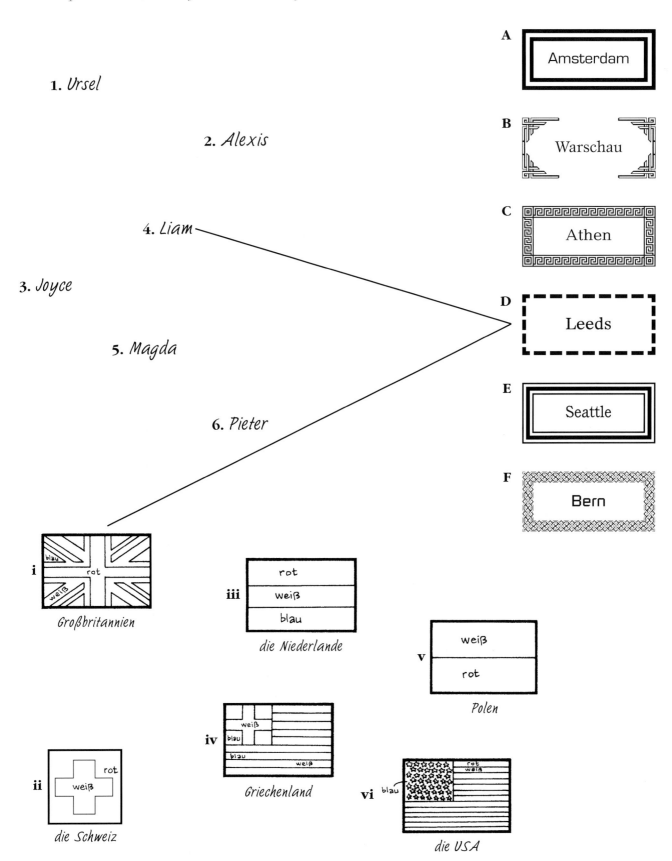

1. *Ursel*

2. *Alexis*

4. *Liam*

3. *Joyce*

5. *Magda*

6. *Pieter*

A Amsterdam

B Warschau

C Athen

D Leeds

E Seattle

F Bern

i Großbritannien (blau, rot, weiß)

iii rot / weiß / blau die Niederlande

v weiß / rot Polen

ii rot / weiß die Schweiz

iv weiß / blau / blau / weiß Griechenland

vi blau / rot / weiß die USA

1.10 Großbritannien

Photocopiable map of the British Isles, with names in German.

1.11 Spiel: Wortsuche

Wie viele Länder kannst du finden?
How many countries can you find?

D	E	U	T	S	C	H	L	A	N	D	T
A	C	G	T	C	E	E	T	W	W	R	H
D	F	G	S	H	P	Z	I	X	C	V	C
B	B	S	B	W	B	O	R	B	B	B	I
N	M	P	M	E	N	G	L	A	N	D	E
I	T	A	L	I	E	N	A	E	I	H	R
P	P	N	P	Z	I	I	N	I	N	N	K
W	E	I	E	S	R	U	D	K	K	J	N
E	S	E	S	F	F	D	U	M	L	N	A
S	X	N	D	D	D	F	U	J	M	H	R
E	D	N	A	L	R	E	D	E	I	N	F

1.12 Spiel: Wo ist die Party?

Find your way to the party. Read the street signs. Go from question to answer.

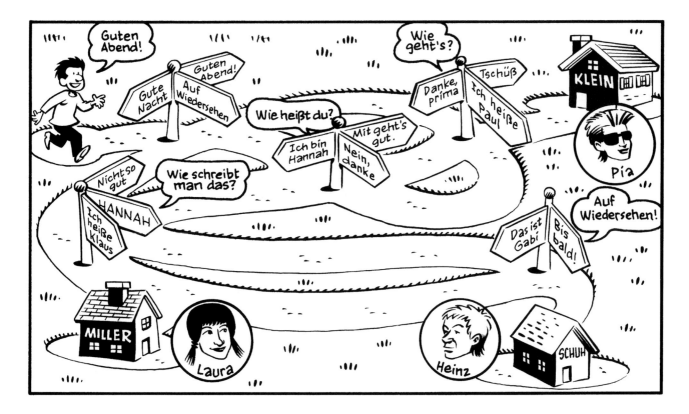

2.1 Schreib was! Wann haben sie Geburtstag?

Beispiel: *Helga hat am zwölften April Geburtstag*

1 Helga   12. April _____

2 Andreas   7. Dezember _____

3 Susanne   1. Mai _____

4 Peter   23. August _____

5 Maria   31.6. _____

6 Jan   7.7. _____

2.2 Was passt zusammen?

Match up the questions and answers

1 Wie geht es dir?   **A** Ich wohne in Hamburg.

2 Woher kommst du?   **B** Ich bin 11 Jahre alt.

3 Wo wohnst du?   **C** Ich heiße Hannah.

4 Wie heißt du?   **D** Ich komme aus der Schweiz.

5 Wo ist das?   **E** Meine Nummer ist 23 66 98.

6 Wie alt bist du?   **F** Das ist im Süden von Österreich.

7 Wie heißen Sie?   **G** Ich bin Frau Meier.

8 Wann ist dein Geburtstag?   **H** Ja, ein bisschen.

9 Wie ist deine Telefonnummer?   **I** Am 12. Februar

10 Sprechen Sie Deutsch?   **J** *Mir geht es gut*

2.3 Hör zu! Mein Geburtstagskalender

Schreib die Geburtstage in den Kalender.

Listen to the cassette and then write the birthdays into the calendar.

Januar	Februar	März
April	**Mai**	**Juni**
Juli	**August**	**September**
Oktober	**November**	**Dezember**

Mama **Papa** **Steffen** **Oma Gitta**

Hassan **Timo** **ich** **Opa**

Oma Birte **Eva** **Luba** **Sascha**

 **Schreib was! Jahreszeiten und Monate**

Welcher Monat gehört zu welcher Jahreszeit? Male ein Bild für jeden Monat.

Which month belongs to which season? Draw a picture for each month.

Frühling	Sommer	Herbst	Winter
März			

Januar	**Februar**	**März**	**April**

Mai	**Juni**	**Juli**	**August**

September	**Oktober**	**November**	**Dezember**

Anstoß 1

2.5 ► Schreib was! Haben oder sein?

haben (to have)	sein (to be)
ich habe	ich bin
du hast	du bist
er / sie / es hat	er / sie / es ist

Schreib das richtige Wort.

Write the correct word.

Beispiel: Wie alt ....du? (hast / bist) *Wie alt **bist** du?*

1 Wann _____ du Geburtstag?
(hast / bist)

2 Wie alt _____ Leah? (hat / ist)

3 Wie _____ deine Telefonnummer?
(bist / ist)

4 Wo _____ die Tasche? (ist / hat)

5 Wer _____ du? (bin / bist)

6 Ich _____ heute Geburtstag!
(habe / hat)

7 Paul _____ im Januar Geburtstag.
(hat / ist)

8 Wann _____ du geboren? (hast / bist)

2.6 ► Gruppenarbeit mit dem Wörterbuch

Finde den Artikel im Wörterbuch und suche im Bild.

Find the gender in your dictionary and look for the object in the picture.

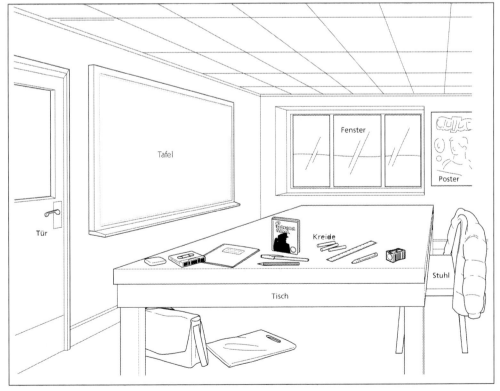

Buch	Kuli	Tasche	Tafel	Poster	Heft	Radiergummi	Lineal	Stuhl
Kassette	Bleistift	Anspitzer	Jacke	Tür	Buntstift	Mappe	Kreide	Fenster

What is **der**, **die** and **das**? Colour the things red, blue or green.

2.7 Spiel: Was ist das?

What is it? Connect the dots and guess the word.
Can you create your own dot-to-dot game?

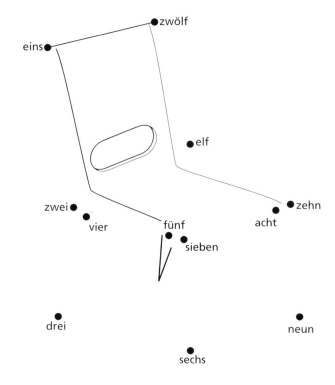

zwölf

eins

elf

zehn

zwei

vier   acht

fünf

sieben

drei   neun

sechs

2.8 Hör zu! Was braucht Peter?

Male die richtigen Sachen bunt. Streiche die falschen Sachen durch.
What does Peter need? Colour in the correct things. Cross out the wrong ones.

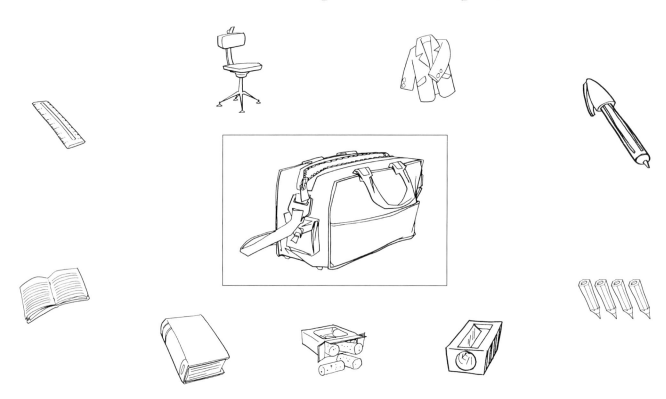

2.9 **Spiel: Piratengold**

Folge den Anweisungen. Sammle die Buchstaben. Wo ist der Schatz?
Follow the instructions. Collect the letters. Where is the treasure?

im Norden

im Westen   im Osten

im Süden

Anfang

F	W	B	R	R
D	K	B	K	T
A	N	G	A	B
E	D	Z	B	C
R	F	B	C	U

1   Gehe drei Schritte nach Osten.

2   Gehe zwei Schritte nach Süden.

3   Gehe zwei Schritte nach Westen.

4   Gehe einen Schritt nach Norden.

5   Gehe drei Schritte nach Süden.

6   Gehe drei Schritte nach Osten.

7   Gehe vier Schritte nach Norden.

8   Gehe einen Schritt nach Süden.

Der Goldschatz ist in:

F								

2.10 Spiel: Schiffe versenken

Play battleships in German and practise numbers and letters.
Place your ships on this grid.

	1	2	3	4	5	6	7	8	9	10	11	12	13	14	15	16	17	18	19	20
A																				
B																				
C																				
D																				
E																				
F																				
G																				
H																				
I																				
J																				
K																				
L																				
M																				
N																				
O																				
P																				
Q																				
R																				
S																				
T																				

meine Schiffe:

3 Schnellboote   **2 Kreuzer**

2 Schlachtschiffe   **1 Flugzeugträger**

Track your opponent's ships on this grid:

	1	2	3	4	5	6	7	8	9	10	11	12	13	14	15	16	17	18	19	20
A																				
B																				
C																				
D																				
E																				
F																				
G																				
H																				
I																				
J																				
K																				
L																				
M																				
N																				
O																				
P																				
Q																				
R																				
S																				
T																				

This is what you say:

Wasser! – water (miss)

Treffer! – hit

versenkt! – sunk

Achtung

Beware of the pronunciation:

A = aah (not like English A)

E = eh (not like English E)

I = eeh (not like English I)

R = air (not like English R)

2.11 Kreuzworträtsel

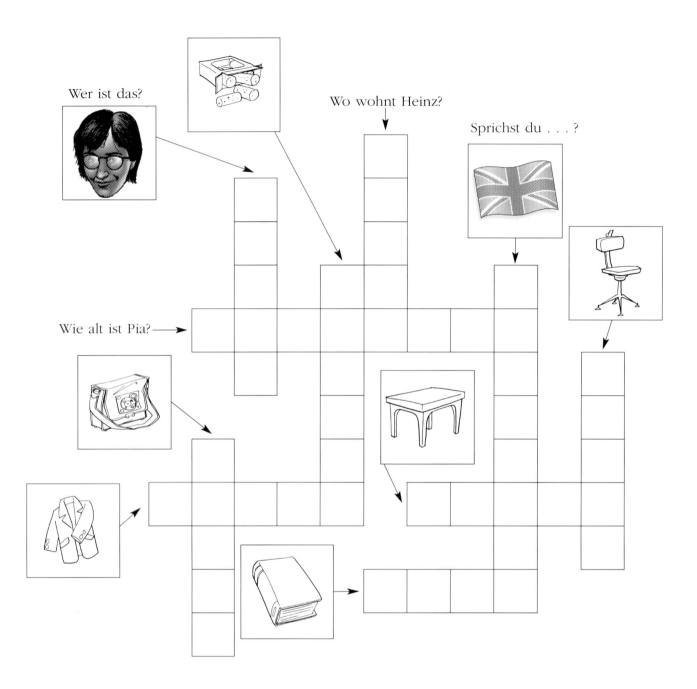

Wer ist das?

Wo wohnt Heinz?

Sprichst du . . . ?

Wie alt ist Pia? →

3.1 Fragebogen: Mein Traum

Wie ist dein Traumboy/Traumgirl? Kreuze an und vergleiche mit deinem Partner.
What is your dream boy/girl like? Put your cross in the boxes and compare with your partner.

Ich bin ein Mädchen ☐ Junge ☐

Mein Traumboy hat

☐ blonde Haare   ☐ braune Haare
☐ keine Haare   ☐ rote Haare
☐ schwarze Haare ☐ grüne Haare

☐ kurze Haare   ☐ lange Haare
☐ glatte Haare   ☐ lockige Haare

☐ blaue Augen   ☐ grüne Augen
☐ braune Augen   ☐ liebe Augen

☐ eine Brille   ☐ einen Bart
☐ ein Auto   ☐ einen Hund

Mein Traumgirl hat

☐ blonde Haare   ☐ braune Haare
☐ schwarze Haare ☐ rote Haare

☐ kurze Haare   ☐ lange Haare
☐ glatte Haare   ☐ lockige Haare

☐ blaue Augen   ☐ grüne Augen
☐ braune Augen   ☐ zwei Augen

☐ eine Brille   ☐ einen Bart
☐ zwei Brillen   ☐ eine hübsche Freundin

Mein Traumboy ist

☐ groß   ☐ klein
☐ dick   ☐ sportlich
☐ doof   ☐ lustig
☐ französisch ☐ reich

Mein Traumgirl ist

☐ groß   ☐ klein
☐ dick   ☐ schlank
☐ intelligent ☐ hübsch
☐ Fotomodell ☐ Anna Meyer

3.2 Spiel: Was passt nicht?

Which is the odd man out?

Beispiel: blond / rot / englisch / braun *englisch (keine Haarfarbe)*

1   kurz / lockig / freundlich / lang _____

2   klein / intelligent / lustig / langweilig _____

3   Mädchen / Junge / Frau / Haare _____

4   sportlich / schlank / groß / lockig _____

5   kurz / blau / blond / braun _____

6   Brille / groß / Bart / Telefonnummer _____

3.3 Schreib was! Grammatik!

Ein oder einen?

Remember: Das ist **ein** Hund.
             Ich habe **einen** Hund.

Beispiel: Hast du _____ Hund?   *Hast du __einen__ Hund?*

1   Ich habe _____ Vogel.

2   Das ist _____ Hamster.

3   Hier ist _____ Fisch.

4   Hast du _____ Vogel?

5   Wo ist _____ Hund?

6   Ich habe _____ Hamster.

7   Sarah hat _____ Fisch und _____ Vogel.

8   Ist das _____ Hamster?

3.4 Lies was! Was ist mein Tier?

Lies den Text und sieh die Bilder an. Welches Tier gehört wem? Schreib den Buchstaben.
Read the text and look at the pictures. Which animal belongs to whom? Write the letter.

A  B  C  D

Mein Tier ist dick und faul. Es ist weiß und nicht alt.

Katja Huber

Mein Tier ist auch dick, aber es ist nicht jung. Es ist auch nicht weiß.

Fridolin Kaiser

Mein Tier ist schwarz und weiß. Es ist sehr lustig.

Birgit Koch

Mein Tier ist klein und weiß. Ich habe keinen Hund.

Hassan Ergül

 **Spiel: Tier–Labyrinth**

Gehe durch das Labyrinth. Welche Tiere trifft Jan? Schreibe die Tiere in die Liste.

Go through the maze. Which animals does Jan meet? Write them on the list.

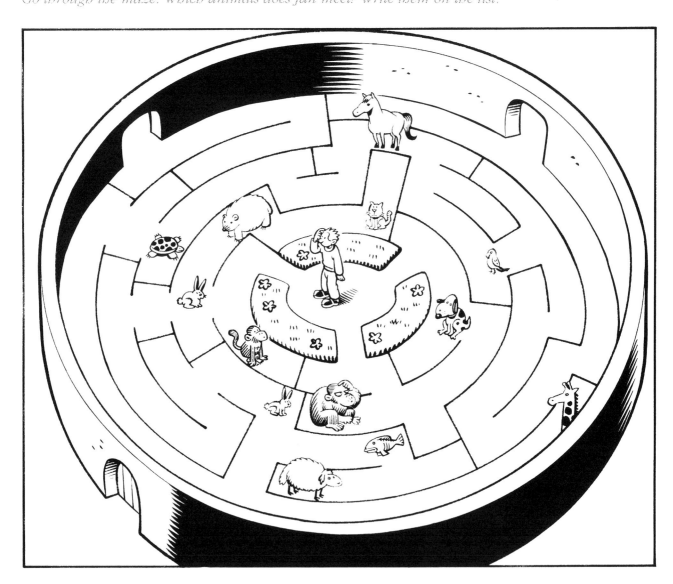

Jans Tiere:

3.6 Spiel: Welches Tier war das?

Which animal left these tracks?

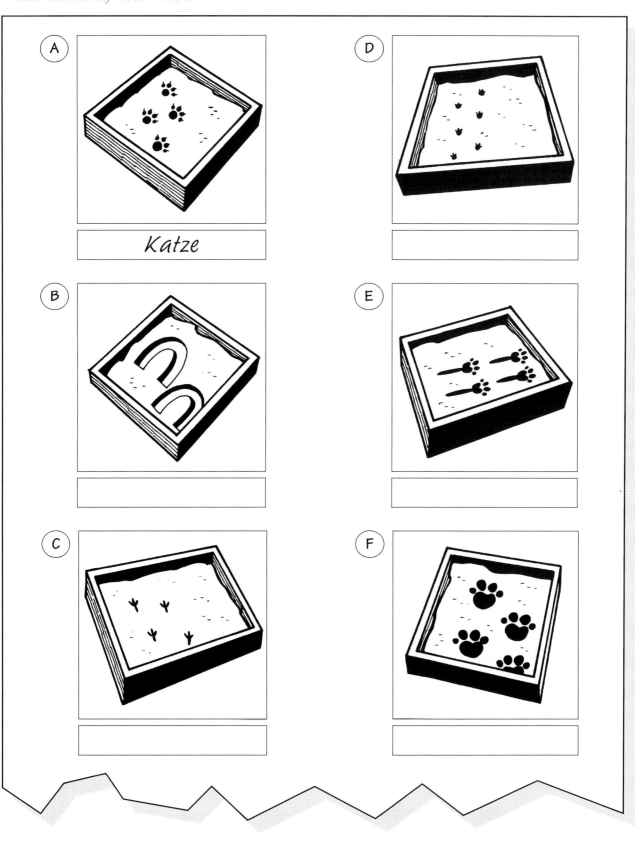

Hund   Pferd   Hamster   ~~Katze~~   Kaninchen   Vogel

3.7 ## Schreib was! Meine oder deine? Wähle das richtige Wort!

Choose the correct word.

mein – my	*sein* – his	*unser* – our
dein – your	*ihr* – her	*Ihr* – polite you
euer – your (plural)	*sein* – its	*ihr* – their

Beispiel: Das ist (my) Freundin Klara. – deine / meine / ihre / Ihre
Das ist meine Freundin Klara.

a) Ist das (your) Katze, Petra? – meine / deine / eure / seine

b) Da ist Jan und da ist (his) Hund. – ihr / euer / mein / sein

c) Wo ist (my) Tasche? – unsere / eure / meine / seine

d) Katja ist 12 und (her) Tante ist 22. – ihre / seine / Ihre / deine

e) Frau Müller, ist das (your) Brille? – ihre / Ihre / deine / unsere

f) Da sind die Geschwister und (their) Eltern. – ihre / Ihre / eure / unsere

g) Hier sind (my) Kaninchen. – unsere / deine / seine / meine

h) Wo hast du (your) Jacke? – meine / deine / seine / ihre

i) Peter nennt (his) Hunde Max und Taps. – meine / deine / ihre / seine

j) Sabine hat (her) Hausaufgaben vergessen. – Ihre / meine / ihre / seine

 3.8 ## Schreib was! Mit oder ohne E?

With or without E?

Das ist	mein Onkel (der)	Das sind	mein**e** Eltern (plural)
	mein**e** Tante (die)		
	mein Pony (das)		

Beispiel: Ist das dein____ Schwester? *deine*

a) Wo ist mein____ Mutter?

b) Sein____ Freundin hat rote Haare.

c) Unser____ Eltern heißen Magda und Klaus.

d) Das ist Steffi. Ihr____ Bruder heißt Maik.

e) Mein____ Vater ist 35 und meine Mutter ist 37.

f) Mein____ Tante hat ein Baby. Ihr____ Baby wurde im Oktober geboren.

g) Hallo, Herr Schulz. Sind das Ihr____ Kinder?

h) Das Mädchen ist mein____ Kind. Die Jungen sind nicht mein____ Kinder.

i) Dein____ Katze ist sehr lieb.

j) Unser____ Hund ist schwarz.

Quiz: Onkel, Mutter, Opa – wer ist das?

Lies die Beschreibung und schreib das richtige Wort.
Read the descriptions and write the correct word.

Hallo! Ich bin Dami. Das ist meine Familie.

● Mein Papa hat dunkle Haut. Er kommt aus Kenia.
● Meine Mama hat blonde Haare. Sie ist sehr hübsch.
● Meine Schwester ist 6 Jahre alt.
● Mein Onkel trägt eine Brille.
● Mein Opa ist sehr dick und lustig. Er kommt aus Berlin.

Vater	Mutter	Schwester	Onkel	~~Großvater~~

A) Ich bin Damis *Großvater*.

B) Ich bin Damis _____.

C) Ich bin Damis _____. **D)** Ich bin Damis _____. **E)** Ich bin Damis _____.

3.10 Kreuzworträtsel

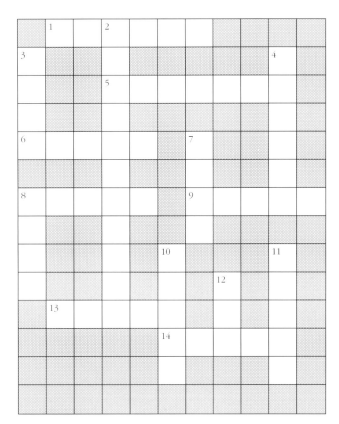

Waagerecht:
Across:

1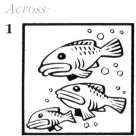

9

5

13

6 brown

8

14

Senkrecht:
Down:

2

3 yellow

4

7 blue

8

10

11

12 red

3.11 # Der Marsmännchen–Rap

Hör zu und male das Marsmännchen bunt.
Listen and colour in the Martian.

 3.12 # Rap: Klaus Chaos sucht eine Brieffreundin

Sieh das Bild an und hör zu. Wer ist wer?
Look at the picture and listen to the song. Who is who?

Oma	Opa	Schwester	Tante	Mutter	Vater	Hamster	Bruder	Onkel	ich

1 *Hamster*	2 _____	3 _____	4 _____
5 _____	6 _____	7 _____	8 _____
9 _____	10 _____		

3.13 Lied: Onkel Jörg hat einen Bauernhof

1

Onkel Jörg hat einen Bauernhof, I-Ei, I-Ei, Oh!
Und auf dem Hof gibt's **einen Hund**, I-Ei, I-Ei, Oh!
Er macht **Wau-Wau** hier und **Wau-Wau** da,
hier ein **Wau**, da ein **Wau**, überall ein **Wau-Wau-Wau**.
Onkel Jörg hat einen Bauernhof, I-Ei, I-Ei, Oh!

2

Onkel Jörg hat einen Bauernhof, I-Ei, I-Ei, Oh!
Und auf dem Hof gibt's **eine Katze**, I-Ei, I-Ei, Oh!
Sie macht **Mi-au** hier und **Mi-au** da,
hier ein **Miau**, da ein **Miau**, . . .

3

Und auf dem Hof gibt's **ein Pferd**, . . .
Es macht **Wieher** hier, . . .

. . . **ein Kaninchen** . . . **Es macht Hoppel** . . .
. . . **einen Fisch** . . . **Er macht Blub-Blub** . . .
. . . **eine Maus** . . . **Sie macht Piep-Piep** . . .

Mi-au

Hoppel

Wau-Wau

Wieher

Blub-Blub

Piep-Piep

3.14 Lied: Bruder Jakob

Bruder Jakob, Bruder Jakob,
Schläfst du noch, schläfst du noch?
Hörst du nicht die Glocken? Hörst du nicht die Glocken?
Ding, ding, dong! Ding, ding, dong!

| Name: | | | | | Klasse: | | | | Datum: | | | |

Meinungsumfrage: Wie gefallen dir deine Schulfächer?

Kreuze auf der Skala von 1–10 an.

Fill in your name and preferences for each subject. Ask your classmates. How does each subject fare across the class?

Fach:_____

Name:												Gesamt-punkte

doof	1-----x-----10	**toll**											
schwierig	1-----x-----10	**einfach**											
langweilig	1-----x-----10	**interessant**											

Ergebnisse

Fach	Gesamt-punkte	Platz
Deutsch		
Englisch		
Französisch		
Mathe		
Physik		
Chemie		
Biologie		
Informatik		

Fach	Gesamt-punkte	Platz
Geschichte		
Sozialkunde		
Technologie		
Religion		
Erdkunde		
Kunst		
Musik		
Sport		

Und du? Was ist dein Lieblingsfach? Warum?

4.2 Hör zu! Wie findest du …?

Verbinde die Bilder.

Connect the pictures.

1

a

A

2

b

B

3

c

C

4

d

D

5

e

E

6

f

F

4.3 Schreib was! Wie spät ist es?

Can you use the 24 hour clock as well as the 12 hour clock?

1	Es ist *drei* Uhr.	6	_____
2	_____	7	_____
3	_____	8	_____
4	_____	9	_____
5	_____	10	_____

4.4 Schreib was! Wann hast du Mathe?

Sieh dir die Bilder an und mache Sätze.
When do you have Maths? Look at the pictures and make sentences.

1
09.00
Um *neun Uhr*
habe ich *Deutsch*.

2
12.00
Um *zwölf* Uhr
habe ich _____

3
08.00
Um _____ Uhr
habe ich _____

4
13.00
Um _____ Uhr
habe ich _____

5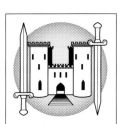
11.00
_____
_____

6
14.00
_____
_____

7
09.00
_____
_____

8
10.00
_____
_____

 4.5 Das Launenbarometer: Wie geht es dir am ...

Macht alle eine Tabelle für die ganze Woche.

Name	Montag	Dienstag	Mittwoch	Donnerstag	Freitag

Schlüssel:

👍 Es geht mir heute gut.

🙂 Es geht.

🙁 Es geht mir heute nicht so gut.

💣 Ich habe heute schlechte Laune.

zzz Ich bin heute müde.

4.6 Schreib was! Wie spät ist es?

1	6:15	6	2:30
2	4:45	7	7:50
3	12:20	8	5:05
4	18:40	9	9:30
5	15:10	10	1:45

1	Es ist *viertel nach sechs*	**6**	
2	Es ist	**7**	
3	Es ist	**8**	
4	Es ist	**9**	
5	Es ist	**10**	

4.7 Schreib was! Tage und Monate

Der Kalender ist durcheinander. Ordne die Tage und Monate.

The calendar got mixed up. Sort out the days and months.

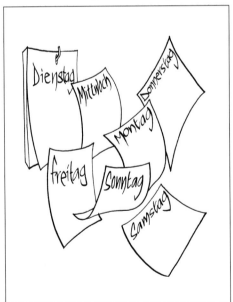

1	*Montag*	**1**	*Januar*	**7**	
2		**2**		**8**	
3		**3**		**9**	
4		**4**		**10**	
5		**5**		**11**	
6		**6**		**12**	
7					

4.8 **Ergänze Yasemins und Claires Stundenpläne**

Yasemin

		Mo.	Di.	Mi.	Do.	Fr.	Sa.
1							
2							
3							
4							
5							
6							
7							

Claire

		Mo.	Di.	Mi.	Do.	Fr.	Sa.
1							
2							
3							
4							
5							
6							
7							

Name:

		Mo.	Di.	Mi.	Do.	Fr.	Sa.
1							
2							
3							
4							
5							
6							
7							

4.9 Grammatik. Schreib was! Ich und du

Schreib das richtige Wort in die Lücke.

Write the correct word into the gap.

| ich | du | er | sie | es | wir | ihr | sie | Sie |

1. _Ich_ heiße Bastian.

4. _____ hat einen Hund.
5. _____ heißt Bello.

8. Das sind Gabi und Anke. _____ sind Schwestern.

2. Wie heißt _____?

6. Sprechen _____ Deutsch?

9. Ich habe ein Kaninchen. _____ heißt Mucki.

3. _____ sind Freunde.

7. Wie findet _____ die neue Lehrerin?

4.10 Schreib was! Finde das richtige Ende

Find the correct ending.

Beispiel: Wo wohn_____ du? Wo wohn*st* du?

1   Wie finde_____ du Mathe?

2   Wo wohn_____ Klaus?

3   Pierre komm_____ aus Frankreich.

4   Ich find_____ Deutsch interessant.

5   Wir wohn_____ in Wien.

6   Ich wohn_____ in Deutschland.

7   Komm_____ du aus England?

8   Ich komm_____ aus der Schweiz.

4.11 ▶ Spiel: Schulrennen

Wie gefällt dir Mathe?	Wie findest du dein(e) Englischlehrer(in)?
Wie findest du Deutsch?	Wie spät ist es?
Was ist dein Lieblingsfach?	Wann beginnt die Schule?
Welches Fach gefällt dir nicht?	Wann ist die Schule aus?
Wer ist dein Lieblingslehrer?	Wann ist Pause?
Wer ist deine Lieblingslehrerin?	Wann hast du Sport?
Wie heißt dein(e) Deutschlehrer(in)?	Wann hast du Kunst?

4.12 Der Schul-Rap – was passiert?

Hör zu und bringe die Bilder in die richtige Reihenfolge.

Listen and put the pictures in the right order.

1  _____

4  _____

7  _____

2  _____

5  _____

8  _____

3  _____

6  _____

Der Schul-Rap. Richtig oder falsch?

Schreibe R (richtig) oder F (falsch).

Beispiel: Es ist Montag. `R`

1 Ich muss zur Schule. ☐

2 Ich bin zu spät. ☐

3 Ich habe meine Hausaufgaben. ☐

4 Um 9 Uhr ist Mathe. ☐

5 Deutsch ist schwierig. ☐

6 Englisch beginnt um 10 Uhr. ☐

7 Pause gefällt mir nicht. ☐

8 Um 2 Uhr ist Musik. ☐

9 Musik ist mein Lieblingsfach. ☐

Test 1

 **Sprechen – Rollenspiele**

1A Student's Role

While on holiday in Germany, a young German asks you some questions about yourself. Your teacher will play the role of your German friend and will speak first.

- Say what nationality you are.
- Say how old you are.
- Ask if he/she has any brother or sisters.
- Say you have a dog and a cat.

1B Teacher's Role

- Bist du Deutscher?
  Allow the student to say what nationality he/she is.
- Wie alt bist du?
  Allow the student to say how old he / she is.
- Ich auch.
  Allow the student to ask if you have any brother or sisters.
- Ja, eine Schwester. Hast du Haustiere?
  Allow the student to say he/she has a dog and a cat.
- Ich auch.

2A Student's Role

While in Germany, your penfriend asks you about your school subjects. Your teacher will play the role of your German friend and will speak first.

- Say what subjects you study at school.
- Say what your favourite subject is.
- Say why it's your favourite subject.
- Say what you think of German.

2B Teacher's Role

- Was lernst du in der Schule?
  Allow the student to say what subjects he/she studies at school
- Was ist dein Lieblingsfach?
  Allow the student to say what his/her favourite subject is
- Warum?
  Allow the student to say why it's his/her favourite subject
- Wie findest du Deutsch?
  Allow the student to say what he/she thinks of German

Further questions for each role play:

- Wie heißt du?
- Wie schreibt man das?
- Woher kommst du?
- Wo wohnst du?

- Wann hast du Geburtstag?
- Wie ist deine Telefonnummer?
- Wie spät ist es?
- Wie viel Uhr ist es?

Lies was! In der Zeitung

Ist doch klar, das ist unser Opa!

Erwin Schindelka der wird heute 65 Jahr'!

Es gratulieren ganz herzlich

Deine Enkelsöhne Jan und Christoph.

Dustin,
wird **ein Jahr**.
Alles Liebe zu deinem
1. Geburtstag
von deiner Mama und Papa
Oma Gaby, Opa Reinhold, Tante
Steffi, Onkel Maik, Uroma Lotte

Hallo

Volker & Bettina

Alles Gute zur Verlobung
und viel Glück
wünschen die
Geschwister

40!

Hallo Norbert

Es gratulieren recht Herzlich zum 40. Geburtstag

Heike, das Tankstellen-Team, Mami, Papi, Susanne, Manfred und Inge

Hallo, ich heiße
Oliver
und bin am 19.2.2001 geboren.
Ich bin 51 cm groß und
wiege 2580 g.
Es freuen sich die Eltern

Bernd und Andrea Wietzke

Richtig oder Falsch?

1 Oliver ist ein Baby. ☐

2 Norbert ist 4 Jahre alt. ☐

3 Volker und Bettina verloben sich. ☐

4 Dustins Uroma heißt Steffi. ☐

5 Erwin Schindelka hat Geburtstag. ☐

Beantworte die Fragen!

1 Wer ist 65 Jahre alt?

_____

2 Wer ist 40 Jahre alt?

_____

3 Wer ist 1 Jahr alt?

_____

4 Wie groß ist Oliver?

_____

5 Wie heißen die Enkelsöhne von Erwin Schindelka?

_____

6 Wie heißen die Eltern von Oliver?

_____

 **Hör zu! Besuch! Schreibe die Worte**

A)   *Your penfriend is coming to visit you. Will you recognise her? Write the words under the name.*

B)   *Your Uncle Bob is coming to visit you. What does he look like? Write the words under the name.*

Sally	Onkel Bob
groß	

Achtung! Zwei Worte sind falsch!

groß, klein, sportlich, lustig

lange, kurze, blonde, glatte, lockige Haare

Brille, Bart, Glatze

braune, blaue, Augen

 **Schreib was!**

Schreib soviel wie möglich!

Write as much as you can about both of these 2 topics

● Meine Familie.
● Meine Schule.

Hör zu! Mein Haus

Wo wohnen sie? Schreibe den Buchstaben.

Where do they live? Write the correct letter.

A

C

B

D

Frau Moser   ☐

Susanne   ☐

Herr Jansen   ☐

Robert   ☐

 **5.2** # Sag was! Was gibt es hier?

einen Garten	einen Balkon	eine Garage	eine Zentralheizung	3 Etagen

1 Mein Haus hat .

2 Unsere Wohnung hat .

3 Es gibt in dem Hochhaus.

4 Ich wohne in einem Wohnblock. Wir haben .

5 Franziska wohnt in einem Wohnblock. Es gibt da .

6 Familie Rodrigez wohnt in einem Wohnblock. Es gibt und .

7 Ich wohne in einem Haus. Es gibt und .

8 Unser Haus hat und .

5.3 Sag was! Beschreibe die Häuser. Was gibt es?

Reihenhaus Wilhelmstraße   Haus Sonnenschein

Hubertushof   Villa Wohngut

Beispiel   Im Reihenhaus Wilhelmstraße gibt es   *eine Zentralheizung, eine Garage und einen Balkon.*

Im Haus Sonnenschein gibt es _____

Im Hubertushof gibt es _____

In der Villa Wohngut _____

5.4 Hör zu! Wo wohnen sie?

Wo wohnen Yasemin, Laura, Matthias und Pierre? Schreibe den Namen unter das Haus.
Where do Yasemin, Laura, Matthias and Pierre live? Write the name under the picture.

1

Hier wohnt _____

3

Hier wohnt _____

2

Hier wohnt _____

4

Hier wohnt _____

5.5 **Hör zu! Ein komisches Haus**

Schreibe die Buchstaben in das Haus.

Write the letters into the plan.

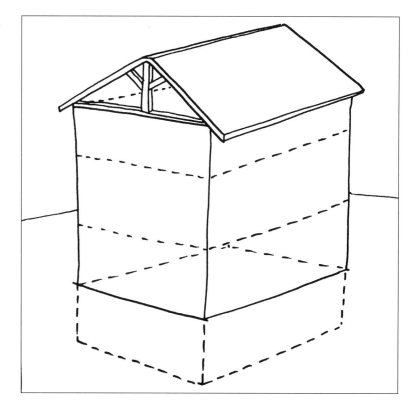

A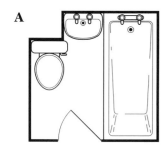

D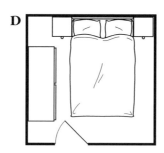

G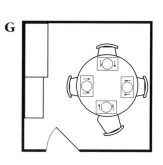

B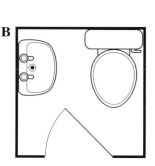

E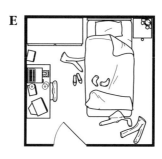

H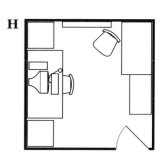

C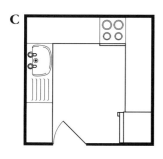

F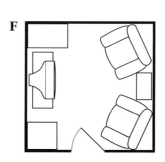

5.6 Gruppenarbeit. Hilf Florian!

Was ist für welches Zimmer? Mache Sätze.
Which item do you think should go in which room? Write full sentences.

Beispiel *Die Waschmaschine ist für die Küche oder das Badezimmer.*
Das Sofa ist für . . .

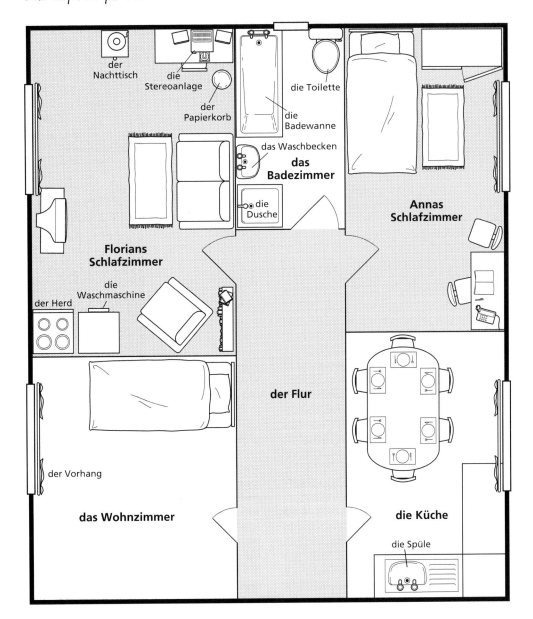

5.7 Sag was! Wo bin ich?

Beschreibe ein Zimmer in der Wohnung. Dein Partner muss raten, wo du bist.
Describe a room in the flat. Your partner has to guess where you are.

Beispiel **A:** Es gibt hier *eine Toilette, eine Badewanne, eine Dusche . . .*
B: Bist du *im Badezimmer?*
A: Ja, richtig!

5.8 Lies was! Zu verkaufen!

Was passt zusammen? Male die Möbel in der richtigen Farbe an.

For sale. Match the ad to the picture. Colour the furniture.

1

2

3 €100

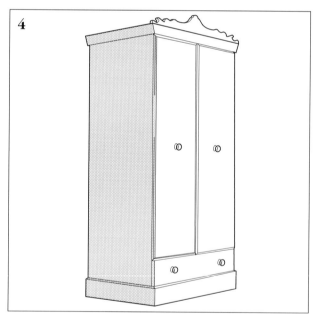

4

A.

Zu verkaufen: **Sofa** – violett, sehr bequem. Nur 120 Euro.

C. **Kleiderschrank**, alt, dunkelgrün und rot, zu verkaufen. Nur 20 Euro.

Billig! Neuer **Schreibtisch**, grau und blau.

B.

Moderner **Sessel**, gelb mit orange, nur 80 Euro.

D.

 **Sag was! In meinem Zimmer gibt es . . .**

Mache Sätze:

Beispiel

In meinem Zimmer gibt es   *einen Sessel, einen Tisch und ein Bett.*

1

_____

_____

4

_____

_____

2

_____

_____

5

_____

_____

3

_____

_____

6

_____

_____

Name:	Klasse:	Datum:

5.10 Meine Laune

A. **WARNING!** Bin schlecht gelaunt!

B. Vorsicht! **ELTERNFREIE ZONE!**

C. **KEEP OUT!** Chaos im Zimmer!

D. Betreten auf eigene **GEFAHR**

E. **FREUNDE UND FANS** willkommen!

F. Psst . . . ! Bitte **NICHT STÖREN!**

G. **RUHE BITTE!** Ich träume!

H. Bin leider nicht da! **BIS SPÄTER!**

Finde im Text:

1 Chaos in the room! _____ *C. Chaos im Zimmer* _____

2 Enter at your own risk! _____

3 I'm in a bad mood! _____

4 Careful! Parent-free zone! _____

5 Quiet please! I'm dreaming! _____

6 Sh! Do not disturb! _____

7 Sorry I am not in! See you later! _____

8 Welcome to friends and fans! _____

5.11 ▸ Schreib was! Er, sie oder es?

Er	Sie	Es

Fülle die Lücken.

Beispiel   Das ist mein Bett. ___ ist sehr bequem. *Es* ist bequem.

1 Hier ist mein Sofa. ___ ist neu.

2 Ich wohne in einer Wohnung. ___ ist sehr schön.

3 Das ist unsere Küche. ___ ist modern.

4 Das sind meine Katzen. ___ sind beide weiß.

5 Wo ist der Hund? ___ ist weg!

6 Wie sieht dein Schrank aus? ___ ist alt.

7 Ich habe einen Schreibtisch. ___ ist braun.

8 Ich habe ein Zimmer. ___ ist klein.

9 Wir haben einen neuen Stuhl. ___ ist blau.

10 Peter hat zwei Sessel. ___ sind sehr modern.

5.12 ▸ Schreib was! Wo sind die Tiere?

Fülle die Lücken.

1 Der Hund ist _____ dem Sofa.

2 Das Pferd ist _____ dem Sofa.

3 Die Katze ist _____ dem Tisch.

4 Der Vogel ist _____ Schrank.

5 Die Maus ist _____ dem Sofa.

6 Die Schlange ist _____ dem Sessel.

vor	unter	auf
neben	hinter	im

5.13 ▸ Schreib was! Bello hat sich versteckt (1)

Der, **dem** oder **den**? Fülle die Lücken.

1   Ist Bello hinter d_____ Schrank?

2   Ist Bello zwischen d_____ Sessel und

    d_____ Sofa?

3   Ist Bello in d_____ Schrank?

4   Ist Bello vor d_____ Tür?

5   Ist Bello neben d_____ Stühlen?

6   Ist Bello unter d_____ Bett?

5.14 ▸ Sag was! Bello hat sich versteckt (2)

Spiele mit einem Partner. Verstecke Bello. Dein Partner muss raten.

Play with a partner. Hide Bello in the picture above. Your partner has to guess where he is hidden by asking you questions.

Beispiel   *A Ist Bello unter dem Schrank?*
                 B Nein, Bello ist nicht unter dem Schrank.

5.15 ▸ Hör zu! Wo ist das Buch?

Male die Gegenstände an die richtige Stelle.

Draw the objects in the correct place.

1

2

3

4

5

5.16 ## Lies was! "Endlich mal Möbel die Fun bringen."

Ich brauche kein Jugendzimmer, sondern einen Raum zum Spaß haben: In dem ich meine Lieblingsmusik höre und in Ruhe Bücher lese. Oder einfach fern sehe und rumhänge.

Ein Zimmer, in dem meine beste Freundin und ich genug Platz zum Rumhüpfen haben, wenn wir Gitarre üben!

Ich will Möbel von hülsta. Sie sehen total gut aus!

Tolle Tips rund um's Wohnen gibt's im Jugend-Wohnbuch von hülsta.

Internet: http://www.huelsta.de

 # Hülsta®

Die Möbelmarke

Das Jugend Wohnbuch

hülsta
Die Möbelmarke.

Erste Hilfe
In Ruhe — in peace
Bücher lesen — read books
fernsehen — watch TV
rumhängen — hang around
rumhüpfen — jump around

Finde im Text:

1 My favourite music _____

2 My best friend _____

3 When we are practising guitar _____

4 They really look good! _____

Beantworte auf Englisch!

1 What does the girl want to be able to do in the room? Give 2 details.

_____

2 What instrument does she play?

_____

3 Why does she want hülsta furniture?

_____

4 What information does the **Jugend Wohnbuch** give?

_____

6.1 Lies was! FUNSTICKER

1	2	3	4	5	6	7
8	9	10	11	12	13	14
15	16	17	18	19	20	21
22	23	24	25	26	27	28
29	30	31				

Super Tag

GUTE ZEITEN
Heute geht's mir richtig gut!

SCHLECHTE ZEITEN
Heute geht's mir ziemlich schlecht!

PARTY!
It's Partytime!

Geburstag von ...

FREI!!
Yeah! Keine Schule!!!

Stress mit ...

Sommerferien!

**Mit diesen Funstickern kannst du ganz besondere Ereignisse und Tage im Kalender
markieren. Viel spass!!!**

6.2 ▸ Schreib was! Verben

Welche Endungen passen zu welchen Verben?

Which endings go with which verbs?

Beispiel: Ich | wohn ⧘ in Schottland, und du?

Ich **wohne** in Schottland, und du?

1 Peter | find ⧘ _____ seine Schultasche nicht.

2 Wir | wach ⧘ _____ jeden Morgen um 7 Uhr auf.

3 Wann | steh ⧘ _____ du morgens auf, Christina?

4 Jan und Emil | zieh ⧘ _____ sich gerade an.

5 Frau Thom | geh ⧘ _____ um halb sieben zur Arbeit.

6 Was | mach ⧘ _____ du da, Martina?

7 Ich | hör ⧘ _____ eine CD von der neuen Band.

8 Wir | lern ⧘ _____ dienstags Deutsch.

⧘en	⧘en	⧘en	⧘st	⧘st	⧘e	⧘e	⧘et	⧘t

6.3 ▸ Schreib was! Starke Verben

Was ist die richtige Verbform?

What is the correct verb form?

Beispiel: Ich (schlafen) jeden Abend um 10 Uhr.

Ich **schlafe** jeden Abend um 10 Uhr.

1 Wann (schlafen) du?

2 (essen) wir bald Mittagessen? Ich habe Hunger!

3 Frau Kasparow (fahren) mit dem Auto zur Arbeit.

4 Ich (sehen) nicht gern fern.

5 Janina (essen) morgens Cornflakes.

6 Ich (fahren) gern Skateboard.

7 Du (sehen) doch auch gern 'Freunde' im Fernsehen, oder nicht?

> ### ⚠ Achtung!
>
> The stem only changes for the **du**, **er**, **sie**, or **es** forms of the verb.
>
> **geben – to give**
>
> | ich gebe | wir geben |
> |---|---|
> | du gibst | ihr gebt |
> | er/sie/es gibt | Sie/sie geben |

isst	essen	siehst	schlafe	sehe	fahre	schläfst	fährt

6.4 ▸ Schreib was! Haben und sein

sein – to be	
ich bin	wir sind
du bist	ihr seid
er/sie/es/man ist	sie/Sie sind

haben – to have	
ich habe	wir haben
du hast	ihr habt
er/sie/es/man hat	sie/Sie haben

Finde die richtige Verbform.

Find the correct verb form.

Beispiel: Wie alt _____ du? (sein)

Wie alt *bist* du?

1   Wir _____ einen MiniDisk-Spieler. (haben)

2   _____ du Engländer? (sein)

3   Ihr _____ beide rote Haare! (haben)

4   Tom _____ mein Freund. (sein)

5   _____ ihr Geschwister? (sein)

6   Katja _____ ihre Hausaufgaben nicht. (haben)

7   Da sind Rebecca und Florian. Sie _____ ein Eis! (haben)

8   Ich _____ eine Katze und einen Hund. (haben)

9   _____ du Haustiere? (haben)

10   Wir _____ Zwillinge. (sein)

11   Ich _____ 12 Jahre alt. (sein)

12   Frau Heinrichs, _____ Sie müde? (sein)

6.5 Schreib was! Übersetze! 🖊

Wie heißt das auf Deutsch?

How do you say this in German? Can you translate the sentences?

1 I live in a flat. _____

2 Where do you live? _____

3 He is living in London. _____

4 What are you doing? _____

5 I am asleep. _____

6 I am sleeping at 11 o'clock. _____

7 Are you asleep at 8 o'clock? _____

8 We go to school. _____

9 Does Tim go to school? _____

10 Are you going to school now? _____

6.6 Schreib was! Mache Sätze! ☺☺ 🖊

Separable verbs. Cut out the boxes and make sentences from the parts.

Ich	ziehst	um 6 Uhr	auf
Wir	mache	ein T-Shirt	fern
Ina	ziehe	um halb sieben	auf
Du	stehen	meine Jacke	aus
Ich	sieht	abends	an

6.7 Partnerarbeit. Was machst du?

- Male die Bilder aus.
- Schneide die Bilder und die Uhren aus.
- Lege eine Uhr neben jedes Bild.
- Wann machst du das? Male die Zeiger auf die Uhr.
- Frage deinen Partner.

- *Colour in the pictures.*
- *Cut out the pictures and clock faces.*
- *Put a clock next to each picture.*
- *When do you do this? Draw the clock bands onto each clock face.*
- *Ask your partner.*

Beispiel: **A** *Wann stehst du auf?* **B** *Um 7 Uhr.*

1

2

3

10

4

9

5

8

7

6

6.8 Schreib was! Mache Sätze.

Reflexive verbs. Make sentences from the words.

uns	duschst	Du
wasche	rasiert	Wir
dich	schminken	euch
kämmen	Ihr	fönt
Sie	sich	Ich
Pedro	mich	sich

6.9 Spiel: Was ziehen sie an?

- Male die Figuren und die Kleidung an und schneide aus.
- Spiele mit einem Partner. Du brauchst einen Würfel.
- Ziehe deine Figur an. Du brauchst mindestens 4 Teile: (Schuhe, Hose oder Rock, Pullover oder T-shirt, Jacke)
- Wer ist zuerst fertig?

- *Colour in and cut out the figures and clothes.*
- *Play with a partner. You need a dice.*
- *Throw the dice. Pick up the item of clothing which matches the number on the dice. You need at least 4 items of clothing (see above). If you already have that piece of clothing, pass the dice on to you partner.*
- *Who is the first to dress their figure(s)?*

1   2

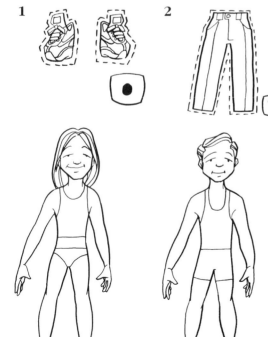

3

4

5

6

6.10 **Hör zu! Der Guten Morgen Rap (3)**

Welche Bilder passen NICHT zum Lied?

passt / passt nicht

passt / passt nicht

passt / passt nicht

passt / passt nicht

passt / passt nicht

passt / passt nicht

passt / passt nicht

passt / passt nicht

6.11 **Gruppenarbeit. Der Guten Morgen Rap (4)**

Was machst du morgens? Kannst du noch mehr Strophen für den Guten Morgen Rap schreiben?
What do you do in the mornings? Can you write any more verses for the rap song?

6.12 **Schreib was! Helfen**

Mache Sätze. Achtung bei trennbaren Verben!

Beispiel: Ich (einkaufen) im Supermarkt.
Ich *kaufe* im Supermarkt *ein*.

1   Meine Mutter (das Essen kochen). _____

2   Mein Bruder (abspülen). _____

3   Du (abtrocknen)! _____

4   Wir (aufräumen) unser Zimmer. _____

5   Meine Eltern (den Rasen mähen). _____

6   Ich (Staub saugen). _____

 **Hör zu! Was hilft Marius? Was hilft Franziska? (2)**

Beantworte die Fragen! Richtig oder Falsch?

1	Marius räumt sein Zimmer auf.	☐
2	Marius mäht den Rasen.	☐
3	Marius spült ab.	☐
4	Marius geht einkaufen.	☐

5	Franziska spült ab.	☐
6	Franziska trocknet ab.	☐
7	Franziska saugt Staub.	☐
8	Franziska kocht das Essen.	☐

6.14 **Schreib was! Verb second**

Ordne die Sätze. Beginne mit dem ersten Wort.

Beispiel: **1** *Morgens gehe ich die Schule.*

1 Morgens | in die Schule | ich | gehe _____

2 Am Nachmittag | ein | kauft | Mutter _____

3 Mein Bruder | auf | nie | räumt | sein Zimmer _____

4 Abends | das Essen | Vater | kocht _____

5 Im Winter | ziehen | einen Mantel | wir | an _____

6 Wie oft | im Haushalt? | hilfst | du _____

7 Meine Schwester | ab und zu | das Abendessen | kocht _____

8 Jeden Tag | ziehst | an | das selbe T-Shirt | du _____

6.15 ▸ Hör zu! Wie kommen sie zur Schule?

Schreibe den richtigen Buchstaben.

1   2   3   4   5

Petra: ☐   Anatole: ☐   Miriam: ☐   Jakob: ☐   Vina: ☐

Mache Sätze!

Beispiel: *Petra fährt mit dem Auto.*

_____

_____

_____

_____

6.16 ▸ Sag was! Wie kommst du zur Schule?

Mache Sätze.

Beispiel: Ich fahre mit *den Inline-Skatern* zur Schule

1   Ich fahre mit _____

_____ zur Schule.

4   Ich fahre mit _____

_____ zur Schule.

2   Ich fahre mit _____

_____ zur Schule.

5   Ich fahre mit _____

_____ zur Schule.

3   Ich fahre mit _____

_____ zur Schule.

6   _____

_____

| Name: _____ | Klasse: _____ | Datum: _____ |

6.17 Hör zu! Mein Wochenende (1)

Was passt zu wem? Schreibe die Buchstaben auf. Achtung, es gibt zu viele Bilder!

A  B  C

D  E  F

G

Eins: _____   Zwei: _____   Drei: _____   Vier: _____

6.18 Hör zu! Mein Wochenende (2)

Richtig oder Falsch? Schreibe R oder F!

1 Nummer eins steht gern früh auf.

5 Nummer drei muss im Haushalt helfen.

2 Nummer eins ist faul.

6 Nummer drei mäht am Samstag den Rasen.

3 Nummer zwei macht Hausaufgaben.

7 Nummer vier findet Videos nicht gut.

4 Nummer zwei hat einen schönen Samstagmorgen.

8 Nummer vier arbeitet Sonntags viel.

7.1 Hör zu! Mein Hobby

My Hobby. Write the right letters in the boxes.

A

B

C

D

E

F

Julia: ☐   Lars: ☐   Jennifer: ☐

Alexeij: ☐   Cheng: ☐   Timo: ☐

Mache Sätze!

Julias Hobby ist _____

Lars' Hobby ist _____

Jennifers Hobby ist _____

Alexeijs Hobby ist _____

Chengs Hobby ist _____

Timos Hobby ist _____

 **7.2** **Schreib was! Sag was! Andere Interessen**

Mache Sätze. Spiele mit einem Partner.
Other interests. Write full sentences. Work with a partner.

Beispiel: ? _____ !

– Interessierst du dich für *das Kino*?   – Nein, ich *spiele* lieber *Fußball*!

1 ?   !

– Interessierst du dich für _____?   – Nein, ich fahre lieber _____!

2 ?   !

– Interessierst du dich _____?   – Nein, ich spiele _____!

3 ?   !

– Interessierst du _____?   – Nein, _____ lieber _____!

4 ?   !

_____?   – Nein, _____!

5 ?   !

_____?   – Nein, _____!

7.3 Spiel: Hobbys raten

Guess the hobby

- Du brauchst 2–6 Spieler.
- Male die Karten an und schneide sie aus.
- Drehe die Karten um und mische sie.
- Nimm eine Karte. Was ist dein Hobby?
- Richtig: Du bekommst die Karte. Falsch: Dein Nachbar darf das Hobby sagen.

- *You need 2–6 players.*
- *Colour in the cards and cut them out.*
- *Turn the cards over and shuffle them.*
- *Take a card. Without looking, guess which hobby is illustrated.*
- *If you're right — you get the card; if you're wrong, don't show you partner — let him/her have a go at guessing.*

Beispiel: Du: *Ich spiele gern Tennis.*   NEIN
Partner: *Ich spiele gern Fußball.*   JA, er / sie bekommt die Karte

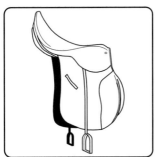
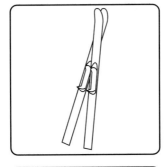

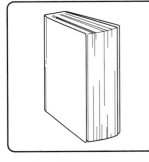

 **7.4** **Spiel: Hobby – Memory**

Memory - cut the words out and put them together with the pictures from PCM 7.3. Shuffle them all, put them face down on a flat surface. Take turns picking up 2 cards. If you get 2 cards with the same hobby, you get to keep the cards. If not, put them back face down.
The winner is the person who has collected the most cards.

Fußball spielen	**Ski fahren**	**Videos sehen**	**Fahrrad fahren**
Tennis spielen	**Rollschuh fahren**	**Lesen**	**Fotografieren**
Tischtennis spielen	**Schwimmen**	**Musik hören**	**Klavier spielen**
Reiten	**Computer spielen**	**Malen**	**Telefonieren**

7.5 Hör zu! Mein Verein

Vier Jugendliche beschreiben ihre Vereine. Schreibe die richtigen Buchstaben.

My club. Four young people are describing their clubs. Write the correct letters.

A

D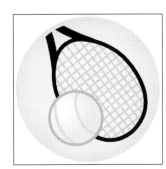

B

E

C

F

Irina: ☐   Martin: ☐   Bettina: ☐   Robert: ☐

7.6 Hör zu! Vereinstermine

Anke ist im Tennisverein. Beantworte die Fragen auf Deutsch!

Anke is in the tennis club. Answer the questions in German.

1 Wie oft spielt Anke Tennis? _____

2 An welchen Tagen spielt sie Tennis? _____

3 Um wie viel Uhr spielt sie samstags Tennis? _____

 **7.7** # Jugend und Sport in der Schweiz

Your friend is visiting Switzerland soon and enjoys sport. Read the text and see if you can help him out by answering the questions below.

Jugend und Sport in der Schweiz

Von Genf bis Rorschach, vom Tessin bis Schaffhausen und vom Engadin bis Basel gibt es hunderte von Vereinen aller Art. Es gibt landauf, landab Jugendklubs, Freizeitzentren usw. Versuch dich doch einmal im Malen und Zeichnen! Es gibt auch Jugend-Theater Vereine, Jugend und Schüler Film-Klubs usw.

Sprecht miteinander über Hobbys. Du weißt was du gern tun willst!

Treibst du gern Sport? Schwimmen, Ballett, Turnen, Tennis, Langlauf, Surfing, Bergsteigen, Segeln, Leichtathletik, Fußball, Laufen, Tauchen usw.

Der SAC (Schweizerische Alpen-Club) hat eine Jugend-Organisation, welche Burschen und Mädchen von 14 bis 22 Jahren offensteht.

Judo ist heute eine sehr populäre Sportart. Man kann in einer der rund 300 Klubs oder in einer Judo-Schule Judo lernen.

Squash ist auch sehr populär unter Jugendlichen. Von den drei Sportarten Badminton, Squash und Tennis ist Squash die bewegungsintensivste! Es macht auch viel Spaß!

Wer regelmäßig Sport treibt, verbraucht Energie z.B.

Sport	Energieverbrauch bei 30minütiger Ausübung
Fahrrad fahren	150 kcal
Tennis spielen	200kcal
Schwimmen	200 kcal
Ski fahren	250 kcal

Erste Hilfe
Bergsteigen — mountaineering
der Bursche — the boy (Swiss German)

Finde im Text

Find in the text the Swiss expression for:

1   of all sorts of clubs _____

2   up and down the country _____

3   talk to each other _____

4   you know what you want to do! _____

5   boys and girls _____

Beantworte auf Englisch!

Answer in English:

1   Give 2 examples of clubs that are mentioned in the first paragraph.

2   Give 3 examples of sports mentioned.

3   What is the age range for the Swiss Alpine Club?

4   How many Judo clubs are there in Switzerland?

5   What does the text say about Squash? Give one example.

6   Which sport requires the most amount of energy according to the table?

7   Which sport requires the least amount of energy according to the table?

7.8   Lied: Der Freizeit Rap (3)

Schreibe Heinz, Pia oder Yasemin.

1   Wer macht Karate?_____

2   Wer telefoniert gern?_____

3   Wer mag sein Bett? _____

4   Wer findet Squash gut? _____

5   Wer mag Bücher?_____

6   Wer schreibt gern Briefe? _____

7   Wer findet fernsehen gut? _____

8   Wer hat Schwimmen als Hobby?_____

7.9   Schreib was! Contracted Prepositions

Fülle die Lücken.
Fill in the gaps.

Beispiel: Ich gehe _____*ins*_____ Haus. (in)

1   Wir wohnen _____ Osten von Berlin (in).

2   Ich stehe _____ Fenster (an).

3   Oma kommt _____ Wohnzimmer (in).

4   Ich gehe _____ Fenster (an).

5   Die Katze geht _____ Dach (auf).

7.10 Schreib was! Dativ oder Akkusativ? (1)

Bewegung = Akkusativ, Ort = Dativ

Schreibe Akkusativ (A) oder Dativ (D)

Write accusative (A) or dative (D).

1   Das Bild hängt an der Wand.   `D`

2   Hänge das Bild an die Wand.

3   Setz dich auf den Stuhl!

4   Ich sitze auf dem Stuhl.

5   Ich wohne in der Stadt.

6   Ich fahre in die Stadt.

7   Der Hund liegt unter dem Tisch.

8   Der Hund geht unter den Tisch.

9   Parke das Auto vor das Haus.

10   Das Auto steht vor dem Haus.

7.11 Schreib was! Dativ oder Akkusativ? (2)

Übersetze!

Translate!

1   The bed is next to the table. (neben)

_____

2   I go into town. (in)

_____

3   I go to bed. (in)

_____

4   I live in a flat. (in)

_____

5   The car is in front of the garage. (vor)

_____

6   I go under the bridge. (unter)

_____

7.12 Schreib was! Mein Terminkalender

Was machst du diese Woche? Trage deine Termine in den Kalender ein.
What are you doing this week? Fill in your diary.

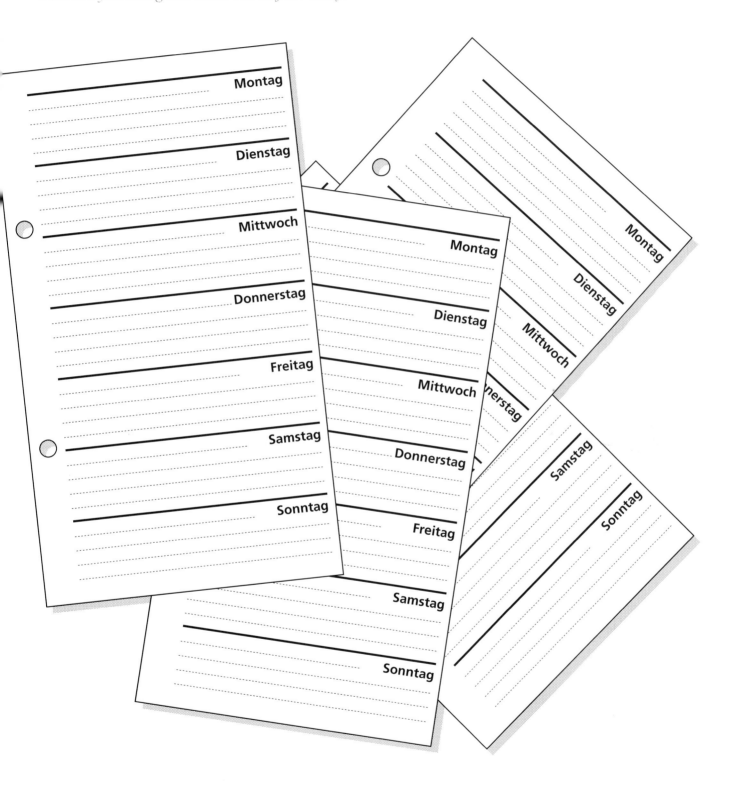

7.13 Rollenspiele: Verabrede dich

Spiele mit einem Partner. Partner A fängt an. Tauscht die Rollen.
Make a date. Play with a partner. Partner A begins. When you have finished swap roles.

1

Partner A

● Ask, if your partner would like to go to the cinema.

● Suggest 9 o'clock.

● Agree. Ask where you shall meet.

● Agree.

Partner B

● Agree. Ask when.

● Say that is too late. Suggest 7 o'clock.

● Suggest your house.

● Say good bye.

2

Partner A

● Greet your partner.

● Say you have some spare time.

● Say, you don't feel like it.

● Ask your partner if (s)he would like to watch TV.

● Suggest your partner's home. Ask when.

● Say that is fine.

Partner B

● Reply. Ask your partner if (s)he's got any spare time.

● Ask if your partner would like to go to town.

● Say, you're sorry.

● Agree. Ask where.

● Suggest this afternoon.

7.14 Hör zu! Einladungen (1)

Wer kommt mit und wer kommt nicht mit? Kreuze an.

Who is coming and who isn't coming with you? Put a cross in the right box.

	Ja	Nein
Klara		
Benjamin		
Maja		

7.15 Hör zu! Einladungen (2)

Hör nochmal zu. Was will der Junge machen? Schreibe den Buchstaben und antworte auf Deutsch.

Listen again. What does the boy want to do? Write the letters and ask in German.

1. Was will der Junge mit Klara machen? *Er will ....* _____

2. Was will der Junge mit Benjamin machen? _____

3. Was will der Junge mit Maja machen? _____

A

D

B

E

C

F

7.16 Lies was! FAHRRAD-VERLEIH

You are travelling in Austria with an English friend who loves cycling.

SPORTHAUS

Alte Straße 3
A-6352 Ellmau
Tirol

FAHRRAD-VERLEIH

1 Stunde	S60,--
jede weitere Stunde	S40,--
Vormittag 9.00–12.00	S100,--
Nachmittag 12.00–18.00	S150,--
1 Tag	S200,--

Wochenende S350,--
1 Woche S750,--

40% Kinderermäßigung

Öffnungszeiten:

Montag-Freitag	Samstag
9.00 Uhr bis 12.00 Uhr	9.00 Uhr bis 12.00 Uhr
15.00 Uhr bis 18.00 Uhr	

Erste Hilfe
Verleih hire
Kinderermäßigung child reduction

Wie viel bezahlen sie?

How much do they pay?

1   Friedl will eine Stunde Rad fahren. _____

2   Susi will Freitagnachmittag Rad fahren. _____

3   Anton will heute Vormittag Rad fahren. _____

4   Stefan will einen Tag Rad fahren. _____

5   Susannah will mit ihrer kleinen Tochter Maria Rad fahren.
    Gibt es eine Kindermässigung? _____

Kann man Fahrräder leihen?   Antworte Ja/Nein

Can you hire a bike?   *Answer yes (Y) or no (N):*

1   Es ist 17.00 Uhr am Freitag. Kann man Fahrräder leihen? ☐

2   Es ist 17.00 Uhr am Samstag. Kann man Fahrräder leihen? ☐

3   Es ist 10.00 Uhr am Sonntag. Kann man Fahrräder leihen? ☐

7.17   Lies was! Was gibt es im Fernsehen? (1)

```
           Teletext - Das Fernsehprogramm nach 20 Uhr

Eins
20.15  Die Landärztin ........................ Liebesfilm (Deutschland, 1958)

ZDF
20.45  Manchester United gegen Lazio Rom ....... Fussball Live

RTL
20.15  Ilona Christen ........................ Talkshow

SAT.1
20.15  Siska ................................. Krimiserie

PRO 7
20.15  Dennis ................................ Komödie (USA, 1993)

SuperRTL
20.15  Micky's fröhlicher Valentinstag ......... Disney Zeichentrickfilm

KABEL 1
 20.15  Südlich von St. Louis ................ Western (USA, 1949)
```

Wo kann man das sehen? Schreibe ganze Sätze.

Beispiel: *Auf Eins kann man einen Liebesfilm sehen.*

1   2   3   4   5

7.18   Lies was! Was gibt es im Fernsehen? (2)

Wie heißt die Sendung? Schreibe den Titel.

1   Hauptkommissar Peter Siska muss in diesem spannenden Mordfall Finderspitzengefühl beweisen.

_____

2   Letzte Folge: "Ilona Spezial". Die Talk-Pionierin nimmt Abschied.

_____

3   Manchester United kann mit David Beckham den 4. Titel in dieser Saison holen.

_____

4   Walt Disney präsentiert ein Special in dem sich alles um die Liebe dreht.

_____

5   Der fünfjährige Dennis ist der Stolz seiner Eltern: blond, frech und voller Energie. Aber der pensionierte Nachbar Mr. Wilson findet den Jungen gar nicht so lustig.

_____

7.19 Sag was! Was gibt es im Fernsehen?

Spiele mit einem Partner. Wähle ein Bild. Mache Sätze.
Work with a partner. Choose a picture. Write sentences.

Beispiel:

A   Was gibt es im Fernsehen?
B   Es gibt einen Western im Fernsehen.

 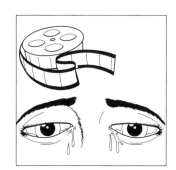 

Hör zu! Was essen sie zum Mittagessen?

Schreibe die richtigen Buchstaben.

What are they eating for lunch? Write the correct letters in the boxes.

A

E

I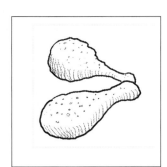

B

F

J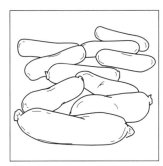

C

G

K

D

H

L

Irene isst:

Irene trinkt:

Paul isst:

Paul trinkt:

8.2 Spiel: Mittagessen

Spiele mit 2 – 6 Spielern. Sammle Karten.

Du brauchst:
- – 1 × Beilage (z.B. Pommes, Nudeln)
- – 1 × Fleisch oder Fisch
- – 1 × Gemüse oder Salat
- – 1 × Getränk
- – 1 × Dessert

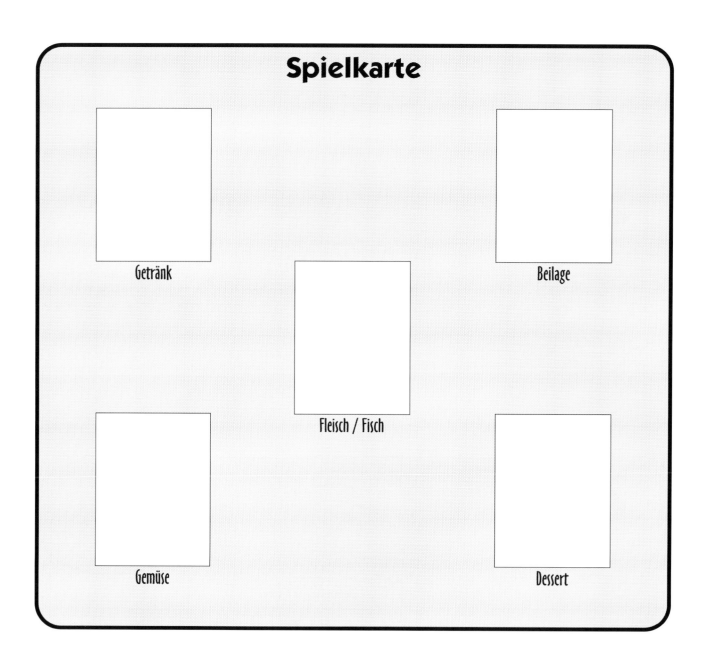

Spielkarte

Getränk

Beilage

Fleisch / Fisch

Gemüse

Dessert

187

8.3 **Hör zu! Es schmeckt uns nicht!**

Famile Schlecker ist im Restaurant.
Leider schmeckt das Essen nicht.
Was passt zusammen?

1   Die Suppe von Herrn Schlecker ist   **a)** zu scharf.

2   Die Bratwurst von Frau Schlecker ist   **b)** lecker, aber zu wenig.

3   Die Nudeln von Jan Schlecker sind   **c)** zu kalt.

4   Das Eis von Ella Schlecker ist   **d)** zu salzig.

8.4 **Schreib was! Personalpronomen im Nominativ**

ich	*I*	wir	*we*
du	*you*	ihr	*you (plural)*
er	*he*	Sie	*you (polite)*
sie	*she*	sie	*they*
es	*it*		

Schreibe die Sätze ganz auf Deutsch.
Write full sentences in German.

Beispiel: (I) esse gern Schokolade.   *Ich* esse gern Schokolade.

1   (We) essen immer um 7 Uhr zu Abend. _____

2   Maria mag keinen Kuchen und (she) isst kein Eis. _____

3   Es ist schon 9 Uhr. (They) sind zu spät! _____

4   Otto kommt heute zu mir. (He) isst mit uns zu Mittag._____

5   Um wie viel Uhr wollt (plural you) kommen? _____

6   Wie spät ist (it)?_____

7   Was magst (you) lieber, Tee oder Kaffee? _____

8   Haben (polite you) Lust, mit in die Stadt zu kommen, Herr Fazal?_____

8.5 ## Schreib was! Personalpronomen im Akkusativ

Fülle die Lücken!

mich	*me*	uns	*us*
dich	*you*	euch	*you (plural)*
ihn	*him, it*	Sie	*you (polite)*
sie	*her, it*	sie	*they*
es	*it*		

Beispiel: Das ist Sabine. Ich kenne ___*sie*___ seit 7 Jahren.

1 Hallo Ali und Naila, ich sehe _____!

2 Das ist mein Kaninchen, Pucki. Ich finde _____ ganz süß!

3 Sprich lauter! Ich kann _____ nicht hören.

4 Wir sind alte Freunde. Wir kennen _____ schon seit 40 Jahren.

5 Da ist Kai. Seine Mutter fährt _____ mit dem Auto zur Schule.

6 Wo sind Tom und Walter. Ich kann _____ nicht sehen?

7 Sagen Sie mal, Frau Jansen, sehen _____ meine Tasche irgendwo?

8 Ich bin hier! Kannst du _____ sehen?

8.6 ## Schreib was! Personalpronomen im Dativ

Fülle die Lücken!

mir	*to me*	uns	*to us*
dir	*to you*	euch	*to you (plural)*
ihm	*to him*	Ihnen	*to you (polite)*
ihr	*to her*	ihnen	*to them*
ihm	*to it*		

Beispiel: Wie geht es ___*dir*___, Dana?

1 Schmeckt es _____, Dana?

2 Wie geht es Paula? Gefällt _____ die neue Schule?

3 Ich will das haben! Gib es _____!

4 Gehst du heute zu Peter? Dann sage _____ bitte, er soll zur Party kommen.

5 Tobias und Jonas lieben das Essen in Italien. Es schmeckt _____ ganz toll!

6 Wir finden den Kuchen lecker. Er schmeckt _____ wirklich gut!

7 Das ist mein Meerschweinchen. Ich gebe _____ jeden Tag frische Möhren.

8 Hallo, Franziska und Julia. Ich habe _____ einen Brief geschrieben.

Gruppenarbeit: Gemischte Pronomen

Wie viele Sätze könnt ihr machen?
How many sentences can you make?

Das Essen	mir	Es	geht
Er	finde	mich	Du
Ich	euch	an	dich
Wir	schmeckt	mag	rufen
ihm	gut	ihn	nicht
Das T-Shirt	gefällt	uns	liebt
sie	Ich	schön	kennst

 Rollenspiel: In der Konditorei

Play with a partner. Partner A begins the conversation.

Partner A

You are a waiter / waitress:

- Greet the customer.
- Ask the customer what (s)he wants to drink.
- Ask what (s)he wants to eat.
- Say here is the menu.
- Ask if with or without whipped cream. (**Schlagsahne**)

Partner B

You are a customer:

- Respond to the greeting and ask for a table for two.
- Say you would like a hot chocolate.
- Say you would like a menu.
- Order a piece of gateau. (**ein Stück Torte**)
- Say with cream.

Sag was! Wie sagt man das auf Deutsch?

How do you say that in German?

1 How could you get the waiter's attention? _____

2 How could you ask for the menu? _____

3 How could you order a hamburger and chips? _____

4 How could you say that something is too cold? _____

5 How could you ask for the bill? _____

6 How could you ask where the toilets are? _____

 Hör zu! Was passt?

Welches Bild passt zu der Situation? Schreibe die Buchstaben.
Which picture goes with which situation? Write the correct letter.

Eins   Zwei   Drei   Vier   Fünf

A

B

C

D

E

8.11 Keldorado

Das familienfreundliche Restaurant

- Ganzjährig geöffnet von 11.00 bis 22.00 Uhr
- Große Panoramafenster zum Schwimmbad
- Sonnenterasse

Auch wenn Sie keine Lust zum Schwimmen haben, besuchen Sie das Keldorado Restaurant

Wir bieten:
- Italienische Spezialitäten
- Fisch- und Fleischgerichte
- Knackige Salate
- Süßes zum Naschen
- Und unsere berühmten Riesenpizzas zu familienfreundlichen Preisen.

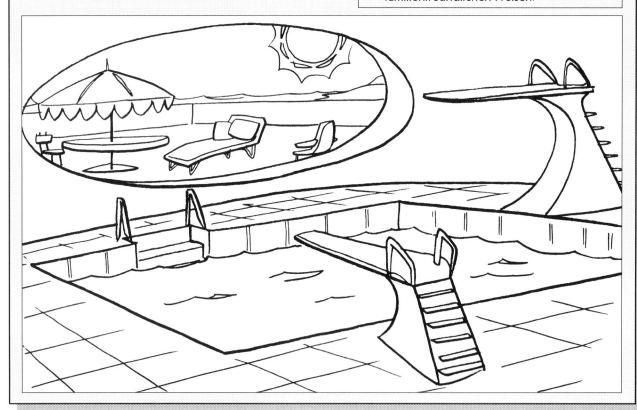

Richtig oder Falsch? Korrigiere die falschen Sätze:

1 Keldorado ist von 11.00 bis 22.00 Uhr geöffnet. _____

2 Keldorado hat kleine Panoramafenster zum Schwimmbad. _____

3 Keldorado hat keine Sonnenterasse. _____

4 Keldorado bietet indianische Spezialitäten._____

5 Keldorado bietet nur Fischgerichte. _____

6 Keldorado bietet knackige Salate._____

7 Keldorado bietet kleine Pizzas. _____

8 Keldorado hat familienfreundliche Preise._____

8.12 # Lies was! Träume in Eis

Bananensplit

Bananenhälfte mit Vanilleeis, Schokosauce

Walnussbecher

Leicht karamelisierte Walnusskerne,
Walnusseiscreme
Mit Eierlikör und Sahne

Coppa Tutti Frutti

Mit frischen Früchten,
Erdbeer-, Vanille-, Zitronen- und Joghurtwaldfruchteis
und Sahne

Schwarzwaldbecher

Schokoladeneiscreme, Morellen,
Kirschwasser und Sahne

Eiskaffee / Eisschokolade

Der klassische Genuss
für Kaffee – und Schokoliebhaber

Heiße Himbeeren mit Vanilleeis und Sahne

Joghurttraum

Mit Joghurtwaldfrucht-, Sahne-Amaretto-, Walnuss- und Vanilleeis,
Naturjoghurt und frischen Früchten

Für unsere kleinen Gäste:

Eisbiene

Erdbeer- und Vanilleeis, Smarties und Schokosauce

Pinocchio

Schoko- und Vanilleeis

Erste Hilfe
die Walnuss   walnut
die Morelle   a type of cherry
die Himbeere   raspberry

Welches Eis? Pass auf! Es gibt manchmal mehrere Antworte

Which ice cream would suit these people? Take care! There is sometimes more than one answer.

1   Anja ist 8 Jahre alt und liebt Smarties. _____

2   Anjas Oma, Johanna, ist Schokoliebhaberin. _____

3   Peter isst gern Himbeeren. _____

4   René ist Kaffeeliebhaber. _____

5   Antonio isst gern frische Früchte und auch Joghurt. _____

6   Chantale isst gern Bananen. _____

7   Andreas Lieblingsessen ist Walnusseiscreme. _____

8   Die kleine Bettina ist erst 7 Jahre alt und isst gern Schokolade. _____

8.13 ▶ Lies was! VEGETARIERREPORTAGE

Ich bin schon seit vielen Jahren Vegetarier. Meine Freunde sagen, dass ich spinne und überhaupt nicht gesund lebe, aber ich sehe es ganz anders. Seit ich einen Film über Tiertransporte gesehen habe, esse ich kein Fleisch mehr!

Marina aus Memmingen

Meine Mutter und ich sind beide Vegetarier und ich kann nicht sagen, dass es uns ohne Fleisch schlecht geht! Tiere sind doch auch Lebewesen, wie wir Menschen!

Regina aus Veitshöchheim

Erste Hilfe

spinnen	to be mad
gesund	healthy
der Tiertransport	animal transport
das Lebewesen	creature

Finde im Text

1 My friends say that I am mad. _____

2 I see it quite differently. _____

3 I cannot say _____

4 Animals are living creatures too. _____

Beantworte auf Englisch!

1 How long has Marina been a vegetarian? _____

2 What do her friends think about this? _____

3 Why did she become a vegetarian? _____

4 Who else in Regina's family is vegetarian? _____

5 Does she think her health suffers because she is vegetarian? _____

6 What does she say about animals? _____

8.14 Lies was! Ein Brief (2)

Servus!

Wie geht's? Wir haben bald Osterferien. Ich freue mich schon auf Ostern!

Karfreitag fahre ich zu meiner Oma. Sie wohnt auf dem Land. Die ganze Familie wird kommen, Onkel, Tanten, Kusinen und Cousins.

Ostersamstag werden wir Eier bemalen und basteln.

Ostersonntag werden wir dann ganz früh aufstehen. Wir werden in Omas Garten Ostereier suchen. Ich mag die Schokoladeneier am liebsten.

Dann wird es das Osterfrühstück geben. Ich hoffe, Oma backt wieder ihre leckeren Osterbrötchen, mmmh!

Nach dem Essen gehen wir alle in die Kirche. Oma ist katholisch.

Am Abend wird es auf dem Dorfplatz ein großes Feuer geben. Ich hoffe, es wird nicht zu kalt sein! Oder noch schlimmer – regnen!

Leider müssen wir Ostermontag schon wieder nach Linz zurück. Aber ich hab zumindest keine Schule!!!

Hast du auch Osterferien? Wie feiert ihr Ostern? Gibt es bei euch auch Ostereier?

Schreib mir bald!

Frohe Ostern!

Deine Katharina

Beantworte die Fragen auf Deutsch!

1 Worauf freut sich Katharina schon?_____ *Auf die Osterferien.* _____

2 Wo wohnt Katharinas Oma?_____

3 Wann wird sie Eier bemalen? _____

4 Wo wird sie Ostereier suchen? _____

5 Was mag sie am liebsten?_____

6 Was ist lecker? _____

7 Wann gibt es ein großes Feuer? _____

8 Wohin fährt Katharina am Ostermontag? _____

8.15 Schreib was! Ein Brief (3)

Beantworte Katharinas Brief. Das will Katharina wissen:

Answer Katharina's letter. She wants to know:

Hast du auch Osterferien?

Wie feiert ihr Ostern?

Gibt es bei euch auch Ostereier?

8.16 Lies was! Das Osterhasenmuseum

Geöffnet: Täglich von 10 bis 18 Uhr (auch Samstag und Sonntag)

Westenriederstraße 41, D-80331 München, Deutschland
80 m vom Isartorplatz – 250 m vom Marienplatz
S-Bahn: Isartorplatz U-Bahn: Marienplatz

Eintritt:

Erwachsene €4,00
Gruppen ab 10 Personen ....€2,50 (pro Person)
Schüler, Studenten €2,50
Gruppen ab 10 Personen..................€1,50 (pro Person)

Beantworte die Fragen auf Englisch!

1   When exactly is the museum open?_____

2   How far is it from Marienplatz?_____

3   Which S-Bahn station is nearest?_____

4   How much would it cost for 2 adults?_____

5   How much would it cost for 3 students?_____

6   How much would it cost for a group of 10 students?_____

8.17 Quiz: Aus welchen Ländern kommt dieses Essen?

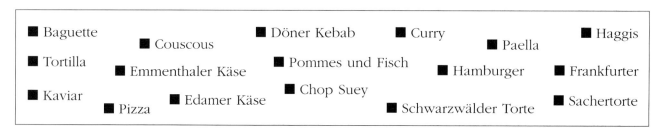

- Baguette
- Couscous
- Döner Kebab
- Curry
- Haggis
- Paella
- Tortilla
- Emmenthaler Käse
- Pommes und Fisch
- Hamburger
- Frankfurter
- Kaviar
- Chop Suey
- Edamer Käse
- Pizza
- Schwarzwälder Torte
- Sachertorte

Beispiel: *Baguette kommt aus Frankreich.*

8.18 Lies was! Ostereier färben

Ostereierfarbe gibt es natürlich im Geschäft zu kaufen. Aber du kannst auch schnell und einfach die Eier selber einfärben. Dazu stellst du einen Topf mit Wasser und etwas Essig auf den Herd. Wenn das Wasser kocht, legst du weiße Eier mit hinein. Zusätzlich zu den Eiern kannst du verschiedene Nahrungsmittel in kleiner Menge dazugeben. Die Eier werden sich entsprechend verfärben.

Zwiebelschalen verfärben die Eier braun

Safran lässt die Eier gelb werden

Spinat gibt den Eiern eine grüne Färbung

Rote Beete lässt die Eier schön rot werden

Blauer Heidelbeersaft gibt ein tolles Blau

Kurkuma ergibt gelbe Eier

Mit Lebensmittelfarben bekommt man tolle knallige Effekte hin!

Erste Hilfe

einfärben	to colour
der Essig	vinegar
der Herd	hob
kochen	to boil
die Zwiebelschale	onion skin
der Safran	saffron
der Spinat	spinach
die Rote Beete	beetroot
Heidelbeeren	blueberries
Kukurma	turmeric
Lebensmittelfarbe	food colouring
knallig	bright

Was macht welche Farbe? Schreibe den richtigen Buchstaben.

braun   *rot*   *gelb*

blau   *grün*

a.   b.   c.

d.   e.   f.

8.19 Gruppenarbeit: Entwirf ein Osterei

Entwirf ein Osterei und mache eine Ausstellung. Beschreibe die Eier.
Design an Easter Egg. Make an exhibition. Describe your egg.

Vokabeltipp Wie sieht es aus

Das Ei ist	_rot_ mit _blau_.	The egg is red and blue.
Das Ei hat	(blaue) Streifen.	The egg has (blue) stripes.
	(gelbe) Punkte.	The egg has (yellow) dots.
Das Ei ist kariert.		The egg has a check pattern.
Auf dem Ei ist ein _____ (+ Akkusativ)		

8.20 # Lies was! Der Osterhase aus Hefe

Here is a recipe – you could try making it!

Zutaten:

1 kg Weizenmehl
2 Hefewürfel
1 Tl. Salz, 100g Zucker
6 EL Speiseöl, 0,5 l warme Milch

Für die Dekoration:

2 Rosinen für die Augen,
2 Mandeln für die Zähne
1 Ei zum Bestreichen

~

Alle Zutaten in einer großen Schüssel mit den Händen zusammenkneten - eventuell Mehl zugeben, wenn der Teig zu klebrig ist. Dann den Teig abdecken und an einem warmen Ort stehen lassen. Sobald der Teig etwa die doppelte Größe erreicht hat, wird er nochmals gut durchgeknetet und auf ein mit Backpapier belegtes Backblech zum Hasenkopf geformt. Dann mit dem verquirlten Ei bestreichen, Rosinen und Mandeln auflegen und bei 160 Grad C ca. 40 Minuten im vorgeheizten Backofen backen.

Test 2

 **Sprechen – Rollenspiele**

1A Student's Role

You are visiting a friend in Austria and you are asked about your school in England. Your teacher will play the role of your Austrian friend and will speak first.

- Say where you live.
- Say what you do before school.
- Say at what time school begins.
- Say what you eat and drink in the lunch break.

1B Teacher's Role

Wir sind in Österreich. Ich bin dein(e) Freund(in).

- Wo wohnst du in England?
  Allow the student to say where he/she lives.
- Was machst du, bevor du zur Schule gehst?
  Allow the student to say what he/she does before school
- Wann beginnt die Schule?
  Allow the student to say at what time school begins.
- Was isst du und was trinkst du in der Mittagspause?
  Allow the student to say what he/she eats and drinks in the lunch break

2A Student's Role

Your German friend is visiting you and he/she asks about your home life. Your teacher will play the role of your friend and will speak first.

- Say where you live.
- Ask him/her if he/she lives in a house or a flat.
- Say what your hobbies are.
- Say what you do to help at home.

2B Teacher's Role

Dein deutscher Freund/Deine deustsche Freundin bleibt bei dir. Ich bin dein(e) Freund(in).

- Wo wohnst du?
  Allow the student to say where he/she lives.
- Du, dein Haus ist so schön!
  Allow the student to ask if you live in a house or a flat.
- Ich wohne in einem Einfamilienhaus. Hast du Hobbys?
  Allow the student to say what his/her hobbies are.
- Hilfst du zu Hause?
  Allow the student to say what he/she does to help at home.

Further questions for each role play:

- Wie heißt du?
- Wie schreibt man das?
- Woher kommst du?
- Wo wohnst du?
- Was für Möbel hast du in deinem Schlafzimmer?

- Wann hast du Geburtstag?
- Wie ist deine Telefonnummer?
- Wie spät ist es?
- Was machst du in der Schule?
- Was machst du nach der Schule?
- Was machst du in deiner Freizeit?

Name: _____	Klasse: _____	Datum: _____

 11a **Lies was! Eine neue Wohnung!**

Your German friend shows you this advert for a new flat he is moving into

Bundesland: Baden Württemberg	
Plz.: 88250	**Ort:** Weingarten
Wohnflächer: 86m²	**Verfügbar ab:** 11. September
Typ: Eigentumswohnung	**Etage:** 1. OG
Zimmer: Küche Balkon Bad Garten Badewanne Garage Dusche Stellplatz WC	
Info: Helle, geräumige 3 Zi. Wohnung, ruhige aber zentrale Lage, Garage, Carport, Stellplatz, Südbalkon.	
Kontaktperson: G. Meier	**E-mail:** meier@weingarten.de

Beantworte auf Englisch!

1 What is the name of the town the flat is situated in? _____

2 What is the postcode? _____

3 How big is the flat? _____

4 When can your friend move in? _____

5 What floor is the flat on? _____

6 Is there anywhere for your friend to park his car? _____

7 How many rooms does the flat have? _____

8 Give 2 details about its location. _____

9 Does the balcony face West? _____

10 How can you contact the owner? _____

Lies was! Mani Privat

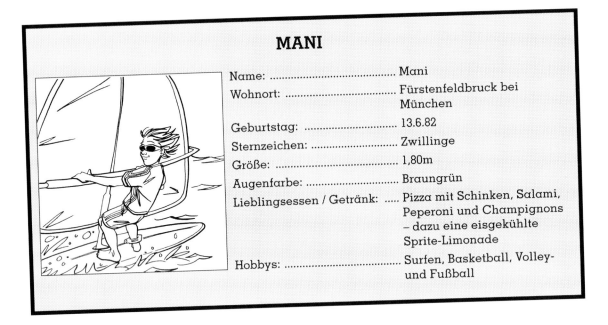

MANI

Name: .... Mani
Wohnort: .... Fürstenfeldbruck bei München
Geburtstag: 13.6.82
Sternzeichen: .... Zwillinge
Größe: 1,80m
Augenfarbe: .... Braungrün
Lieblingsessen / Getränk: ..... Pizza mit Schinken, Salami, Peperoni und Champignons – dazu eine eisgekühlte Sprite-Limonade
Hobbys: .... Surfen, Basketball, Volley- und Fußball

Beantworte auf Deutsch!

1 Wo wohnt Mani? _____

2 Wann ist Mani geboren? _____

3 Was ist sein Sternzeichen? _____

4 Wie groß ist er? _____

5 Was ist sein Lieblingsessen? _____

6 Was ist sein Lieblingsgetränk? _____

7 Was sind seine Hobbys? _____

Lies was! Vereine

Was ist los?

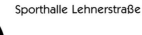

Hallenhockey

HTC Uhlenhorst

Neue Mitglieder immer willkommen!

Jugendtraining: Di., Do. 16 – 18 Uhr

Senioren: Di., Do. 18 – 20 Uhr, Sa. 10 – 12 Uhr.

Sporthalle Lehnerstraße

Fußball

VfB Speldorf

Sa. Und So. 9 – 15 Uhr, Stadion am Blötteweg.

Verschiedene Altersgruppen.

Bitte informieren Sie sich telefonisch: 0208 – 503 503

Handball

HSV Dümpten

Frauenmannschaft: Mo, Mi. Sa. 17 – 20 Uhr

Herrenmannschaft: Di. Do. Fr. 17 – 20 Uhr.

Sporthalle Boverstraße

Kegeln

Kegelverein Fortuna sucht neue Mitglieder

Männer und Frauen zwischen 30 und 50 gesucht.

Wir treffen uns jeden ersten Dienstag im Monat
ab 19.30 Uhr.

Interessenten wenden sich bitte an:
Frau Schösser 0208-44 12 52

Ja oder nein? Beantworte die Fragen in ganzen Sätze!

Beispiel: Können Frauen Handball spielen?
Ja, Frauen können Handball spielen

Sollen Kegelfreunde Frau Schösser schreiben?
*Nein, Kegelfreunde sollen Frau Schösser **nicht** schreiben. Sie sollen anrufen.*

1   Möchte der HTC Uhlenhorst neue Hockeyspieler?

_____

2   Können Jugendliche dienstags und donnerstags Hockey spielen?

_____

3   Dürfen Mädchen beim HSV Dümpten Fußball spielen?

_____

4   Kann man im Stadion Blötterweg kegeln?

_____

5   Sollen im Kegelverein Männer und Frauen anrufen?

_____

6   Kann man einmal pro Woche kegeln?

_____

7   Kann man nur am Wochenende Fußball spielen?

_____

8   Kann man morgens Handball spielen?

_____

 **III** **Hör zu! Meine Freizeit**

Hör zu und beantworte die Fragen!

1 Was sind deine Hobbys?

Meine Hobbies sind . . .
_____

2 Bist du in einem Verein?

Ja / Nein . . .
_____

3 Siehst du gern fern?

Ja / Nein, ich sehe (nicht) gern fern.
_____

4 Hast du einen eigenen Fernseher?

Ja / Nein . . .
_____

5 Wie oft siehst du pro Tag fern?

Ich sehe . . . Stunden pro Tag fern.
_____

6 Was für Sendungen siehst du gern?

Ich sehe gern . . .
_____

7 Wie heißt deine Lieblingssendung?

Meine Lieblingssendung heißt . . .
_____

8 Welche Sendung findest du doof?

Ich finde . . . doof.
_____

9 Wie heißt dein Lieblingsschauspieler?

Mein Lieblingsschauspieler heißt . . .
_____

10 Wie heißt deine Lieblingsschauspielerin?

Meine Lieblingsschauspielerin . . .
_____

 **Schreib was!**

Schreib so viel wie möglich!

- Mein Haus.
- Ein Schultag.
- Meine Hobbys.
- Diese Woche. Schreib was du diese Woche machst.

_____

_____

_____

_____

_____

_____

_____

_____

_____

_____

_____

_____

_____

_____

_____

_____

_____

_____

_____

_____

_____

_____

_____

_____

_____

_____

Action Plan

German

Test number: ....

My mark: ....   Average mark for my class: ....

Corrections:

....

....

....

....

....

....

....

....

....

....

....

1   Am I happy with my progress? What did I do well?

....

2   How could I improve my work?

Example: *Don't panic! Write neatly and give all the information I am asked to give.*

....

3   What things did I do to prepare for this test?

Example: *Noting down and learning vocabulary regulary*

....

4   What things should I have done to prepare for this test?

....

Student Profiles

Kapitel 1

I can	Student	Teacher
● greet people		
● ask people how they are		
● say how I am		
● give my name		
● ask people their name		
● say the alphabet		
● spell my name		
● understand some useful classroom phrases		
● say where I live		
● ask where someone lives		

Kapitel 2

I can	Student	Teacher
● say the numbers 1–31		
● say the months and the seasons		
● say how old I am		
● ask how old someone is		
● say when my birthday is		
● ask when someone's birthday is		
● give a telephone number		
● ask for someone's telephone number		
● say the names of classroom objects		
● ask where something is		

Kapitel 3

I can	Student	Teacher
● describe someone		
● ask what someone looks like		
● describe someone's character		
● ask what sort of character someone has		
● ask whether someone has any pets		
● say whether I have any pets		
● describe pets		
● talk about my relatives		
● talk about my family tree		
● ask someone about their family		
● say the numbers 30–100		
● write an e-mail to a penfriend		
● write a short letter in German		

Kapitel 4

I can	Student	Teacher
● say which school subjects I study		
● say what I think of these subjects		
● say what my favourite subjects are		
● ask what the time is		
● say what the time is		
● say the days of the week		
● say when school starts		
● say when school finishes		
● say what lessons I have		
● say when I have lessons		
● say some useful classroom phrases		

Kapitel 5

I can	Student	Teacher
● say where I live		
● understand people describing the area in which they live		
● describe the area that I live in		
● describe what sort of a house / flat I live in		
● describe the outside of my house e.g. garden etc.		
● name the rooms of the house		
● ask about someone else's house		
● understand descriptions of houses		
● say whether I like / dislike my house		
● understand someone describing their bedroom		
● describe my bedroom		
● describe furniture in my bedroom		
● describe where the furniture is		
● say whether I like / dislike my room and furniture		

Kapitel 6

I can	Student	Teacher
● understand someone describing their day		
● describe what I do each school day		
● describe what I do on a day when I am not at school		
● ask what someone else does each day		
● describe what someone else does each day		
● describe how I travel to school		
● understand what someone does to help at home		
● describe what I do / do not do to help at home		
● ask someone how they help at home		
● say what someone does to help at home		
● understand a short text message in German		
● write a short text message in German		

Kapitel 7

I can	Student	Teacher
● understand someone describing their hobbies		
● describe my hobbies		
● ask what someone else's hobbies are		
● say what someone else's hobbies are		
● say I would like to meet up with someone		
● arrange a time to meet		
● arrange a place to meet		
● understand where and when to meet someone		
● understand a short text message arranging a meeting		
● write a short text message to arrange a meeting		
● ask what sort of film is on TV		
● say what sort of film is on TV		
● say what I like to watch on TV		

Kapitel 8

I can	Student	Teacher
● say what foods I like		
● say what I like to drink		
● say I am hungry / I am thirsty		
● understand people talking about food and drink		
● say what other people like to eat / drink		
● say what I prefer to eat / drink		
● describe the taste of something		
● say if I'm allergic to a certain food		
● ask if someone else is allergic to a certain food		
● say if someone else is allergic to a certain food		
● understand a basic menu		
● order a meal / drink		
● ask for the bill		
● understand the bill		
● ask where the toilet is		
● order a takeaway		
● understand information about celebrations in Germany (e.g. Easter)		

Certificate Master

Anstoß

This is to certify that

....

has successfully completed

Anstoß 1

Signature ....
German Teacher

Date ....

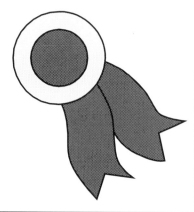

I can:

- greet people and ask their name and how they are; give my name and say how I am.
- say the alphabet, spell my name, understand some useful classroom phrases.
- ask where someone lives; say where I live.
- say the numbers 1–1000, the months and the seasons.
- ask how old someone is; say how old I am.
- ask when someone's birthday is; say when my birthday is.
- ask for someone's telephone number; give a telephone number.
- say the names of classroom objects; ask where something is.
- describe someone; describe someone's character; ask what sort of character someone has.
- ask whether someone has any pets; say whether I have any pets; describe pets.
- ask someone about their family; talk about my family and relatives.
- write an e-mail or a short letter to a penfriend in German.
- say which school subjects I study and what I think of these subjects.
- ask what time it is; say what time it is and what day it is.
- say when school starts/finishes; what lessons I have; when I have lessons.
- understand people describing the area in which they live.
- describe the area that I live in; describe what sort of a house/flat I live in.
- describe the outside of my house; name the rooms of the house.
- ask about someone else's house; understand descriptions of houses.
- say whether I like/dislike my house.
- understand someone describing their bedroom; describe my bedroom.
- describe furniture in my bedroom; say whether I like/dislike my room and furniture.
- understand someone describing their day; describe what I do each school day.
- describe what I do on a day when I am not at school.
- ask what someone else does each day; describe what someone else does each day.
- describe how I travel to school; understand what someone does to help at home.
- describe what I do/do not do to help at home; ask someone how they help at home.
- understand/write a short text message in German.
- understand someone describing their hobbies; describe my hobbies.
- ask what someone else's hobbies are; say what someone else's hobbies are.
- say I would like to meet up with someone; arrange a time to meet.
- arrange a place to meet; understand where and when to meet someone.
- understand a short text message arranging a meeting.
- write a short text message to arrange a meeting.
- ask what sort of film is on TV; say what sort of film is on TV; say what I like to watch on TV.
- say what foods I like; say what I like to drink.
- say I am hungry/I am thirsty.
- understand people talking about food and drink; say what other people like to eat/drink.
- say what I prefer to eat/drink; describe the taste of something.
- say if I'm allergic to a certain food.
- ask/say if someone else is allergic to a certain food.
- understand a basic menu, order a meal/drink/takeaway; ask for the bill.

Appendix A Mapping grid for National Curriculum

The following grid shows how the core activities of *Anstoß 1* map against the attainment targets and levels from the National Curriculum.

Please Note: Where an activity functions at two levels within the same attainment target, the higher level is listed.

KAPITEL 1: HALLO				

Einheit A – Wie geht's?	AT1	AT2	AT3	AT4
1. Die Geburtstagparty (1)	1			
2. Lies den Cartoon und hör zu noch einmal.	2		2	
3. Hör zu Guten Tag!	1	1		
4. Hör zu Was sagt man?	2	2		
5. Schreib was! Anagramme				1
6. Hör zu! Wie geht's?	1	1		
7. Hör zu! Wie geht's?	2			
8. Partnerarbeit: Sag was!		2		
9. Schreib was! Füll die Lücken im Cartoon.			2	2

Einheit B – Wie heißt du?	AT1	AT2	AT3	AT4
1. Die Geburtstagsparty (2)	1		2	
2. Lies den Carton noch mal. Wie sagt man das auf Deutsch?			2	
3. Schreib was!				2
4. Schreib was und sag was!		1		1
5. Hör zu und schreib was! Wie heißt du?	2			
6. Hör zu! Wie heißt du? oder: Wie heißen Sie?	2			
7. Quiz: Wie heißen Sie?		1		
8. Hör zu! Das Alphabet	1	1		
9. Hör zu! Lied: ABC	1			
10. Hör zu – Am Telefon	2			
11. Partnerarbeit. Du bist dran: Sag was!:		2		
12. Gruppenarbeit: Autos		2		
13. Schreib was! Dialog			2	2

Einheit C – Wo wohnst du?	AT1	AT2	AT3	AT4
1. Die Geburtstagparty (3)	2			
2. Partnerarbeit: Laura und Matthias		2		
3. Woher kommen sie?			3	1
4. Gruppenarbeit:Ortsnamen				
5. Sag was! Partnerarbeit: Wo ist…?		2		
6. Hör zu! Wo wohnt er? Wo wohnt sie?	3			
7. Sag was! Du bist dran! Wo wohnst du?		2		
8. Hör zu!: Hallo!	2			
9. Quiz: Deutschsprachige Länder			2	
10. Quiz: Woher kommt das Auto? Buchstabiere!				2
11. Schreib was!				3
12. Schreib was! Verben				3
13. Partnerarbeit: Sag was! Ein Interview		3		
Leseseiten			3	

National Curriculum PoS statements covered in Kapitel 1.
1a, 1b, 2a, 2b, 2c, 2e, 2h, 3a, 3c, 4a, 4c, 5a.

KAPITEL 2: WIR LERNEN UNS KENNEN

Einheit A – Zahlen und Daten	AT1	AT2	AT3	AT4
1. Lies den Cartoon und hör zu. Die Telefonnummer	2			
2. Partnerarbeit: Wie sagt man das auf Deutsch?	2	2		
3. Hör zu! ie oder ei?	2			
4. Sag was! Wie viele?		2		
5. Hör zu: Die Fußballergebnisse	2			
6. Hör zu: Die Rakete	1	1		
7. Partnerarbeit: Sag was!		2		
8. Gruppenarbeit: Nationale Telefonnummern				
9. Hör zu!: Wie alt ist…		3		2
10. Hör zu! Lied: Monate	1			
11. Sag was! Wann hast du Geburtstag?		2		
12. Quiz: Wann ist Ihr Geburtstag?		2		
13. Hör zu! Lied: Geburtstagslied	1			
14. Sag was! Heinz und Band auf Tour		2		
15. Hör zu: Die Top Ten in Deutschland	2			
16. Hör zu: Lotto	2			
17. Lies was! Eine E-Mail aus Deutschland			3	
18. Schreib was! Eine E-Mail an Katja				2
19. Lied: Der Heinz- und Pia-Rap	3			

Einheit B – Wo ist es?	AT1	AT2	AT3	AT4
1. Lies den Cartoon und hör zu! Lauras Traum	2			
2. Gruppenarbeit: Sieh dir Bild 6 im Cartoon auf Seite 30 an.		1		
3. Finde den Artikel im Wörterbuch und suche im Bild.			2	
4. Sag was! Ist das ein...		2		
5. Was sucht der Lehrer? Hör zu und kreuze an.	1			
6. Partnerarbeit: Sag was!		3		
Leseseiten			3	
Aussagesätze				2

National Curriculum PoS Statements covered in Kapitel 2:

1a, 1b, 2a, 2b, 2c, 2e, 2h, 3a, 3d, 4c, 5a, 5h,

KAPITEL 3: FREUNDE UND FAMILIE

Einheit A – Wie siehst du aus?	AT1	AT2	AT3	AT4
1. Lies den Cartoon und hör zu! Der Telefonanruf	2		2	
2. Partnerarbeit. Leute beschreiben		2	2	
3. Sag und schreib was! Mein Lieblingsstar		2		3
4. Hör zu! Kriminelle gesucht.	3			
5. Sag was! Zeugen		3		
6. Sag was! Wie siehst du aus?		3		
7. Schreib was! Wer ist das?				3
8. Schreib was! Sieh die Bilder an.			2	2
9. Spiel: Zwanzig Fragen		2		
10. Hör zu! Danas Freunde.	3			
11. Schreib was! Wie ist er? Wie ist sie?				3
12. Ganz oder gar nicht?			2	2
13. Hör zu! Meine Traumfrau.	3			

Einheit B – Haustiere	AT1	AT2	AT3	AT4
1. Lies den Cartoon und hör zu! Der Spazierang im Park	2		2	
2. Haustiere beschreiben		2	2	
3. Hör zu! Tiere	2			3
4. Schreib was! Wie heißt der Plural?				3
5. Hör zu. Meine Haustiere	3			
6. Lies was. Vermisst!			3	
7. Schreib was! Mach ein Poster.				4
8. Sag was! Tiere		3		
9. Sag was! Du bist dran.		4		
10. Spiel: Wortschlange			1	

Einheit C – Meine Familie	AT1	AT2	AT3	AT4
1. Lies den Cartoon und hör zu! Tante Anna	3		3	
2. Lies was! Matthias' Stammbaum			3	
3. Schreib was! Matthias' Familie			3	
4. Schreib was! Was sehen sie? Füll die Lücken aus				4
5. Sag was! Wie alt sind sie?	3			3
6. Schreib was! Ergänze die Sätze.			2	2
7. Schreib was! Beschreib Matthias' Familie.				3
8. Sag was! Beschreibe deine Familie.		3		
9. Schreib was! Mache Sätze!				2
10. Schreib was! ist oder sind?				4
11. Schreib was! Mann und Frau. Was passt zusammen?				1
12. Hör zu. Welche Familie ist es? Trag die richtige Zahl in dein Heft ein	3			
13. Hör zu! Pias Familie	4			2
14. Schreib was! Ergänze Pias Stammbaum			3	1
15. Schreib und sag was! Meine Familie.		4		4

Einheit D – Brieffreunde	AT1	AT2	AT3	AT4
1. Lies den Cartoon und hör zu! Brieffreundin gesucht	3		3	
2. Schreib was! –er, –e, –es, –en oder keine Endung?				4
3. Schreib was! Schreibe einen Brief. Fülle die Lücken aus.				4
4. Schreib was! Groß oder klein?				4
5. Schreib was! sie, sie oder Sie?			4	4
6. Der Marsmännchen-Rap	3			
7. Mach selber einen Rap		3		
Leseseiten			2	

National Curriculum PoS Statements covered in Kapitel 3:

1a, 1b, 1c, 2a, 2b, 2c, 2e, 2f, 2h, 2j, 3a, 3b, 3c, 3d, 4a, 4c, 5a, 5h.

KAPITEL 4: IN DER SCHULE

Einheit A – Meine Fächer	AT1	AT2	AT3	AT4
1. Mein Lieblingsfach.	3		3	
2. Schreib was! Pias Fächer.			3	2
3. Hör zu! Welche sechs Schulfächer sind das?	1			
4. Schreib was! Richtig oder falsch?			3	3
5. Sag was! Wie gefallen dir deine Schulfächer?		3		
6. Sag was! Was magst du lieber?		3		
7. Hör zu: Mein Lieblingsfach.	3			
8. Sag was! Was ist dein Lieblingsfach?		3		
9. Hör zu. Warum?	4			
10. Sag was! Mach einen Dialog nach dem Modell oben.		4		
11. Wie viel Uhr ist es in…?		2		
12. Lied: Laurenzia	3		2	
13. Das Launenbarometer: Wie geht es dir am …?		3		

Einheit B – Mein Schultag	AT1	AT2	AT3	AT4
1. Heinz ist spät dran	3		3	
2. Schreib was! Uhr oder Stunde? Fülle die Lücken				1
3. Lies was! Pias Stundenplan			2	
4. Sieh dir Pias Stundenplan an. Wann sind die Stunden?			2	2
5. Sieh dir Pias Stundenplan an und fülle die Lücken: „beginnt" oder „endet"?			2	2
6. Hör zu! Schule in Deutschland und England.	4			4
7. Ergänze die Stundenpläne.	4			2
8. Sag was! Stundenpläne.		4		
9. Schreib was! Ergänze die Sätze!				4
10. Schreib was! Bilde Sätze (1)				4
11. Schreib was! Bilde Sätze (2)				4
12. Hör zu. Welcher Tag ist es?	3			
13. Sag was! Beschreib den Stundenplan.		4		
14. Sag was! Mein Traumstundenplan.		3		
15. Hör zu: Umlaut?				
16. Hör zu! Welches Bild passt?	3			
17. Spiel: Bitte!.	3			
18. Wortschlange: Finde die Schulfächer. Was bleibt übrig?			1	
19. Hör zu! Lied: Der Schul-Rap	4		3	
Leseseiten			4	

National Curriculum PoS statements covered in Kapitel 4:

1a, 1b, 1c, 2a, 2b, 2c, 2d, 2e, 2f, 2h, 3a, 3b, 3c, 3d, 4c, 4d, 5a, 5b, 5c, 5f.

KAPITEL 5: MEIN ZUHAUSE

Einheit A – Mein Haus	AT1	AT2	AT3	AT4
1. Ich wohne hier	3		3	
2. Gruppenarbeit			4	
3. Schreib was! Wo wohnt Heinz?				4
4. Lies was! Wer wohnt hier?			3	
5. Schreib was! Kreuze an: Was hat das Haus?			1	
6. Sag was! Hat dein Haus…?		3		
7. Schreib was! Wo wohnst du?				1
8. Lies was! Wer wohnt hier?			4	
9. Sag was! Beschreib ein Haus.		4		
10. Hör zu! Wo wohnen sie?	4			
11. Lies den Cartoon und hör zu! Der Umzug	3		2	
12. Hör zu! Wo sind ihre Zimmer?	3			
13. Schreib was! Sag was! Wo wohnen die Familien?	2			2
14. Schreib was! Zimmer im Haus			3	3
15. Sag was! Was für Zimmer gibt es?		4		
16. Hör zu! Unser Haus	4			
17. Schreib was! Mein Haus				4
18. Lies was! Zu vermieten!			3	
19. Schreib was! Beschreib das Haus jetzt richtig!				4
20. Hör zu und sing mit: Der Wohn-Rap	4			
21. Schreib was! Wie wohnen Sie?			4	
22. Gruppenarbeit: Mach selber einen Wohn-Rap.				4
23. Hör zu und sing mit: Mein Haus – dein Haus	4			
24. Was passt zum ersten Haus / zum zweiten Haus?			4	3
25. Mal ein Bild von den Häusern im Lied.	4		3	

Einheit B – Mein Zimmer	AT1	AT2	AT3	AT4
1. Schreib was! Florians Möbel				2
2. Sag was! Was gibt es in Florians Zimmer? Mach Sätze		3		
3. Hör zu! Heinz' Möbel	4			
4. Schreib was! Was gibt es in deinem Traumzimmer?				4
5. Schreib was! Ein Möbelkatalog				3
6. Sag was! Anna und die Möbel.		3		
7. Hör zu! Der Sessel 1	4			
8. Hör zu! Der Sessel 2	4			
9. Lies den Cartoon und hör zu! Florians Sofa	3		3	
10. Schreib was! Richtig oder falsch?			3	1
11. Hör zu! Pia hat ihre Schultasche vergessen.	4			
12. Lies was! Julias Zimmer			4	
13. Schreib was!				3
14. Lied: So richtig nett ist's nur im Bett	3			
15. Hör zu und beantworte die Fragen	4		4	4
Leseseite			4	

National Curriculum PoS statements covered in Kapitel 5:

1a, 1b, 1c, 2a, 2b, 2c, 2e, 2f, 2h, 3a, 3b, 3c, 3d, 4b, 4c, 4d, 5a, 5c, 5f.

KAPITEL 6: MEIN TAG

Einheit A – Was machst du?	AT1	AT2	AT3	AT4
1. Ein toller Morgen	3		3	
2. Schreib was! David, der Popstar I			2	2
3. Schreib was!				4
4. Schreib was! Was machst du, Beate?				4
5. Sag was! Beates Tag.		2		
6. Schreib was!				4
7. Hör zu! Rennfahrer Rudi Raser: Mein Morgen	3			
8. Schreib was! David, der Popstar (2)				4
9. Lies was! Didi Disko (1)			4	
10. Didis Kalender				2
11. Sag was! Didi Disko (2)		4		
12. Hör zu! Was ziehen sie an?	2			
13. Hör zu und lies! Susi Schön und Fritz Faul I	3		2	3
14. Sag was! Susi Schön und Fritz Faul II		4		
15. Schreib was! Susi Schön und Fritz Faul III				4
16. Lied: Der Guten Morgen Rap 1	4		3	
17. Der Guten Morgen Rap 2				4

Einheit B – Hilfst du mit?	AT1	AT2	AT3	AT4
1. Das Handy	3		3	
2. Sag was! Was macht Pierre?		2		
3. Hör zu! Was passiert hier?	2			
4. Sag was! Wer hilft zu Hause?		4		
5. Schreib was! Was machen Pia und ihre Mutter?				4
6. Sag was! Wie oft hilfst du mit?		4		4
7. Hör zu: Was hilft Marius? Was hilft Franziska? (1)	3			2
8. Meinungsumfrage (1): Wie sieht dein Morgen aus?		3	3	
9. Sag was! Meinungsumfrage (2)		4		
10. Meinungsumfrage: Wie kommst du zur Schule?		4		
11. Lies was! Ich bin ein Schlüsselkind			4	
12. Schreib was! Jonas, das Schlüsselkind				4
13. Schreib was! Beantworte Jonas Brief.				4
14. Spiel: Pantomime		3		
15. Lied: Fleißige Leute	3		4	
Leseseite			4	4

National Curriculum PoS statements covered in Kapitel 6:

1a, 1b, 1c, 2a, 2b, 2c, 2e, 2f, 2h, 3a, 3b, 3c, 3d, 4c, 4d, 5a, 5d, 5f.

KAPITEL 7: FREIZEIT UND HOBBYS

Einheit A – Mein Hobby	AT1	AT2	AT3	AT4
1. Ein Super-Date – Teil 1	3		3	
2. Lies den Cartoon!			4	3
3. Lies was! Stars und ihre Hobbys			3	
4. Sag was! Meine Hobbys		3		
5. Persönlichkeitstest: Was für ein Freizeittyp bin ich?			4	
Mein Freizeittyp			4	
6. Hör zu! Unsere Lieblingshobbys I	4			
7. Schreib was! Unsere Lieblingshobbys II				3
8. Lies was! Vereine			4	
9. Sag was! Bist du im Verein?		3		
10. Quiz – Sport			1	
11. Sportarten und Länder		2		2
12. Lied: Der Freizeit Rap (1)	4			4
13. Lied: Der Freizeit Rap (2)	4			

Einheit B – Einladungen	AT1	AT2	AT3	AT4
1. Ein Super-Date - Teil 2	3		3	
2. Lies was!			4	
3. Beantworte die Fragen.				3
4. Schreib was! SMS – Nachrichten I				4
5. Sag was! Nach der Schule.		3		
6. Hör zu! Eine Verabredung	4			
7. Logikrätsel Wer trifft wen?			2	3
8. Schreib was! Mein Terminkalender				2
9. Sag was! Verabrede dich.		4		
10. Hör zu! Was für ein Film ist das?	4			
11. Hör zu! Mein Lieblingsfilm (1)	3			
12. Sag was! Mein Lieblingsfilm (2)		3		
13. Wann siehst du fern?			4	3
14. Lied: TV-Total	4		4	
15. Sag was! Meine Freizeit		4		
Leseseite			4	

National Curriculum PoS statements covered in Kapitel 7:

1a, 1b, 1c, 2a, 2b, 2c, 2d, 2e, 2f, 2h, 3a, 3b, 3c, 3d, 3e, 4a, 4c, 4d, 5a, 5b, 5c, 5e.

KAPITEL 8: ESSEN UND TRINKEN

Einheit A – Lecker!	AT1	AT2	AT3	AT4
1. Liebe geht durch den Magen Teil 1	3		3	
2. Sag was! Fragen zum Cartoon.			4	
3. Sag was! Was isst die Familie Gruber?		4		4
4. Sag was! Was isst du?		4		4
5. Lied: Wir haben Hunger!	3		3	
6. Mein Lieblingsessen (1)	4			
7. Mein Lieblingsessen (2)	4			3
8. Mein Lieblingsessen (3)		3		2
9. Schreib was! Wie schmeckt das?				3
10. Lies was! Das darf ich nicht essen (1)			4	
11. Schreib was! Wer darf was nicht essen? Es gibt mehrere Möglichkeiten.			4	
12. Das darf ich nicht essen (2)		3		

Einheit B – Ich möchte etwas bestellen!	AT1	AT2	AT3	AT4
1. Liebe geht durch den Magen - Teil 2	3		3	
2. Schreib was!			4	3
3. Hör zu und schreib was! Im Restaurant	3			3
4. Schreib was! Was bestellen Sie?			3	3
5. Hör zu! Stimmt das?	4			
6. Sag was! Im Restaurant.				
7. Hör zu! Frühstück bei Familie Schuh	4		4	
8. Sag was! Wie sagt man das?		2		2
9. Rollenspiel		4		4
10. Hör zu! Eine Telefonbestellung	4			3

Einheit C – Ich möchte etwas bestellen!	AT1	AT2	AT3	AT4
1. Sag was! Osterbilder		2		
2. Lies was! Ein Brief (1)			5	
3. Hör zu! Ostern mit der Band	4			
4. Der Wettbewerb	4		3	
5. Beantworte die Fragen auf Englisch!			3	
6. Beantworte die Fragen auf Deutsch!			3	3
7. Lied: Der Anstoß-Rap (Ein Lied für Berlin)	4		4	
Leseseite			4	

National Curriculum PoS statements covered in Kapitel 8:

1a, 1b, 1c, 2a, 2b, 2c, 2d, 2e, 2f, 2g, 2h, 3a, 3b, 3c, 3d, 3e, 4a, 4c, 4d, 5a, 5b, 5c, 5d, 5f, 5h.

Appendix B Mapping grid for Scottish Curriculum

The following grid shows how the core activities of *Anstoß 1* map against the main skills and levels from the 5–14 guidelines.

Please Note:

- *List = Listening; Spk = Speaking; Read = Reading; Writ = Writing*
- *Where an activity functions at two levels within the same attainment target, the higher level is listed.*

KAPITEL 1: HALLO

Einheit A – Wie geht's?	List	Spk	Read	Writ
1. Die Geburtstagparty (1)	A			
2. Lies den Cartoon und hör zu noch einmal.	B		B	
3. Hör zu Guten Tag!	B	A		
4. Hör zu Was sagt man?	B	A		
5. Schreib was! Anagramme				A
6. Hör zu! Wie geht's?	A	A		
7. Hör zu! Wie geht's?	B			
8. Partnerarbeit: Sag was!		C		
9. Schreib was! Füll die Lücken im Cartoon.			B	A

Einheit B – Wie heißt du?	List	Spk	Read	Writ
1. Die Geburtstagparty (2)	A		B	
2. Lies den Carton noch mal. Wie sagt man das auf Deutsch?			B	
3. Schreib was!				B
4. Schreib was und sag was!		A		B
5. Hör zu und schreib was! Wie heißt du?	B			
6. Hör zu! Wie heißt du? oder: Wie heißen Sie?	C			
7. Quiz: Wie heißen Sie?				
8. Hör zu! Das Alphabet	A			
9. Hör zu! Lied: ABC	A			
10. Hör zu – Am Telefon	C			
11. Partnerarbeit. Du bist dran: Sag was!		C		
12. Gruppenarbeit: Autos		B		
13. Schreib was! Dialog			B	B

Einheit C – Wo wohnst du?	List	Spk	Read	Writ
1. Die Geburtstagparty (3)	B			
2. Partnerarbeit: Laura und Matthias		B		
3. Woher kommen sie?			B	A
4. Gruppenarbeit:Ortsnamen				
5. Sag was! Partnerarbeit: Wo ist...?		B		
6. Hör zu! Wo wohnt er? Wo wohnt sie?	C			
7. Sag was! Du bist dran! Wo wohnst du?		B		
8. Hör zu!: Hallo!	C			
9. Quiz: Deutschsprachige Länder			C	
10. Quiz: Woher kommt das Auto? Buchstabiere!				B
11. Schreib was!				B
12. Schreib was! Verben				B
13. Partnerarbeit: Sag was! Ein Interview		C		
Leseseiten			B	

KAPITEL 2: WIR LERNEN UNS KENNEN

Einheit A – Zahlen und Daten	List	Spk	Read	Writ
1. Lies den Cartoon und hör zu. Die Telefonnummer	B			
2. Partnerarbeit: Wie sagt man das auf Deutsch?	B	A		
3. Hör zu! ie oder ei?	A			
4. Sag was! Wie viele?		A		
5. Hör zu: Die Fußballergebnisse	B			
6. Hör zu: Die Rakete	A	A		
7. Partnerarbeit: Sag was!		A		
8. Gruppenarbeit: Nationale Telefonnummern		A		
9. Hör zu!: Wie alt ist…		B		A
10. Hör zu! Lied: Monate	A			
11. Sag was! Wann hast du Geburtstag?		B		
12. Quiz: Wann ist Ihr Geburtstag?		B		
13. Hör zu! Lied: Geburtstagslied	A			
14. Sag was! Heinz und Band auf Tour		B		
15. Hör zu: Die Top Ten in Deutschland	B			
16. Hör zu: Lotto	B			
17. Lies was! Eine E-Mail aus Deutschland			C	
18. Schreib was! Eine E-Mail an Katja				C
19. Lied: Der Heinz- und Pia-Rap	C			

Einheit B – Wo ist es?	List	Spk	Read	Writ
1. Lies den Cartoon und hör zu! Lauras Traum	B			
2. Gruppenarbeit: Sieh dir Bild 6 im Cartoon auf Seite 30 an.		B		
3. Finde den Artikel im Wörterbuch und suche im Bild.			B	
4. Sag was! Ist das ein...		C		
5. Was sucht der Lehrer? Hör zu und kreuze an.	A			
6. Partnerarbeit: Sag was!		C		
Leseseiten			C	
Aussagesätze				A

KAPITEL 3: FREUNDE UND FAMILIE

Einheit A – Wie siehst du aus?	**List**	**Spk**	**Read**	**Writ**
1. Lies den Cartoon und hör zu! Der Telefonanruf	B		B	
2. Partnerarbeit. Leute beschreiben		A	B	
3. Sag und schreib was! Mein Lieblingsstar		B		C
4. Hör zu! Kriminelle gesucht.	C			
5. Sag was! Zeugen		C		
6. Sag was! Wie siehst du aus?		C		
7. Schreib was! Wer ist das?				C
8. Schreib was! Sieh die Bilder an.			C	C
9. Spiel: Zwanzig Fragen		B		
10. Hör zu! Danas Freunde.	B			
11. Schreib was! Wie ist er? Wie ist sie?				B
12. Ganz oder gar nicht?			C	B
13. Hör zu! Meine Traumfrau.	C			

Einheit B – Haustiere	**List**	**Spk**	**Read**	**Writ**
1. Lies den Cartoon und hör zu! Der Spazierang im Park	B		B	
2. Haustiere beschreiben		A	B	
3. Hör zu! Tiere	B			B
4. Schreib was! Wie heißt der Plural?				B
5. Hör zu. Meine Haustiere	C			
6. Lies was. Vermisst!			B	
7. Schreib was! Mach ein Poster.				C
8. Sag was! Tiere		B		
9. Sag was! Du bist dran.		B		
10. Spiel: Wortschlange			A	

Einheit C – Meine Familie	**List**	**Spk**	**Read**	**Writ**
1. Lies den Cartoon und hör zu! Tante Anna	C		C	
2. Lies was! Matthias' Stammbaum			C	
3. Schreib was! Matthias' Familie			C	
4. Schreib was! Was sehen sie? Füll die Lücken aus				B
5. Sag was! Wie alt sind sie?		B		B
6. Schreib was! Ergänze die Sätze.			B	A
7. Schreib was! Beschreib Matthias' Familie.				A
8. Sag was! Beschreibe deine Familie.		C		
9. Schreib was! Mache Sätze!				B
10. Schreib was! ist oder sind?				B
11. Schreib was! Mann und Frau. Was passt zusammen?				A
12. Hör zu. Welche Familie ist es? Trag die richtige Zahl in dein Heft ein	C			
13. Hör zu! Pias Familie	C			B
14. Schreib was! Ergänze Pias Stammbaum			C	A
15. Schreib und sag was! Meine Familie.		C		C

Einheit D – Brieffreunde	**List**	**Spk**	**Read**	**Writ**
1. Lies den Cartoon und hör zu! Brieffreundin gesucht	D		D	
2. Schreib was! –er, –e, –es, –en oder keine Endung?				C
3. Schreib was! Schreibe einen Brief. Fülle die Lücken aus.				C
4. Schreib was! Groß oder klein?				C
5. Schreib was! sie, sie oder Sie?			C	B
6. Der Marsmännchen-Rap	C			
7. Mach selber einen Rap		C/D		
Leseseiten			B	

KAPITEL 4: IN DER SCHULE

Einheit A – Meine Fächer	List	Spk	Read	Writ
1. Mein Lieblingsfach.	B		B	
2. Schreib was! Pias Fächer.			B	A
3. Hör zu! Welche sechs Schulfächer sind das?	B			
4. Schreib was! Richtig oder falsch?			C	C
5. Sag was! Wie gefallen dir deine Schulfächer?		C		
6. Sag was! Was magst du lieber?		C		
7. Hör zu: Mein Lieblingsfach.	C			
8. Sag was! Was ist dein Lieblingsfach?		B		
9. Hör zu. Warum?	D			
10. Sag was! Mach einen Dialog nach dem Modell oben.		D		
11. Wie viel Uhr ist es in…?		B		
12. Lied: Laurenzia	E		E	
13. Das Launenbarometer: Wie geht es dir am …?		C		

Einheit B – Mein Schultag	List	Spk	Read	Writ
1. Heinz ist spät dran	B		B	
2. Schreib was! Uhr oder Stunde? Fülle die Lücken				A
3. Lies was! Pias Stundenplan			B	
4. Sieh dir Pias Stundenplan an. Wann sind die Stunden?			C	A
5. Sieh dir Pias Stundenplan an und fülle die Lücken: „beginnt" oder „endet"?			B	B
6. Hör zu! Schule in Deutschland und England.	E			E
7. Ergänze die Stundenpläne.	C			C
8. Sag was! Stundenpläne.		C		
9. Schreib was! Ergänze die Sätze!				B
10. Schreib was! Bilde Sätze (1)				C
11. Schreib was! Bilde Sätze (2)				C
12. Hör zu. Welcher Tag ist es?	C			
13. Sag was! Beschreib den Stundenplan.		C		
14. Sag was! Mein Traumstundenplan.		C		
15. Hör zu: Umlaut?	C			
16. Hör zu! Welches Bild passt?	C			
17. Spiel: Bitte!.				
18. Wortschlange: Finde die Schulfächer. Was bleibt übrig?			B	
19. Hör zu! Lied: Der Schul-Rap	D		D	
Leseseiten			E	

KAPITEL 5: MEIN ZUHAUSE

Einheit A – Mein Haus	List	Spk	Read	Writ
1. Ich wohne hier	C		C	
2. Gruppenarbeit			C	
3. Schreib was! Wo wohnt Heinz?				C
4. Lies was! Wer wohnt hier?			C	
5. Schreib was! Kreuze an: Was hat das Haus?			B	
6. Sag was! Hat dein Haus…?		C		
7. Schreib was! Wo wohnst du?				A
8. Lies was! Wer wohnt hier?			D	
9. Sag was! Beschreib ein Haus.		B		
10. Hör zu! Wo wohnen sie?	D			
11. Lies den Cartoon und hör zu! Der Umzug	C		C	
12. Hör zu! Wo sind ihre Zimmer?	C			
13. Schreib was! Sag was! Wo wohnen die Familien?	B			B
14. Schreib was! Zimmer im Haus			C	C
15. Sag was! Was für Zimmer gibt es?		C		
16. Hör zu! Unser Haus	E			
17. Schreib was! Mein Haus				C
18. Lies was! Zu vermieten!			C	
19. Schreib was! Beschreib das Haus jetzt richtig!				C
20. Hör zu und sing mit: Der Wohn-Rap	D			
21. Schreib was! Wie wohnen Sie?			C	
22. Gruppenarbeit: Mach selber einen Wohn-Rap.				C
23. Hör zu und sing mit: Mein Haus – dein Haus	D			
24. Was passt zum ersten Haus / zum zweiten Haus?			C	C
25. Mal ein Bild von den Häusern im Lied.	C		C	

Einheit B – Mein Zimmer	List	Spk	Read	Writ
1. Schreib was! Florians Möbel				A
2. Sag was! Was gibt es in Florians Zimmer? Mach Sätze		B		
3. Hör zu! Heinz' Möbel	C			
4. Schreib was! Was gibt es in deinem Traumzimmer?				C
5. Schreib was! Ein Möbelkatalog				B
6. Sag was! Anna und die Möbel.		B		
7. Hör zu! Der Sessel 1	C			
8. Hör zu! Der Sessel 2	C			
9. Lies den Cartoon und hör zu! Florians Sofa	C		C	
10. Schreib was! Richtig oder falsch?			C	A
11. Hör zu! Pia hat ihre Schultasche vergessen.	E			
12. Lies was! Julias Zimmer			D	
13. Schreib was!				D
14. Lied: So richtig nett ist's nur im Bett	C			
15. Hör zu und beantworte die Fragen	C		C	C
Leseseite			D	

KAPITEL 6: MEIN TAG

Einheit A – Was machst du?	List	Spk	Read	Writ
1. Ein toller Morgen	C		C	
2. Schreib was! David, der Popstar I			C	B
3. Schreib was!				B
4. Schreib was! Was machst du, Beate?				C
5. Sag was! Beates Tag.		C		
6. Schreib was!				B
7. Hör zu! Rennfahrer Rudi Raser: Mein Morgen	C			
8. Schreib was! David, der Popstar (2)				C
9. Lies was! Didi Disko (1)			D	
10. Didis Kalender				B
11. Sag was! Didi Disko (2)		B		
12. Hör zu! Was ziehen sie an?	C			
13. Hör zu und lies! Susi Schön und Fritz Faul I	C		B	C
14. Sag was! Susi Schön und Fritz Faul II		C		
15. Schreib was! Susi Schön und Fritz Faul III				B
16. Lied: Der Guten Morgen Rap 1	C		C	
17. Der Guten Morgen Rap 2				B

Einheit B – Hilfst du mit?	List	Spk	Read	Writ
1. Das Handy	C		C	
2. Sag was! Was macht Pierre?		B		
3. Hör zu! Was passiert hier?	A			
4. Sag was! Wer hilft zu Hause?		C		
5. Schreib was! Was machen Pia und ihre Mutter?				B
6. Sag was! Wie oft hilfst du mit?		C		C
7. Hör zu: Was hilft Marius? Was hilft Franziska? (1)	C			A
8. Meinungsumfrage (1): Wie sieht dein Morgen aus?		B	B	
9. Sag was! Meinungsumfrage (2)		C		
10. Meinungsumfrage: Wie kommst du zur Schule?		C		
11. Lies was! Ich bin ein Schlüsselkind			E	
12. Schreib was! Jonas, das Schlüsselkind				D
13. Schreib was! Beantworte Jonas Brief.				C
14. Spiel: Pantomime		B		
15. Lied: Fleißige Leute	C		C	
Leseseite			C	B

KAPITEL 7: FREIZEIT UND HOBBYS

Einheit A – Mein Hobby	List	Spk	Read	Writ
1. Ein Super-Date – Teil 1	B		C	
2. Lies den Cartoon!			D	D
3. Lies was! Stars und ihre Hobbys			D	
4. Sag was! Meine Hobbys		C		
5. Persönlichkeitstest: Was für ein Freizeittyp bin ich?			C	
Mein Freizeittyp			E	
6. Hör zu! Unsere Lieblingshobbys I	C			
7. Schreib was! Unsere Lieblingshobbys II				C
8. Lies was! Vereine			D	
9. Sag was! Bist du im Verein?		C		
10. Quiz – Sport			B	
11. Sportarten und Länder		C		A
12. Lied: Der Freizeit Rap (1)	D			D
13. Lied: Der Freizeit Rap (2)	D			

Einheit B – Einladungen	List	Spk	Read	Writ
1. Ein Super-Date - Teil 2	B		C	
2. Lies was!			D	
3. Beantworte die Fragen.				C
4. Schreib was! SMS – Nachrichten I				C
5. Sag was! Nach der Schule.		C		
6. Hör zu! Eine Verabredung	C			
7. Logikrätsel Wer trifft wen?			C	B
8. Schreib was! Mein Terminkalender				C
9. Sag was! Verabrede dich.		D		
10. Hör zu! Was für ein Film ist das?	C			
11. Hör zu! Mein Lieblingsfilm (1)	C			
12. Sag was! Mein Lieblingsfilm (2)		C		
13. Wann siehst du fern?			D	C
14. Lied: TV-Total	C		D	
15. Sag was! Meine Freizeit		D		
Leseseite			D	

KAPITEL 8: ESSEN UND TRINKEN

Einheit A – Lecker!	List	Spk	Read	Writ
1. Liebe geht durch den Magen Teil 1	B		C	
2. Sag was! Fragen zum Cartoon.		C		
3. Sag was! Was isst die Familie Gruber?		D		D
4. Sag was! Was isst du?		C		C
5. Lied: Wir haben Hunger!	C		C	
6. Mein Lieblingsessen (1)	C			
7. Mein Lieblingsessen (2)	C			C
8. Mein Lieblingsessen (3)			C	C
9. Schreib was! Wie schmeckt das?				B
10. Lies was! Das darf ich nicht essen (1)			E	
11. Schreib was! Wer darf was nicht essen? Es gibt mehrere Möglichkeiten.			E	
12. Das darf ich nicht essen (2)		D		

Einheit B – Ich möchte etwas bestellen!	List	Spk	Read	Writ
1. Liebe geht durch den Magen - Teil 2	C		C	
2. Schreib was!			C	C
3. Hör zu und schreib was! Im Restaurant	D			C
4. Schreib was! Was bestellen Sie?			C	B
5. Hör zu! Stimmt das?	C			
6. Sag was! Im Restaurant.		D		
7. Hör zu! Frühstück bei Familie Schuh	D		C	
8. Sag was! Wie sagt man das?		C		B
9. Rollenspiel		D		D
10. Hör zu! Eine Telefonbestellung	C			C

Einheit C – Ich möchte etwas bestellen!	List	Spk	Read	Writ
1. Sag was! Osterbilder		B		
2. Lies was! Ein Brief (1)			E	
3. Hör zu! Ostern mit der Band	E			
4. Der Wettbewerb	D		D	
5. Beantworte die Fragen auf Englisch!			D	
6. Beantworte die Fragen auf Deutsch!			D	C
7. Lied: Der Anstoß-Rap (Ein Lied für Berlin)	D		D	
Leseseite			D	